OFFICE PROCEDURES

FOURTH EDITION

John Harrison

LONGMAN

Addison Wesley Longman
Addison Wesley Longman Limited,
Edinburgh Gate, Harlow,
Essex CM20 2JE, England
and associated companies through the world

First published 1984
Fourth edition 1996

British Library Cataloguing in Publication Data
A catalogue entry for this title is available from the British Library

ISBN 0–582–29341–3

Library of Congress Cataloging-in-Publication Data
A catalog entry for this title is available from the Library of Congress

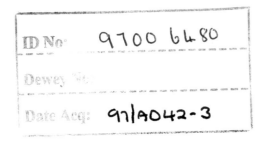

Typeset by 36 in New Baskerville
Printed in Great Britain by Henry Ling Ltd., at the Dorset Press, Dorchester, Dorset

Contents

Preface vii

Acknowledgements ix

Assessment chart xi

Section A
INDUCTION 1
1 The role and the relationship of office workers in the organisation 1

Section B
OFFICE SYSTEMS, PROCEDURES AND RECORDS 12

2 Buying and selling 12

3 Stock control 28

4 Receipts and payments 34

5 Petty cash 47

6 Wages and salaries 51

7 Filing 68

8 Incoming and outgoing mail 78

9 Work planning and scheduling 88

Section C
OFFICE TECHNOLOGY 97

10 Computer systems and terminology 97

11 Reprography 105

12 Calculators 114

13 Health and safety 117

Section D
COMMUNICATIONS 129

14 Oral communication 131

15 Written communication 140

16 Mail services 151

17 Receiving and assisting visitors 159

18 Travel arrangements 166

19 Organising meetings and other events 172

20 Sources of information 180

Section E
STUDENT'S GUIDE TO ASSESSMENT 188

Answers to progress checks 192

Index 201

Preface

Office Procedures is an introductory study of office practice, with topics specially selected for the new entrant to the office. The breadth of content is well illustrated in the assessment chart (page xi) which sets out the NVQ Level 1 and 2 elements of competence and the Pitman Qualifications Office Procedures Level 1 and 2 sections which are developed in each unit of this book. The book also assists students preparing for GNVQ Business Intermediate, GCSE Business Studies and similar examinations in other countries.

The key concepts of learning in this book are:

- it is up to date, featuring the latest developments in information technology, new mail services, and telecommunication services
- it has been brought into line with the latest NVQ criteria, with new units in work planning and scheduling, travel arrangements, and organising meetings and other events – providing the necessary background knowledge.
- it is clearly written and well illustrated in order to be of the greatest assistance to students in learning and understanding the subject
- it helps to develop essential core skills in communication, application of number, information technology, personal and interpersonal skills, and problem solving through the medium of practical office procedures
- the progress checks at the end of each unit with the multiple choice and short answer questions provide an easy means of monitoring progress
- helpful advice is given in Section E on tackling assignments and preparing for examinations
- the accompanying book *Practical Office Procedures* provides realistic and effective learning resource material for each of the units in this book. These include:
  - a series of practical activities centred around four case studies
  - recent Pitman Qualifications (formerly PEI) Office Procedures examination questions
  - work experience tasks to co-ordinate the activities in the classroom with the workplace
  - tasks for completion by computer or word processor
  - a comprehensive bank of copiable specimen documents specially designed for use with the tasks

Students enjoy and benefit from taking part in both their learning and assessment. The multiple choice and short answer questions set in the progress checks enable students to be actively involved in this process. The questions are easy to mark, in fact students should be encouraged to do this for themselves, thus providing them with instant knowledge of results and progress. The answers are given on page 192. The student faced with a multiple choice question must choose the correct answer and consider the reasons why the other answers are unacceptable. In this all important process of thinking the student gains a better understanding of the topic. Many of the short answer questions have been set in past examinations for the Pitman Qualifications Office Procedures Level 1 examination and this will be beneficial for students preparing for this and similar examinations.

Other forms of assessment are, of course, essential for the development of the competences given at the beginning of each unit and a good selection of these are provided in the companion to this book *Practical Office Procedures*. The two books together are a complete learning package designed to provide students with the skills and related knowledge essential for employment in business and success in examinations.

JH

Acknowledgements

The author and publishers wish to thank the following for permission to reproduce photographs, forms and other documents:

Acco Rexel Ltd
Alliance & Leicester Giro
Barclays Bank plc
Bell & Howell Ltd
British Airways
British Telecom
James Burn International Ltd
Computing Plus
Elite Manufacturing Co Ltd
Flexiform Business Furniture Ltd
GBC (United Kingdom) Ltd
Hampshire Fire and Rescue Service
Hengstler Flextime Ltd
Hewlett Packard Ltd
Kardex Systems (UK) Ltd
Larkins Security Ltd
Midland Bank plc
Minolta (UK) Ltd
Neopost Ltd
Parcelforce
Pitney Bowes plc
The Post Office
QAS Systems Ltd
Rank Xerox (UK) Ltd
Red Star Parcel Delivery Service
Ricoh UK Ltd
Royal Mail
Samsung Electronics (UK) Ltd
3M United Kingdom plc
Vickers plc
Warwick Time Stamping Co Ltd
Mrs J Wyeth of Eastleigh College

The competences featured in this book are reproduced by kind permission of the Administration Lead Body.
Crown copyright material is reproduced with the permission of the controller of Her Majesty's Stationery Office.

Assessment Chart

Office Procedures Unit	NVQ Level 1 Element	NVQ Level2 Element	PQ OP1 Sec	PQ OP2 Sec
1 The role and relationship of office workers in the organisation	4.1	4.1	1	1
2 Buying and selling	–	7.2 10.1	3	4
3 Stock control	9.1/2	9.1/2	3	4
4 Receipts and payments	–	7.2 10.2	3	4
5 Petty cash	5.3	10.2	3	–
6 Wages and salaries	–	7.2	–	–
7 Filing	6.1/2	5.1/2	4	5
8 Incoming and outgoing mail	8.1/2	8.2	3/5	1
9 Work planning and scheduling	1.1/3	1.1/3 3.1/2	–	–
10 Computer systems and terminology	7.1	6.1/3	5	3
11 Reprography	7.2 3.1/2	3.3	5	3
12 Calculators	5.3	–	–	–
13 Health and safety	2.1/2	2.1	1	1
14 Oral communication	5.1/2	8.1	2	2
15 Written communication	5.2	7.1/2 8.1	2	2
16 Mail services	8.1/2	8.2	3	1
17 Receiving and assisting visitors	4.2 2.3	4.2 2.2	2	2
18 Travel arrangements	–	11.1/2	–	6
19 Organising meetings and other events	–	12.1/3	–	6
20 Sources of information	5.2/3	5.2	–	5

Section A
INDUCTION

Unit 1
The role and relationship of office workers in the organisation

Competence developed in this unit:

- Establish and maintain working relationships with other members of staff

(NVQ2)

So you want to work in an office ... this unit sets the scene for your course in office procedures by introducing you to the different types of organisation you may work for; how they are organised; the role and relationship of office workers in the organisation; and the documents involved in employing staff. By studying office procedures and gaining office skills you are taking the first important step towards an office career.

The office is essential to any organisation as it provides the means by which information is received, processed, recorded, controlled and transmitted. Fig 1.1 shows what is involved at each stage of the office procedure.

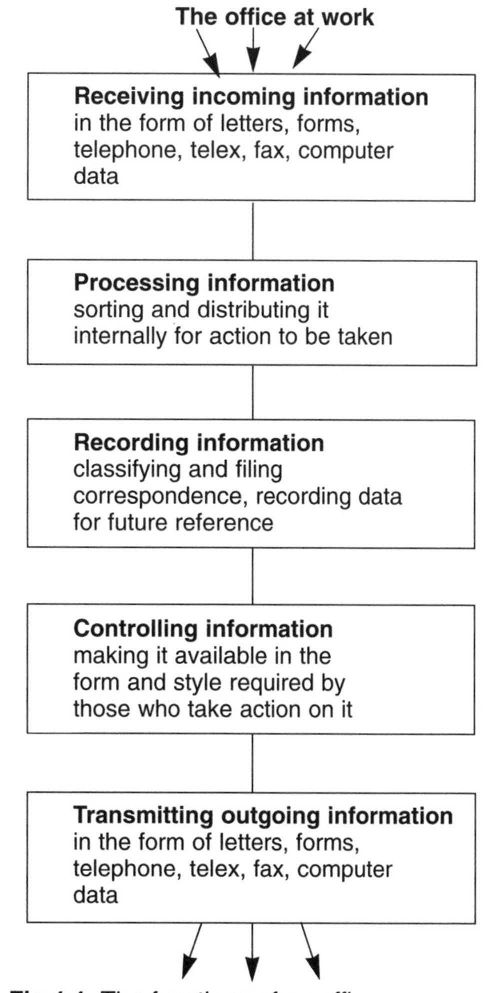

The office at work
Receiving incoming information
in the form of letters, forms, telephone, telex, fax, computer data
Processing information
sorting and distributing it internally for action to be taken
Recording information
classifying and filing correspondence, recording data for future reference
Controlling information
making it available in the form and style required by those who take action on it
Transmitting outgoing information
in the form of letters, forms, telephone, telex, fax, computer data

Fig 1.1 The functions of an office

▶ OFFICE SERVICES

Office services are necessary for every type of organisation, however large or small, or whatever activities are performed. The number and different types of organisation are vast but the functions of the office are basically common to all. You will be acquainted with many of the office services in this book such as filing, mail handling, communicating messages and letters and using the telephone, receiving visitors and keeping records of financial transactions. It is often advantageous for some office services such as typing, filing, reprographics, mailing, control of stationery, reception and the telephone system to be organised centrally. This means, for example, that an information processing centre provides all departments with secretarial services; instead of each department keeping its own files, there is a central section where all paperwork is filed together; a reprographics centre supplies the copying and printing needs of all departments; all mail is received and despatched by one central mailing section.

The advantages gained from centralisation are:

- economy of staff, equipment and office space
- better control over quality and standardisation of work
- more even distribution of work
- more flexible use of staff
- better systems and equipment
- more effective training and supervision

On the other hand, some departments have special requirements which do not lend themselves to centralisation, for example:

- some departments need information close at hand
- personnel files are confidential and should be kept within the personnel department
- some departments require constant access to a copier
- heads of department may require the services of a secretary within their own departments
- direct telephone lines may be needed in offices where calls are received out of normal office hours

A certain amount of flexibility is, therefore, essential in most organisations where it is normal to centralise the main services such as keyboarding, reprographics, reception, telephone, while providing limited departmental services where necessary, eg where there is a centralised print room, each department may have a small copier for urgent work.

▶ TYPES OF ORGANISATION

The three main types of organisation are:

- manufacturing and industrial
- commercial
- services

These organisations are illustrated in Fig 1.2 and in the following table.

Manufacturing/ industrial	Commercial	Services
Organisations producing raw materials or manufacturing them into finished goods	Organisations distributing goods from the manufacturer to the consumer or providing aids to trade	Organisations providing social and personal services
Examples	*Examples*	*Examples*
farming	retailing	schools
mining	wholesaling	hospitals
building	transporting	doctors
manufacturing:	advertising	police
cars,	banking	solicitors
office machines,	insurance	leisure pursuits:
furniture,		sport, music,
chemicals,		drama etc
clothes, books		youth clubs
etc		hotels

▶ BUSINESS UNITS

'Business unit' is the term used to indicate the way in which an organisation is owned and how it receives the necessary capital to set up in business. The private sector (ie organisations privately owned) includes the following different types of business unit:

Sole trader

One person, known as the proprietor, owns and runs the business, receiving all profits and being responsible for any losses incurred.
Examples: small retailers, hairdressers, plumbers

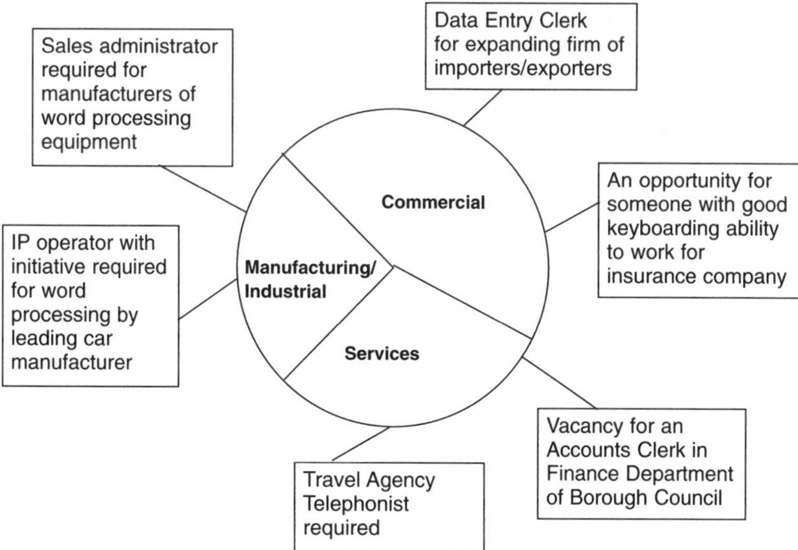

Fig 1.2 Advertisements for office jobs and their organisation classifications

Partnership

At least two but not more than twenty people, known as partners, share in the ownership of the firm, with the exception of solicitors and accountants who can have more than twenty partners. As with the sole trader the partners receive all profits and are liable to meet fully any debts incurred.
Examples: solicitors, doctors, accountants

Private limited company (Ltd)

At least two people, known as shareholders, contribute funds to provide share capital in a 'family type' business which is controlled by a board of directors. Shares are negotiated privately and not publicly through the stock exchange. The liability of each shareholder is limited to the amount of share capital contributed, hence the term 'limited'.
Examples: small manufacturers/traders, medium-sized retailers, builders and garages

Public limited company (PLC)

At least two people contribute funds to provide the share capital which must have at least £50,000 or the minimum amount of capital as specified by the Companies Act 1980. The company is controlled by a board of directors. All shareholders have limited liability, ie in the case of a loss they cannot be held responsible for more than their share capital. Shares in a public limited company can be bought and sold by the public on the stock exchange.
Examples: multiple stores (such as Marks and Spencer and J Sainsbury), industrial/manufacturing concerns (such as Tate & Lyle and Jaguar Cars)

Private and public companies may be referred to as joint stock companies as the assets are contributed jointly by several shareholders.

Holding companies

A public company which controls the activities of other companies (known as subsidiaries) by acquiring more than 50 per cent of their voting shares is known as a holding (or parent) company. Holding companies may operate within one country or within many different countries (in which case they may be called multinational companies or corporations).
Examples: ICI and Unilever

Multinational companies

A 'multinational' is a group of companies operating with subsidiaries in several parts of the

world. The operations of the subsidiary companies are controlled by the parent company. Each subsidiary company normally has a board of directors, appointed by the parent company, to be responsible for the conduct of its local affairs, but reports to the parent company on important policy matters.
Examples: IBM and Exxon/Esso

The different types of organisation in the public sector (ie those publicly owned and run) are:

Central government departments

Departments responsible for a government service and headed by a minister who is a member of parliament.
Examples: Department of Social Security, Department for Education and Training

Local government

Councillors elected at local government elections serve on committees responsible for public services such as education, roads, housing etc. Local government officers are appointed as permanent officials to administer the services.
Examples: county council, district council

▶ INTERNAL STRUCTURE OF THE ORGANISATION

This explains the way in which an organisation operates and shows:

- The different levels of staff, eg the proprietors, executives, supervisors etc (see next column), providing lines of authority. In the organisation chart on page 5 the cashiers are each responsible for an area of work and report to the chief cashier, who in turn reports to the chief accountant for all aspects of cash control.
- The division of work, ie it makes clear how the work is allocated to the different departments, sections and staff.
- The grouping of functions into departments with related activities such as production, buying, personnel etc.

The internal structure varies considerably with the nature of the organisation, ie whether it is manufacturing goods or providing personal services; the type of business unit such as a sole trader compared with a government department; and the size of its operations. A useful aid to the internal structure is an organisation chart such as the one illustrated in Fig 1.3. It shows the proprietors, executives and staff of a typical medium-sized trading concern, together with the main office functions and documents associated with each of the departments.

▶ LEVELS OF RESPONSIBILITY

1 Proprietors
The owners, ie the shareholders in the organisation chart (Fig 1.3).

2 Executives
The management team. These are the senior staff with their leader or co-ordinator, the general manager, responsible for managing the firm and implementing the major policy decisions made by the board of directors.

3 Supervisors
Responsible to the executives for the work of a section consisting of several members of staff.

4 Office staff
Administrative, clerical and secretarial staff responsible to the supervisors for the day to day office services.

▶ SIZE OF ORGANISATION

Your work, surroundings and relationships will vary according to the size of the organisation, as illustrated in the following comparisons between large and small organisations:

- A large organisation will normally be a limited company or a public authority, whereas a small firm will be a sole trader, partnership or private company.
- In a small organisation most, if not all, staff will have direct contact with the owner or manager, but in a large organisation there will be much less personal contact with the proprietors.
- A large organisation will be sectionalised and

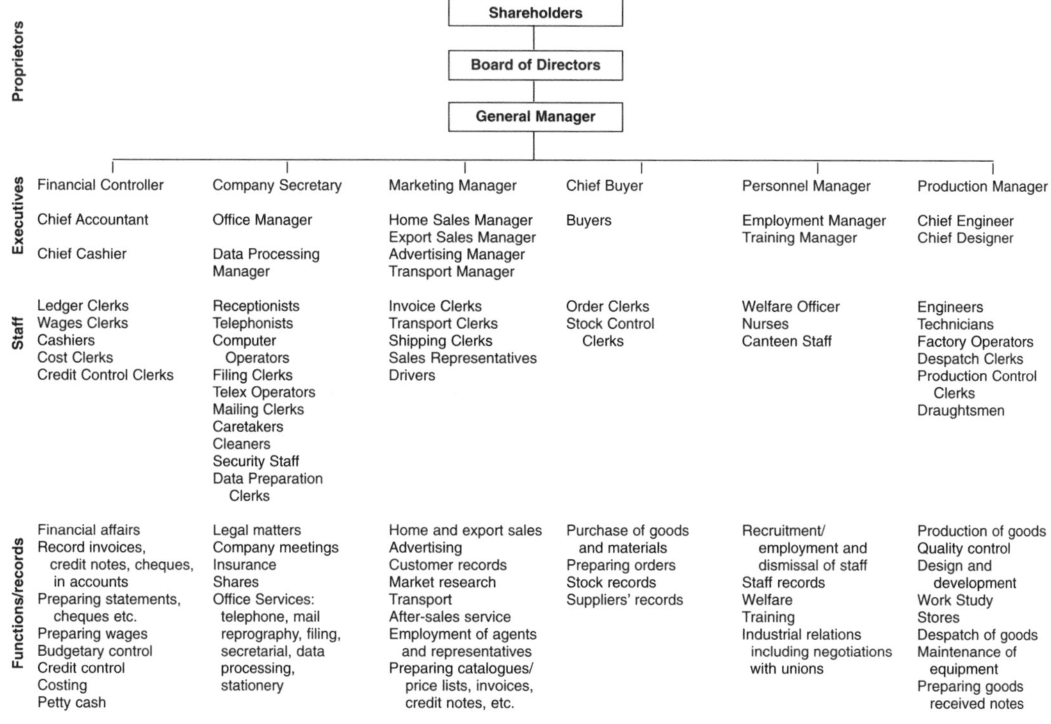

Fig 1.3 Organisation chart for a medium-sized manufacturing organisation (Note: Keyboard operators, secretaries and clerical staff are attached to all departments.)

departmentalised and work will be related to one aspect of the business, whereas in a small organisation the work is likely to be more varied and relate to a wider range of the firm's activities (*see* Figs 1.3 and 1.4).

- There is greater specialisation of staff in a large organisation, eg sales staff will specialise in one branch of the department such as home sales, exporting, market research, etc. Such specialisation will not be possible in a small organisation.
- In a small organisation there are fewer opportunities for training, staff development, social activities, etc, whereas in a large organisation these will be highly organised within its Personnel Department.
- Large organisations will normally be better equipped with the latest office technology and sophisticated systems which are not normally possible in a small business.

▶ INTERPERSONAL RELATIONSHIPS

It is important that office employees establish and maintain good relationships with staff at all levels and with members of the public. Office staff should assist and co-operate with their supervisors by:

- accepting requests courteously
- listening properly and giving feedback to show understanding
- anticipating likely questions and having answers ready
- offering suggestions and help
- requesting any assistance required politely
- discussing any difficulties concerning working relationships and resolving or reporting

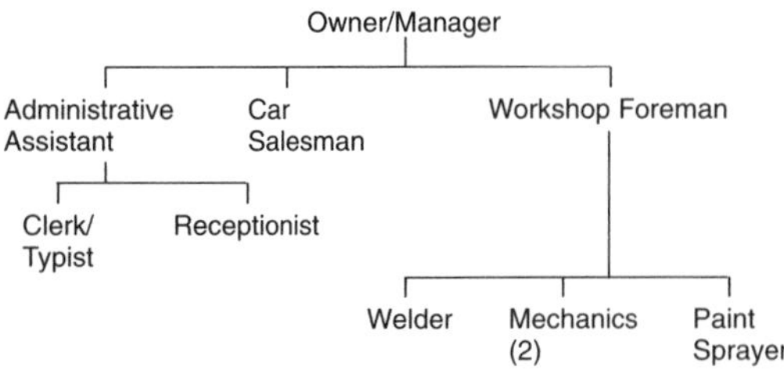

Fig 1.4 Organisation chart for a small business – a garage

them accurately and promptly

- making constructive criticisms of current or proposed work systems

Good relations with colleagues at the same level are also crucial in creating a happy and trouble-free environment. It is in relationships with colleagues that the office worker must guard against divulging confidential information. The employee should refrain from entering into gossip and wasting valuable time in the office. A good working relationship is a contributory factor in gaining the full support and co-operation of other members of staff.

Communications with the public, such as customers or clients on whom the business may rely for its livelihood, are of great importance in enhancing the company's reputation, goodwill and public esteem. Good relations are established when:

- effective working relationships are maintained with colleagues and external contacts
- the public is greeted promptly and politely and its needs identified
- the required information is supplied clearly, accurately, promptly and in a friendly manner
- any reasons for a delay in supplying or non-availability of information are explained politely
- any requests for information or advice outside the employee's responsibility are passed to an appropriate member of staff promptly and accurately
- dress and appearance conform to the accepted standards of the organisation

See also Unit 14 Oral communication.

▶ THE OFFICE WORKER'S ROLE

We will now take a look at the place of office staff in an organisation and the jobs and responsibilities of a sales clerk. Junior staff normally begin with jobs which are fairly routine, but with experience and further training they can progress to more demanding tasks later. The range of tasks which the new entrant may be required to perform is often dependent upon the size of the organisation in which they work, and is also affected by the office systems and equipment used. When you apply for a job you should be given a job description (*see* Fig 1.5) which lists the tasks involved in the job and identifies the position of the job in the organisation.

The job description can be used as a basis for

- deciding what qualities and qualifications are needed for new applicants for a post
- job evaluation, ie determining the grade or rate of pay for a job
- induction of new staff to inform them of their duties and the work of others
- identifying training needs
- supervisory purposes

▶ ADVERTISING JOBS

Selecting the newspaper or journal

- choose publications which will be read by the people the advertisement aims to reach
- before placing an advertisement, compare costs of various publications and find out the time required for booking space and delivering the copy
- decide whether to advertise with the journal direct or use the services of an advertising agency

When drafting the advertisement

- use words sparingly, selecting only those which give the salient facts and attract the attention of readers (*see* Fig 1.6)
- create interest by including information which encourages readers to respond to the advertisement, eg aspects of the work which give job satisfaction, salary offered, etc
- state clearly any basic requirements, eg competence in keyboarding skills, so that only those qualified will apply

JOB DESCRIPTION

Post:	Sales clerk
Scale:	2
Department:	Marketing
Section:	Home Sales
Accountable to:	Sales supervisor

Duties:

General — Clerical services associated with issuing quotations and receiving orders from customers

Specific

- accept orders by post, telephone, telex or fax from a customer direct or from a sales representative and complete the necessary documentation, taking into account customer records and previous orders
- file sales correspondence and retrieve files/documents when required
- update and access computer records
- maintain customer record cards
- prepare and despatch quotations
- deal with telephone enquiries and relay messages accurately and promptly to the people concerned
- transmit and receive messages by telex
- transmit and receive information using fax
- deal with enquiries at the enquiry desk
- comply with the company's health, safety and security regulations
- such other office duties as may be required in the Home Sales Section

Date: 1 January 199–

Fig 1.5 Job description

- display the draft in a suitable style and in the manner required for publication, emboldening and enlarging text to give prominence to any eye-catching information
- ensure that the advertisement sets out clearly the contact name and address or telephone number for replies
- when submitting the advertisement to the newspaper or journal state:
  i the type of advertisement required, ie *classified* (the cheapest form of advertising as it is grouped with other advertisements under headings without any form of display)
  semi-displayed (more expensive but set apart from other advertisements and usually displayed in a box)
  displayed (the most expensive form in which the advertisement will be fully displayed with different typefaces and may be illustrated)
  ii the amount of space required
  iii the date(s) of publication
  iv the number of entries required

SALES CLERK

required by manufacturers of office furniture

Interesting and varied work in a post which calls for good administrative ability and tact. We are looking for a well-motivated person who enjoys working with people and has good keyboarding skills

Salary: £8000 per annum

Please telephone Pauline Adams on 0193 384192 or write with CV to Systems Furniture plc, Brookfield Industrial Estate, Twyford TD3 2BS

Fig 1.6 Advertisement example

▶ JOB APPLICATIONS

An application form may be supplied in response to a job advertisement. This provides the employer with the essential information about each applicant.

The way in which the application form is completed is very important as it may well determine which applicants are invited to attend an interview for a job.

When completing a job application form check that you have:

- entered the information:
  as requested and that it is clear and concise;
  in the format required, eg block capitals;
  neatly;
  with a black pen (desirable when photocopies have to be taken)
- attached a supplementary sheet if there is insufficient space on the form for any of the information requested or if you wish to supply additional relevant information
- obtained permission, in advance, to use the referees you mention, and that you have supplied their full names and addresses (including their positions held, eg Head of Business Studies
- retained a copy of the form for future reference
- no spelling or grammatical errors on the form or on supplementary sheets

If an application form is not provided, it is a good idea to send a neatly written or typed curriculum vitae (CV) (*see* Fig 1.7).

A letter should accompany the application form or CV expressing your interest in the post and your keenness to attend an interview.

Induction course

This provides the means of introducing new employees to their company in order to assist them to be effective in their jobs as quickly as possible. The following items might be included in an induction course:

Information about the company

- an outline of the background to the company and its structure, organisation, products and markets. It is useful to issue employees with an organisation chart
- main lines of communication within the company, including arrangements for consultation, grievance procedures and membership of trade unions
- health and safety regulations
- security regulations
- social facilities
- a tour of the premises. The new entrants should have their attention drawn to points of safety, such as the location of fire alarms, fire equipment, fire escapes and first-aid personnel and equipment

Individual information

- personnel policies relating to conditions of employment including salaries, pensions, hours of work, holidays, etc
- career development: training programmes and opportunities for further education
- training for the job and an introduction to colleagues in the workplace
- training on company equipment, ie telephone, fax, copier and computer

▶ PROGRESS CHECK

Multiple choice questions

1 Which of the following services are performed by the office in the overall functioning of an organisation?
a manufacturing goods for sale
b transporting goods to customers
c receiving and processing information concerning the sale of goods
d designing new products for manufacture

CURRICULUM VITAE

Name:	Kate Louise Johns
Address:	Crossways, 18 Parkway Gardens, Twyford, Westshire TD3 2BS
Telephone:	0193 621895
Date of birth:	14 March 1978
Nationality:	British
Next of kin:	Mr P L Johns (my father)
Education:	
Sept 1990–July 1995	Twyford Comprehensive School Post of responsibility held: Member of School Council
Sept 1995–June 1996	Twyford College Administration NVQ 2

Qualifications gained:

Subject	Examination	Grade	Date
Art and Design	GCSE	3	1995
English	"	1	"
French	"	4	"
Home Economics	"	2	"
Human Biology	"	1	"
Mathematics	"	2	"
Social and Economic History	"	2	"
Business Administration	NVQ Level 2	Pass	1996

Work experience:	
Sept 1995–June 1996	J Sainsbury plc, Twyford Part-time Sales Assistant
April 1996	Plessey Electronics plc Office duties in all major departments
Interests:	Cinema, swimming, tennis, travelling abroad
Referees:	Mr J R Turner Head of Business Studies Twyford College Park Avenue Twyford TD3 4AW
	Mrs G Smart Manager J Sainsbury plc The Square Twyford TD4 6AT
Other information:	I am able to commence work in July 19–

14.6.19–

Fig 1.7 A curriculum vitae

2 Which of the following is a joint stock company?
- **a** Gray & Robson (Stockbrokers)
- **b** Dorset County Council
- **c** Barclays Bank plc
- **d** Renshaw & Crew (Stocktakers)

3 Which of the following positions is likely to be included in the blank space on the organisation chart in Fig 1.8?
- **a** financial controller
- **b** factory manager
- **c** general manager
- **d** personnel manager

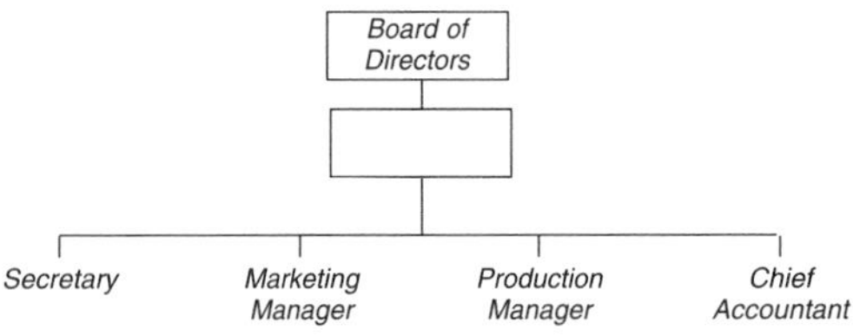

Fig 1.8 Organisation chart

4 The capital of a sole trader belongs to its:
- **a** debtors
- **b** proprietor
- **c** creditors
- **d** chief accountant

5 The person to whom an employee is accountable is stated in:
- **a** a job advertisement
- **b** an application form
- **c** a job description
- **d** a curriculum vitae

6 The marketing department of a company is responsible for:
- **a** organising the production of goods to be sold
- **b** buying raw materials for manufacture
- **c** controlling the stock levels of finished goods
- **d** forecasting the demand for products

7 An induction course is an in-house scheme for:
- **a** introducing new staff to a company
- **b** inducing staff to join the company's pension scheme
- **c** promoting staff
- **d** selecting and engaging new staff

8 A customer telephones to complain about the delay in supplying an order. Would you:
- **a** advise the customer to place an order with another firm
- **b** note the customer's complaint and offer to ring back when you have checked on the delivery position
- **c** explain that it is not your fault and that the caller should speak to the sales manager
- **d** suggest that the customer should allow more time as delays frequently occur?

9 Rearrange the categories of personnel in the correct order according to the usual line of authority (the most senior first):

a executives	**c** proprietors
b office staff	**d** supervisors

10 Pair the two lists of words. Note that there is a surplus item in the second column.

Business unit	Organisation
a sole trader	**a** Home Office
b partnership	**b** painter and decorator
c central government	**c** accountant
d public limited company	**d** Lancashire County Council
	e furniture manufacturer

Short answer questions

State the missing words or phrases.

11 One of the functions of an office is to process..

12 When centralised, a reprographics centre supplies the .... needs of all departments.

13 A sole trader ....and runs the business, receiving all profits and being responsible for any losses incurred.

14 A despatch clerk is employed in the .... department.

15 When receiving telephone calls from customers, greet them promptly and ....

Supply brief answers to the following questions:

16 Name three documents used in the process of employing new staff:
a..
b..
c..

17 Give an example of each of the following organisations:
a Industrial ....
b Commercial..
c Service..

18 Suggest three characteristics of working in a large organisation:
a..
b..
c..

19 List three factors which establish good relations between staff and customers:
a..
b..
c..

20 State three items of information which should be given in a job description:
a..
b..
c..

Section B
OFFICE SYSTEMS, PROCEDURES AND RECORDS

Unit 2
Buying and selling

Competences developed in this unit:

- Prepare a variety of documents
- Order goods and services

(NVQ2)

Fig 2.1 shows the documents which flow between a purchaser and seller in a credit transaction and the departments and sections involved in the process. This is explained in more detail in the following pages as we see how OP Electronic Services set about purchasing three desks for their word processing operators.

The transaction begins with the supervisor in the word processing centre completing and issuing a requisition (Fig 2.2).

▶ REQUISITION

Purpose: to request goods to be drawn from stock or purchased; a stock requisition is used for requesting goods from stock and a purchases requisition is used when goods are not in stock and have to be purchased
Prepared by: person in department requesting goods to be purchased and countersigned, ie authorised, by a supervisor or head of department; it may also be prepared by the storekeeper when stocks need replenishing
Distribution: storekeeper or buyer

▶ SALES ENQUIRIES

There are several ways in which buyers can find out about the price and other details of the goods they wish to purchase. They may send a letter of enquiry and receive in return a catalogue and price list, a quotation, a firm offer or an estimate. The information might also be obtained by telephone; telex; fax; one of the televised information services such as Prestel or Ceefax or by visiting a showroom where the goods can be seen.

Letter of enquiry

Letters of enquiry may be sent to several suppliers to provide the buyer with a selection of offers. The letter must explain clearly what range and type of goods you are enquiring about and what information you are requesting from the supplier, for example:

- price
- whether price includes VAT
- discounts given
- delivery date
- whether delivery charges are made
- any modifications to be made to the standard models

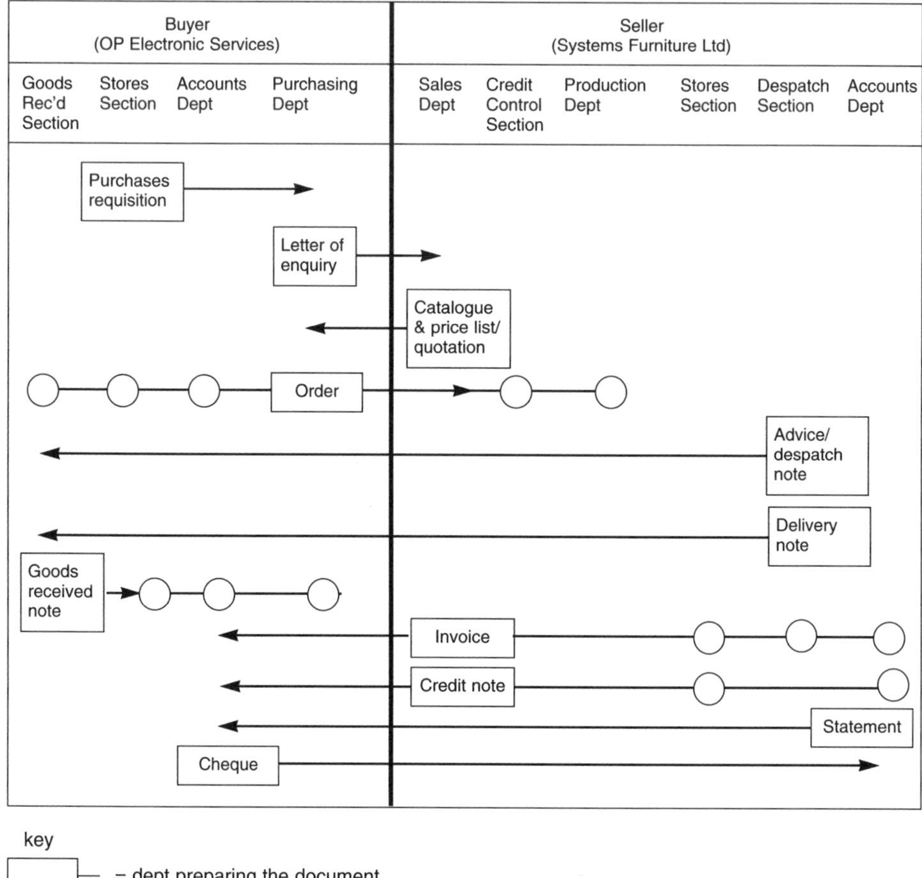

Fig 2.1 Documents used in buying and selling

PURCHASES REQUISITION

No 64

Date 1-3-9

Quantity	Description	Supplier's Cat No	Purchase Order No	Supplier
3	Systems desks 1050mm x 750mm x680mm	AS2	489	Systems Furniture
3	3 drawer pedestals (mobile)	AP4	"	– " –

Signed J Hobbs

Approved J. Edmondson
Buyer

Authorised S Docherty

Fig 2.2 Requisition

- how the information should be supplied, eg:
  - catalogue and price list
  - quotation
  - estimate
  - letter

Fig 2.3 is an example of a letter of enquiry to Systems Furniture plc requesting a quotation for an executive desk. The reply is given in Fig 2.6.

Catalogue

This usually consists of a printed pamphlet giving a description of goods offered for sale; catalogues are normally illustrated with photographs or drawings (Fig 2.4). Instead of including prices in their catalogues, suppliers frequently decide to issue separate price lists. The catalogue and price list do not constitute a definite promise to sell as the goods are offered subject to stocks being available at the time the order is received.

Price list

This contains a short description and the current prices of goods offered for sale; illustrations are not normally given in price lists (Fig 2.5).

Quotation

A buyer requesting goods which require modifications and are not included in the standard range will normally receive a quotation. This may be sent in a letter or it may be a standard

OP ELECTRONIC SERVICES

OP House, PO Box 19, Bracknell, Berks, RG21 3PT

Tel: 01344 61839 Telex: 487361 Fax: 01344 82193

26 February 199-

Systems Furniture plc
Brookfield Industrial Estate
TWYFORD
Westshire
TD3 2BS

Dear Sirs

We are interested in purchasing an executive desk made in mahogany with a 3-drawer fixed pedestal to a modified size as given in the attached drawing and would be pleased to receive your quotation. Please supply details of your price including VAT, discount given and any delivery charges made, together with delivery date and terms of payment.

An early reply would be appreciated.

Yours faithfully
OP ELECTRONIC SERVICES

J Edmondson

J EDMONDSON
BUYER

Fig 2.3 Letter of enquiry

Chess office furniture is the award-winning, innovative new range from Flexiform which has been designed to be flexible and increase the efficiency of your office accommodation.

The range offers desking, screening and personal storage solutions to suit different applications, tasks and budgets.

Chess is complemented by Flexiform's comprehensive range of storage and filing systems which are attractive, save staff time and up to 60 per cent of floor space.

Using the very latest CAD software Flexiform offers expertise in interior design, office planning and filing audits.

All products carry a five-year warranty and are designed to comply with all relevant British and European Standards for safety and performance.

Visit Flexiform's Bradford, London or Edinburgh showroom to view our complete range of business furniture.

Head Office, Showroom and Sales Centre
The Business Furniture Centre,
1392 Leeds Road,
Bradford, BD3 7AE
Telephone 01274 656013
Fax 01274 665760

London Showroom and Sales Centre
Business Design Centre,
52 Upper Street, Islington Green,
London N1 0QH
Telephone 0171 226 9955
Fax 0171 226 6552

Edinburgh Showroom and Sales Centre
Kirkbrae House,
43 Lasswade Road, Liberton,
Edinburgh, EH16 6TD
Telephone 0131 664 4747
Fax 1031 664 4310

Fig 2.4 Catalogue page

form such as that illustrated (Fig 2.6). It should be noted that the price and terms are offered for a stated period.

The quotation is typed in duplicate with a copy filed in the customer's file in the Sales Department. If an order has not been received within 14 days of sending the quotation, a follow-up letter or telephone call will be made to the customer, asking if the quote was acceptable and offering to supply any further information that may be required.

Firm offer

If the seller decides to give the prospective buyer a special price for his goods he writes a letter containing a firm offer. This offer is usually only open to the buyer for a certain period of time.

Estimate

An estimate differs from a quotation in that the ultimate cost can vary from the price 'estimated' and it is usually supplied when work such as building or repairing has to be undertaken.

Tender

If a local authority or other public body requires goods or services to be supplied it will advertise for tenders to be submitted by a certain date. The tender is another method of offering to supply goods or to carry out work at a specific price and is similar to an estimate.

Choosing the supplier

You may have to consider the offers made by several suppliers and, if so, the key factors in

SYSTEMS FURNITURE plc

Brookfield Industrial Estate, Twyford, Westshire TD3 2BS

Tel: 0193 384192 | Telex: 342689 | Fax: 0193 219673

PRICE LIST

Cat No	Description	Price (ex-warehouse) £
OFFICE FURNITURE		
	Systems desks – for keyboards and VDUs – with pencil drawers in sizes:	
AS1	1200mm wide 750mm deep 680mm high	300
AS2	1050mm wide 750mm deep 680mm high	280
AS3	750mm wide 750mm deep 680mm high	260
	Systems desks (split level) with pencil drawers in sizes:	
AS4	1200mm wide 750mm deep 720/680mm high	320
AS5	1050mm wide 750mm deep 720/680mm high	300
	Executive desks with pencil drawers in sizes:	
AE1	1800mm wide 850mm deep 720mm high	400
AE2	1500mm wide 850mm deep 720mm high	360
AP1	Fixed pedestal – 2 drawer	80
AP2	Fixed pedestal – 3 drawer	100
AP3	Mobile pedestal – 2 drawer	100
AP4	Mobile pedestal – 3 drawer	120

Note: All prices exclude VAT

Fig 2.5 Price list

selecting the one to receive the order should be based on:

- price of the goods
- quality of the goods
- delivery costs, if any
- delivery date
- VAT – is it included in the price?
- trade discount – this is an allowance from the invoice or list price of goods; it is deducted on the invoice and it does not depend on the time of payment. It is given as an allowance for a large order, an agent's profit, trade allowance or as a correction of the list price
- cash discount – this is an allowance made for the prompt settlement of an account within a stated period; it is deducted when payment is made
- guarantee
- after-sales service
- reputation of the firm, ie your previous experience with the firm

In the transaction we are following in this book,

QUOTATION

No 222

From: Systems Furniture plc
Brookfield Industrial Estate, Twyford, Westshire TD3 2BS

Tel: 0193 384192
Telex: 342689
Fax: 0193 219673

Bankers: Midland Bank plc, Twyford
National Giro Account No 6/143/2169

Date: 1 March 19-

To: OP Electronic Services
OP House
PO Box 19
Bracknell
Berkshire RG21 3PT

In reply to your enquiry dated 26 February 19- we have pleasure in quoting you for the following:

Supplying one executive desk with 3-drawer fixed pedestal to a modified size as per your drawing @ £560.00. (Offer valid for two months from this date.)

Terms:
Net cash within one month after delivery.
Price includes delivery costs but excludes VAT.
Trade discount: 10%
Delivery: 6 weeks on receipt of order

We look forward to receiving your instructions which will receive our prompt attention.

L A Scott
Sales Manager

Fig 2.6 Quotation

Systems Furniture plc were selected because we were satisfied with the furniture supplied previously; they were able to deliver the goods without any delay; delivery costs were included in the price and a 10% trade discount was offered.

▶ ORDER

Purpose: to request the seller to supply goods (Fig 2.7)
Prepared by: buyer
Distribution: *1* supplier
2 accounts department – for checking invoice
3 stores section – for recording on the stock record card
4 goods received section – notification of goods to be received
5 buyer – file copy

The order form should be completed neatly and accurately with the following details:

- name and address of supplier
- date of order
- quantity, description, cat. no. and price of each item
- method of delivery
- delivery address

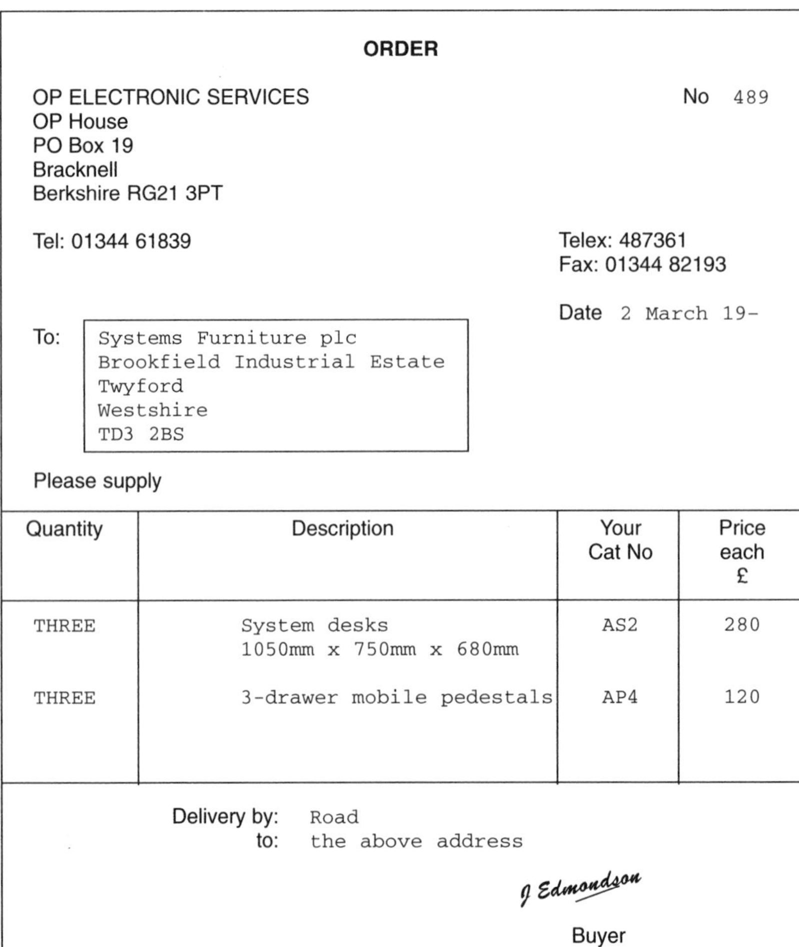

ORDER

OP ELECTRONIC SERVICES
OP House
PO Box 19
Bracknell
Berkshire RG21 3PT

No 489

Tel: 01344 61839

Telex: 487361
Fax: 01344 82193

Date 2 March 19-

To: Systems Furniture plc
Brookfield Industrial Estate
Twyford
Westshire
TD3 2BS

Please supply

Quantity	Description	Your Cat No	Price each £
THREE	System desks 1050mm x 750mm x 680mm	AS2	280
THREE	3-drawer mobile pedestals	AP4	120

Delivery by: Road
to: the above address

J Edmondson
Buyer

Fig 2.7 Order

Each order will be allocated a serial number which is normally pre-printed on the form. When the order form has been checked with the price list, quotation, etc, it is signed by the buyer, the top copy is despatched to the supplier and the remaining four copies distributed as indicated above.

▶ ADVICE/DESPATCH NOTE

Purpose: to inform the customer that the order has been despatched or is ready for despatch (Fig 2.8)
Prepared by: despatch clerk
Distribution: customer

▶ DELIVERY NOTE

Purpose: to serve as an advice of goods delivered (for customer) and a receipt for goods delivered (for supplier) (Fig 2.9)
Prepared by: despatch clerk
Distribution: *1* driver
2 customer

▶ GOODS RECEIVED NOTE

Purpose: to notify internal departments of the arrival of a consignment and the condition of the goods (Fig 2.10)

ADVICE/DESPATCH NOTE

From: SYSTEMS FURNITURE plc
Brookfield Industrial Estate, Twyford, Westshire TD3 2BS

Tel: 0193 384192

Telex: 342689
Fax: 0193 219673
Date: 9 March 19–

To
OP Electronic Services
OP House
PO Box 19
Bracknell
Berkshire RG21 3PT

Your Order No 489

Your Order dated 2 March 19– has been/~~is ready to be~~ despatched

Quantity	Description	Cat No
3	Systems desks	AS2
3	Mobile pedestals	AP4

for SYSTEMS FURNITURE plc

R. Page

Fig 2.8 Advice/despatch note

Prepared by: goods received section
Distribution:
1 accounts department – for checking the invoice
2 stores section – for entering their receipt on the stock record card
3 buyer – notification that the goods have arrived

▶ INVOICE

Purpose: to inform the customer of goods purchased and the amounts charged in a credit transaction, ie one to be paid for in the future – in this case within one month after delivery (Fig 2.11)

Prepared by: sales department (invoice section)
Distribution:
1 customer
2 accounts department – for entering in accounts
3 stores section – for recording on stock control card
4 despatch section – for delivery of goods
5 sales department – file copy

<table>
<tr><td colspan="5">DELIVERY NOTE   No 346
TWYFORD CARRIERS LIMITED
Southdown Road, Twyford, Westshire TD4 8AR</td></tr>
<tr><td colspan="2">Delivered to:</td><td colspan="3">OP Electronic Services
OP House
PO Box 19
Bracknell
Berkshire RG21 3PT</td></tr>
<tr><td colspan="2">By order of:</td><td colspan="3">Systems Furniture plc
Brookfield Industrial Estate
Twyford
Westshire TD3 2BS</td></tr>
<tr><td colspan="2">Date despatched:</td><td colspan="3">9 March 19-</td></tr>
<tr><td rowspan="2">No of packages</td><td rowspan="2" colspan="2">Description</td><td colspan="2">Order</td></tr>
<tr><td>No.</td><td>Date</td></tr>
<tr><td>3
3</td><td colspan="2">Desks
Pedestals }</td><td>489</td><td>2.3-</td></tr>
<tr><td colspan="5">Received in good order and condition
but not examined
Customer's signature T Parrick</td></tr>
</table>

Fig 2.9 Delivery note

Value added tax

VAT is a tax on the supply of certain goods and services (including carriage). Whenever traders buy goods or services to which VAT apply, they receive from the supplier a tax invoice indicating the cost of the goods and the VAT charged on them. When, in turn, the traders supply taxable goods and services to their customers, they charge them tax at the same rate. Every quarter the traders make a tax return to HM Customs and Excise showing the tax charged to them (input tax) and the tax they have charged to their customers (output tax). They will then pay the difference. If their input tax is greater than their output tax, they are entitled to claim a refund of the difference. VAT is added to the net value of the goods, ie after deducting discounts, to arrive at the net value of the invoice. In the invoice (Fig 2.11), 17½% of the net value of £1080, ie £189, is added to arrive at a net invoice price of £1269.

Purchase invoices

When an invoice is received from a supplier the following procedure is carried out:

- A check is made to ensure that the goods stated in the invoice have been delivered and that they were satisfactory. Source of reference: goods received note
- The price and terms are checked. Source of reference: copy of the order

GOODS RECEIVED NOTE

No 116

Supplier Systems Furniture plc
Brookfield Industrial Estate
Twyford
Westshire TD3 2BS

Date received: 9 March 19-

Quantity	Description	Order No
3	Systems desks	489
3	Mobile pedestals	489

Carrier	Received by	Checked by	Bay No
Twyford Carriers Ltd	T Parrick	J Butterworth	5

Condition of goods Satisfactory except for one pedestal which has been badly scratched

Distribution: Accounts ✓
Stock Control
Buyer

Fig 2.10 Goods received note

- The extensions are checked – extensions are the various calculations including:
  - ○ quantity of goods multiplied by the rate per article
  - ○ addition of the different items
  - ○ addition of carriage
  - ○ calculation and deduction of trade discount
  - ○ calculation and addition of VAT
- If all of the above are correct, the invoice is stamped 'checked' and passed to the purchases ledger clerk who enters it in the purchases day book and authorises it for payment by the cashier
- If there is an error, the invoice is returned to the supplier with the request that an amended invoice should be issued or a credit note or debit note prepared to correct the error.

Sales invoices

Checklist for calculating and completing invoices

Transfer data from related documents:

- advice note/despatch note
- quotation
- order

to the invoice recording:

INVOICE

No 1431

From: SYSTEMS FURNITURE plc
Brookfield Industrial Estate, Twyford, Westshire TD3 2BS

Tel: 0193 384192
VAT Registration No 3027560 21

Telex: 342689
Fax: 0193 219673
Date: 10 March 199-

To: OP Electronic Services
OP House
PO Box 19
Bracknell
Berkshire RG21 3PT

Terms: Net cash within one month after delivery
Delivered to Bracknell

Completion of Order No 489 dated 2 March 19-

Quantity	Description	Cat No	Price each £	Cost £	VAT rate %	VAT amount £
3	System desks	AS2	280	840.00		
3	3-drawer mobile pedestals	AP4	120	360.00		
				1200.00		
	Less trade discount	10%		120.00		
				1080.00	$17^1/_2$	189.00
	Plus VAT			189.00		
				1269.00		

Delivered on: 9.3.-
by: Twyford Carriers Ltd

Fig 2.11 Invoice

- customer's name and address
- date of invoice
- terms of payment agreed
- order details
- quantity, description, catalogue no. and price of each item
- delivery date and address

Calculate and record:

- cost of each item
- total gross cost of all items
- trade discount (deducted)
- cost of carriage – if charged (added)
- VAT (added)
- net invoice total

A print calculator is useful for making these calculations.

▶ CREDIT NOTE

Purpose: to notify the customer of a reduction in the amount charged on an invoice because of goods being damaged or lost in transit; an error being made in the price quoted in an invoice; the wrong quantity or type of goods being sent or faulty goods being sent (Fig 2.12)
Prepared by: sales department (invoice section)
Distribution: *1* customer
2 accounts department – for entering in accounts

CREDIT NOTE

No 12

From: SYSTEMS FURNITURE plc
Brookfield Industrial Estate, Twyford, Westshire TD3 2BS

Tel: 0193 384192

Telex: 342689
Fax: 0193 219673
Date: 16 March 19

VAT Registration No 3027560 21

To:
OP Electronic Services
OP House
PO Box 19
Bracknell
Berkshire RG21 3PT

Ref: Invoice No 1431
dated 10.3-

Quantity	Description	Price each £	Cost £	VAT rate %	VAT amount £
1	Defective pedestal (3-drawer mobile) damaged in transit	120	120.00		
	Less trade discount		12.00		
			108.00	$17\frac{1}{2}$	18.90
	Plus VAT		18.90		
			126.90		

Fig 2.12 Credit note

3 stores section – for recording on stock control card
4 sales department – file copy

The credit note is calculated from the invoice to which it relates and the entries relating to the returned or reduced item are similar to those for an invoice, including the deduction of trade discount and addition of VAT.

▶ STATEMENT

Purpose: to inform the customer of the total amount owing and to request payment; it is a copy of the customer's account in the sales ledger containing a record of all transactions for a given period, usually a month (Fig 2.13)
Prepared by: accounts department (sales ledger clerk)
Distribution: *1* customer
2 accounts department – file copy

The statement may begin with a balance brought forward from the previous period and followed by the net amount of each transaction carried out in the current period. These transactions are entered as follows:

- invoices for sales are entered in the Dr column and added to the balance
- credit notes for sales returns (cancellation of sales) and cheques received are entered in the Cr column and deducted from the balance
- the balance column is updated after every entry, the last amount in the balance column being the amount owing at the end of the period covered by the statement

STATEMENT

From: SYSTEMS FURNITURE plc
Brookfield Industrial Estate, Twyford, Westshire TD3 2BS

Tel: 0193 384192

Telex: 342689
Fax: 0193 219673

VAT Registration No: 3027560 21

Date: 31 March 19--

To:
OP Electronic Services
OP House
PO Box 19
Bracknell
Berkshire RG21 3PT

Terms: Net cash within one month after delivery

Date 19--	Details	Ref No	Dr £	Cr £	Balance £
March 10	Sales	1431	1269.00		1269.00
March 16	Returns	12		126.90	1142.10

The last amount in the balance column is the amount owing.

Please return this statement with your remittance.

2.13 Statement

The transaction is completed when the purchaser sends a cheque to the seller, received in the accounts department.

▶ COMPUTERISED PROCEDURES FOR BUYING AND SELLING

- A word processor can be used to prepare letters of enquiry or any standard letters using texts stored on a disk. Also the suppliers' names and addresses can be merged from a mailing list file to a text file to provide automatic typing in one operation of both letter and address.
- All forms used in buying and selling can be completed on a word processor, the machine tabulating to the correct positions on the forms and automatically reproducing any standard data.
- Suppliers' and customers' records can be filed on a computer disk providing a rapid

means of locating and printing details from them.

- To order goods by computer:
  a the operator keys in catalogue/part numbers to reveal on the terminal screen:
    i a description of the item
    ii the preferred supplier and any other suitable suppliers
    iii the current price
    iv discounts allowable
    v carriage charges
    vi normal delivery time
  b the operator keys in details of the order placed to:
    i record it in the purchase record file
    ii print the order at the end of the day
    iii sort the orders by supplier to enable all the orders for one supplier to be printed on the same form
- To prepare invoices and statements by computer:
  a the operator keys in the code number of the customer to print out the customer's name and address on the invoice form
  b the operator keys in the product code number and the quantity for each item ordered to print out the type and quantity of goods with their unit and total prices
  c when the last item has been entered the computer calculates and prints the gross total price of goods ordered, discounts, VAT and the net invoice price
  d when all of the invoices for a day have been completed the computer can be instructed to print out:
    i the daily total of sales and if necessary the total sales for each country, region or division
    ii the totals of each product sold
    iii the totals of each product remaining in stock after the day's sales
  e at the end of the month the statements are printed automatically from the data entered into the sales record file when the invoices and credit notes are prepared
- If terminals are 'on line' to a computer the following tasks are carried out automatically:
  a when the order clerk keys in details of an order, the computer stores it on the purchase record file.
  b when the goods received clerk keys in the details of goods received the computer checks whether these agree with the data supplied in *a* on the purchase record file
  c when the accounts clerk keys in details from the supplier's invoice the computer checks these with the data supplied in *a* and *b* on the purchase record file and then enters the results in the supplier's account

▶ PROGRESS CHECK

Multiple choice questions

1 An internal request for goods to be drawn from stock should be in the form of:
a a stock card
b a goods received note
c an order
d a requisition

2 Which one of these documents used in a business transaction is out of order?
a quotation
b goods received note
c order
d advice note

3 The net amount of the invoice in Fig 2.14 is:
a £94.05
b £133.95
c £148.05
d £103.95

4 A goods received note is completed when:
a goods are checked against the advice note
b goods are ordered
c goods are ready to be despatched
d goods are invoiced

5 Rearrange the following quotations in price order, beginning with the cheapest (assume a carriage charge of £25):
a £800 excluding VAT carr paid
b £800 including VAT ex-works
c £800 excluding VAT carr fwd
d £800 including VAT carr paid

INVOICE Terms: 5% trade discount Carriage paid Net one month					
Quantity	Description	Cat No	Price each £	Total £	VAT @ 17½% £
20	Ream of white copying paper	X100	6		

Fig 2.14 Extract from invoice

6 A customer telephones to ask for the list price (Fig 2.5) of the largest split level systems desk you manufacture.
Would you say:
a £260
b £300
c £320
d £400?

7 The purpose of an invoice is to:
a charge the customer for goods supplied
b inform the customer of the total amount owing at the end of the month
c give the estimated cost of goods ordered
d allow the customer credit for goods returned

8 The net amount of the invoice on p. 22 will be payable to:
a Systems Furniture plc
b HM Customs & Excise
c Twyford Carriers Ltd
d OP Electronic Services

9 Rearrange the following documents in the order in which they are prepared with the first at the top:
a statement
b quotation
c invoice
d order

10 Pair the following lists of words (note that there is a surplus item in the second column):

Business document	Explanation
a price list	**a** internal document prepared before order
b delivery note	**b** internal document prepared after order
c goods received note	**c** document sent before order
d requisition	**d** document sent after order
	e internal document prepared at the same time as the invoice

Short answer questions

State the missing words or phrases:

11 A/an .... is sent to a customer at the end of the accounting period showing the total amount owed.

12 In order to encourage customers to pay promptly, a firm may offer a/an........
....

13 The document a firm will send to a customer if there has been an overcharge is a/an...

14 Give the name of the document which informs the customer that goods have been sent. ....

15 VAT is .... the discounted price of goods, in order to arrive at the net invoice price.

Supply brief answers to the following questions:

16 Explain three ways in which trade discount differs from cash discount:
a ....
b ....
c ....

17 Suggest three documents which enable buyers to find out about the price and other details of the goods they wish to purchase:
a ....
b ....
c ....

18 State departments or sections to which copies of a goods received note would be sent and the reasons why each require those copies.
a ....
b ....
c ....

19 State three extensions which have to be checked on an invoice.
a ....
b ....
c ....

20 For what purposes are each of the following documents used by the buyer?
a quotation: ....
b order: ....
c invoice: ....

Unit 3
Stock control

Competences developed in this unit:

- Order, monitor and maintain stock
- Issue stock items on request

(NVQ2)

Equipment and materials for the factory and offices must be carefully controlled so that they are always available in the stores when they are required. A stock control card (or bin card as it is sometimes called) is kept for each item giving a record of receipts and issues together with the maximum, minimum and re-order levels.

► MAXIMUM STOCK

The maximum stock figure is the largest quantity of stock which should be held at any one time to avoid over-stocking. It ensures that capital is not tied up in excessive amounts of stock, that valuable store-room space is not used unnecessarily and that the stock does not deteriorate or become obsolete in the store room.

► MINIMUM STOCK

The minimum stock figure is the smallest quantity which should be maintained to prevent stocks from running out and, in order to allow the buyer time to replenish the stock before the balance in hand is used up, a re-order level is given to remind the buyer to place a further order.

► RE-ORDER LEVEL

This is the level at which stock should be re-ordered and is determined as follows:

$$\text{daily usage} \times \text{number of days for delivery} + \text{minimum, stock level}$$

For example, in the case of the headed A4 bond paper it is estimated that half a ream is used daily, 20 days are required for orders to be delivered and the minimum stock level is 10. The re-order level is, therefore:

$$\tfrac{1}{2} \times 20 + 10 = 20$$

When the amount of stock has been reduced to the re-order level the stock control clerk knows that a further quantity of the item must be ordered. The clerk is guided in the amount of the order as the total of the balance in stock and the new order must not exceed the maximum stock figure.

Stocktaking takes place at regular intervals, when a physical check is made of all items in stock. These are recorded on a stock list (*see* Fig 3.1) and the total in stock should agree with the balance stated on the stock control card (*see* Fig 3.2), eg 25 reams of headed A4 bond paper were in stock on 1 January and this figure appears on the stock list and on the stock control card for this item. Every receipt, issue or order placed is recorded on the stock control card. In the example given, on 2 January, P Sherwin requested and was issued with 3 reams of paper on requisition No 141, reducing the balance to 22. On 5 January L Tyler requested and was issued with 2 reams of paper on requisition No 159, and this further reduced the balance to 20. This last issue brought the balance down to the re-order level and so an order (No 123) was placed with a supplier for another 30 reams. Note that the amount ordered and the existing stock balance should not exceed the maximum of 50. When the order was received on 15 January the date was entered in the 'on order' column and the date, quantity, invoice no and new balance,

STOCK OF STATIONERY AT 1 JANUARY 19—							
Ref No	Item	Location	Unit Size	Maximum	Re-order Level	Minimum	Balance in stock
100	Headed bond paper A4	A1	ream	50	20	10	25
101	Headed bond paper A5	A2	ream	50	20	10	44
102	Plain bond paper A3	A3	ream	30	10	5	12
103	Plain bond paper A4	A4	ream	60	20	10	52
104	Plain bond paper A5	A5	ream	50	20	10	28
105	Bank paper A3	A6	ream	30	10	5	28
106	Bank paper A4	A7	ream	60	20	10	54
107	Bank paper A5	A8	ream	50	20	10	18
108	Memo forms A4	A9	ream	20	6	4	10
109	Memo forms A5	A10	ream	20	6	4	14
110	Postcards	A11	50 pkt	20	6	4	12
111	Compliment slips	A12	50 pkt	20	8	6	12
112	Envelopes C3	B1	25 pkt	10	5	3	8
113	Envelopes C4	B2	25 pkt	20	6	4	14
114	Envelopes C5	B3	25 pkt	30	10	5	20
115	Envelopes C6	B4	25 pkt	40	12	8	38

Fig 3.1 stock list

STOCK CONTROL CARD

Item: Headed A4 bond paper

Store ref: 100
Location: A1

Maximum: 50
Re-order level: 20
Minimum: 10
Unit: Ream

Date	Receipts		Issues			Balance in stock	On order			
	Quantity	Inv No	Quantity	Reqn No	Dept/ staff		Date ordered	Quan- tity	Order No	Date rec'd
19--							19--			19--
Jan 1						25	Jan 5	30	A123	Jan 15
" 2			3	141	P Sherwin	22				
" 5			2	159	L Tyler	20				
" 8			2	163	P White	18				
" 15	30	S193				48				

Fig 3.2 Stock control card

now 48, in the receipts column.

The stock list may also be called a stock inventory. If, as a result of stock-taking, there is a discrepancy between the amount of stock in hand on the inventory with the amount recorded on the control card, an adjustment is made to the stock control card figure. For example, if stock-taking on 15 January revealed a stock figure of 46 reams instead of the 48 reams recorded, the balance on the stock control card would be adjusted by the following entry:

'Jan 15 Stock check Balance: 46'

▶ ADVANTAGES OF STOCK CONTROL

An effective stock control system should enable a firm to:

- keep an accurate check on the quantities of stock issued and avoid pilferage
- ensure that production is not stopped as this would happen if the stores ran out of stock
- minimise the space occupied by stock
- avoid deterioration or goods becoming obsolete

▶ RECEIPT OF GOODS

When receiving goods into stock, the stock control clerk should ensure that they are supplied in accordance with the order and that the seller has complied with the conditions laid down in the Sale of Goods Act 1979, for example that the goods are of 'merchantable quality', ie fit for the purpose intended and that they correspond with their description.

▶ INVENTORY

Whereas the purchase of consumables are recorded on stock record cards, the purchase of non-consumables, ie machinery, fixtures and fittings and furniture are recorded in an inventory which is a record for audit purposes of assets acquired. An inventory contains the following information:

- inventory serial number
- description of asset
- serial number of asset
- cost of asset
- name of supplier
- date received
- location of asset

▶ STOCKROOM ORGANISATION

Key factors for the efficient organisation of a stationery stockroom:

- Appoint one person to be in charge of issuing and ordering stationery.
- Allocate a central store room for housing stationery supplies.
- Allocate regular times for the issue and collection of supplies.
- Arrange the stationery neatly in cupboards or on shelves with clear labels at the front.
- Place heavy items on the lower shelves and arrange the items used frequently in the most accessible positions.
- Store any highly inflammable materials in sealed containers and preferably in a metal cupboard or cabinet.
- Prohibit smoking in the storeroom.
- Adopt a FIFO (first in, first out) system for issuing stock to avoid deterioration.
- Check that every issue of stock is covered by a requisition, authorised by a supervisor.
- Enter every issue and receipt on a stock control card, keeping a watchful eye on stock levels.
- When stock levels reach the re-order level, order up to the maximum figure.

▶ COMPUTERISED STOCK CONTROL

Computers can be used to maintain stock records from the minimum and maximum levels stored in their memories. When receipts and issues are entered on the keyboard the balance of stock is automatically updated and the screen shows the operator when the minimum figure has been reached, thus indicating the need for re-ordering. Stock valuations can also be seen and/or printed out as the stock prices are stored on disk.

Many large retail establishments commonly

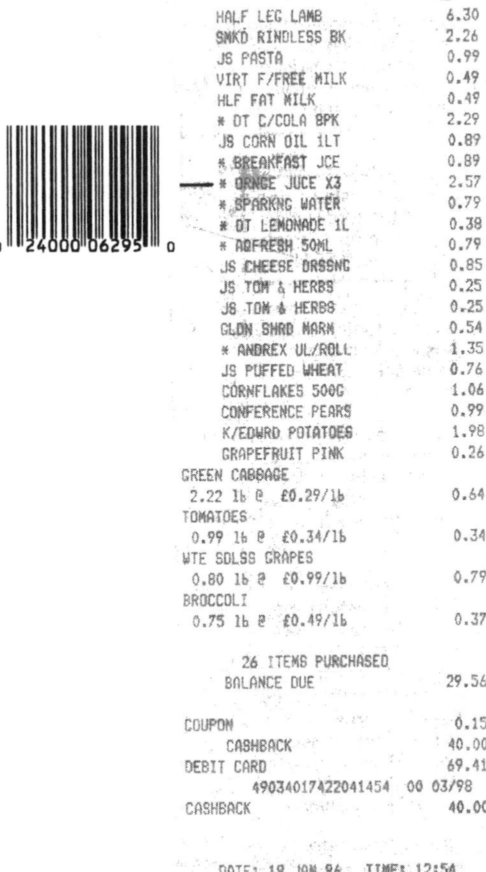

0 24000 06295 0
£
HALF LEG LAMB 6.30
SMKD RINDLESS BK 2.26
JS PASTA 0.99
VIRT F/FREE MILK 0.49
HLF FAT MILK 0.49
* DT C/COLA 8PK 2.29
JS CORN OIL 1LT 0.89
* BREAKFAST JCE 0.89
* ORNGE JUCE X3 2.57
* SPARKNG WATER 0.79
* DT LEMONADE 1L 0.38
* AQFRESH 50ML 0.79
JS CHEESE DRSSNG 0.85
JS TOM & HERBS 0.25
JS TOM & HERBS 0.25
GLDN SHRD MARM 0.54
* ANDREX UL/ROLL 1.35
JS PUFFED WHEAT 0.76
CORNFLAKES 500G 1.06
CONFERENCE PEARS 0.99
K/EDWRD POTATOES 1.98
GRAPEFRUIT PINK 0.26
GREEN CABBAGE
2.22 lb @ £0.29/lb 0.64
TOMATOES
0.99 lb @ £0.34/lb 0.34
WTE SDLSS GRAPES
0.80 lb @ £0.99/lb 0.79
BROCCOLI
0.75 lb @ £0.49/lb 0.37
26 ITEMS PURCHASED
BALANCE DUE 29.56
COUPON 0.15
CASHBACK 40.00
DEBIT CARD 69.41
49034017422041454 00 03/98
CASHBACK 40.00
DATE: 19 JAN 96 TIME: 12:54
LOC: 022 OP: 196 TRANS: 2525

Fig 3.3 Bar coding and receipt (extract)

use bar coding (Fig 3.3) for printing receipts and controlling stocks. When an item is passed over a scanner at the checkout, a computer reads the description and price of the item and relays it back to the checkout where it is displayed on a panel and printed on the customer's receipt. In addition, every item scanned in this way is automatically deducted from the total stock figure to provide instant access to the stock levels of every commodity and, if necessary, create requisitions and orders for further goods to be supplied.

▶ PROGRESS CHECK

Multiple choice questions

1 Which of the following documents provide information for stock control cards?
- **a** statement
- **b** advice note
- **c** cheque
- **d** requisition

2 A stock control card may also be called a:
- **a** bin card
- **b** ledger card
- **c** clock card
- **d** follow-up card

3 A company does not wish to hold too much stock at any one time because:
- **a** more capital than is necessary is tied up in stock
- **b** more storekeepers have to be employed
- **c** better discount rates can be secured by ordering smaller quantities at frequent intervals
- **d** transport charges are lower for small consignments

4 The department of a firm responsible for stock control is:
- **a** sales
- **b** accounts
- **c** buying
- **d** company secretary

5 The balance of stock on the stock control card in Fig 3.4 after the issue on 18 February is:
- **a** 12
- **b** 56
- **c** 30
- **d** 40

6 When restocking the C6 envelopes on the stock control card in Fig 3.4 on 18 February the buyer would order:
- **a** 30
- **b** 12
- **c** 40
- **d** 28

STOCK CONTROL CARD

Ref: 115 Item: C6 envelopes

Location: B4 Maximum: 40
Unit: Pkt Re-Order Level: 12
(containing 25) Minimum: 8

Date	Ref	In	Out	Balance
19--				
Jan 1				38
" 5	Reqn 23		8	
" 17	Reqn 46		20	
" 24	Inv 1178	30		
Feb 2	Reqn 53		14	
" 9	Reqn 74		10	
" 18	Reqn 80		4	

Fig 3.4 Stock control card

7 If two articles of a stock item are used daily, 14 days are required to acquire additional stock and the minimum stock figure is 50, the re-order level would be:
- **a** 100
- **b** 64
- **c** 66
- **d** 78

8 The reason for issuing stationery from stock on a FIFO basis is to:
- **a** avoid deterioration of stationery while in stock
- **b** dispose of recent acquisitions first
- **c** allow stock to appreciate in value
- **d** save valuable store room space

9 Bar coding is a means of:
- **a** controlling stocks of wines and spirits in public houses and restaurants
- **b** printing receipts and controlling stocks
- **c** allocating code numbers to stock cards
- **d** printing statements for goods supplied on credit

10 Pair the following lists of words (note that there is a surplus item in the second column):

a stock record card	**a** computerised stock control
b order	**b** internal request for stock
c bar code	**c** list of stock items
d requisition	**d** bin card
	e external request for stock

Short answer questions

State the missing words or phrases:

11 Bar coding is a means of printing .... and controlling stocks.

12 New items of machinery, fixtures, fittings and furniture are recorded on a/an ....

13 An internal request for goods to be drawn from stock is in the form of a/an ....

14 A/an .... is used to record the receipt and issue of stationery and other items.

15 Re-order level of stock is daily usage × number of days for delivery+ ....

Supply brief answers to the following questions:

16 In stock control what is meant by the following?
- **a** Maximum stock figure: ....
- **b** Minimum stock figure: ....
- **c** Re-order level:....................................

17 List three advantages of an effective stock control system:
- **a**..
- **b**..
- **c**..

18 Office consumable stock should be kept in a cupboard or room which is:

a..

b..

c..

19 Give three reasons for having a maximum stock level of stationery items:

a..

b..

c..

20 The following are automatically revealed in a computerised stock control system:

a..

b..

c..

Unit 4
Receipts and payments

Competences developed in this unit:

- Prepare a variety of documents
- Process claims for payment

(NVQ2)

▶ RECEIVING AND RECORDING PAYMENTS

The cashier lists remittances received in a Cash Receipts Journal, making certain that the cheques are in order. The following points should be checked:

- cheques contain current dates
- the amounts in words and figures are the same
- the payee's name is correct
- the cheques are signed
- any alterations on the cheques are clear and are signed

Any errors on cheques or postal orders should be reported to the supervisor. If a cheque has not been crossed the cashier will cross it with two parallel lines before paying it into the bank. When this has been done the remittances are checked carefully with the cash receipts journal. The use of a print calculator simplifies this work as a tally roll is supplied and the total calculated automatically. The customers' accounts in the sales ledger are credited with the receipts.

▶ RECEIPTS FOR CASH PAYMENTS

Strict security procedures should be observed with the handling of money received in the office. A cheque passing through a bank provides sufficient evidence of payment and receipts are not normally issued where payment is made by cheque, although the receipt or payment of cash requires some form of docu-

CASH RECEIPT	**SYSTEMS FURNITURE plc** **Brookfield Industrial Estate,** **Twyford, Westshire TD3 2BS**	No. 123
Date:	1 April 19-	
	Description	£
One Fixed Pedestal (2 drawer) Cat. No. AP1		80.00
	VAT @ 17½%	14.00
TOTAL		94.00
RECEIVED WITH THANKS		
from:	Mr T W Perkins	
P. T. Watkins Cashier		**VAT Registration no 302 7560 21**

Fig 4.1 Receipt

mentary evidence.

The payer (or remitter) requires a receipt (as in Fig 4.1) to provide written evidence of the payment made. In addition to substantiating the payment of cash, a receipt provides information relating to any VAT which may have been charged for a claim on Customs and Excise.

The payee, when receiving the cash, issues a receipt and keeps a duplicate copy as a source document for recording the remittance in the accounts. The receipt copy also provides evidence of any VAT for which the payee may be accountable to Customs and Excise.

▶ PAYING MONEY INTO THE BANK

The cashier is responsible for checking all remittances received, recording them and paying them into a current account at a bank. The bank supplies a paying-in book (*see* Fig 4.2) for the purpose of recording payments made into an account. Each page is divided into two parts by perforated lines. The bank clerk checks the cash etc and ticks off the amounts on the page, checks the additions and initials the counterfoil which is handed back to the cashier.

An alternative method of paying money into a bank account is to use the bank giro credit slips which are inserted towards the end of cheque books.

▶ POST OFFICE PAYMENTS

The following Royal Mail services are available for the payment of money:

- registration
- postal orders
- cash on delivery

Registration

The Royal Mail Registration Services can be used for posting sums of money and other valuables for next-day delivery. Compensation for loss or damage up to £500 is provided in the Registration Service and up to £2200 in the Registration Plus Service.

If the optional facility of consequential loss insurance is taken out compensation up to £10,000 can be obtained. A consequential loss is a loss to the sender arising out of some failure in the postal service and is over and above the actual value of the articles lost, damaged or delayed, eg a delayed contract might result in the loss of a valuable sale.

The amounts of the registration fee and insurance charge vary according to the value of the articles and compensation required. The fees payable and the compensation limits are given in the *Mailguide*. First-class postage rates are also payable.

Registered and Registered Plus labels must be prepared in the following way:

1 Detach and stick the top portion of the label to the top left-hand corner of the envelope.

Midland Bank plc / first direct

Date 4 May 19- Sortcode

Credit Systems Furniture plc

Account Number

	£	p
£50 Notes		
£20 Notes		
£10 Notes	40	00
£5 Notes	25	00
£1	8	00
S & I Notes	-	-
50p	1	50
20p	-	80
Silver	-	35
Bronze	-	10
Total Cash	75	75
Cheques P.O.s etc.	122	25
	198	00

COUNTER CREDIT

Date 4 May 19-

Cashier's Stamp

Forms for use with other banks are available on request

bank giro credit

Bank	**Midland Bank plc / first direct**	Delete as appropriate
Branch	Twyford	
Customer's Account	Systems Furniture plc	
Paid in by	N Tilling	
Address		

Number of cheques 3

SORTING CODE NUMBER 40 – 24 – 01

ACCOUNT NUMBER 21357603

	£	p
£50 Notes		
£20 Notes		
£10 Notes	40	00
£5 Notes	25	00
£1	8	00
S & I Notes	-	-
50p	1	50
20p	-	80
Silver	-	35
Bronze	-	10
Total Cash	75	75
Cheques P.O.s etc.	122	25

£ 198 00

70

Fig 4.2 Paying in book

2 Enter the sender's name and address on the middle portion of the label which contains the bar coding. Detach and affix it to the reverse of the envelope.
3 Fill in the name and address of the recipient on the remaining portion of the label.
4 Affix postage stamps to the envelope for the total cost of the service (as above).
5 Hand in the label and envelope at a post office or give it to the Royal Mail driver who collects the mail. The label will be date-stamped and initialled for the sender to keep as a receipt.

It is important to ensure that the envelope is strong enough to hold the contents. The package should be sealed with gum or other adhesive substance. The sender should make sure that the contents cannot be removed without breaking a seal, tearing the wrapper or forcing two adhesive surfaces apart. If adhesive tape is used it must be marked with a stamp or a signature.

If several Registered or Registered Plus packets are to be sent, they should be accompanied by a list, in duplicate, of the names and addresses; one list is retained at the post office and the other, when completed and signed, is returned to the sender. These are usually kept in book form and are obtainable from the Royal Mail Customer Service Centre. A signed receipt of delivery may be requested for an additional fee. Confirmation of delivery can be obtained on the day after delivery is due by telephoning 01645–272100 and quoting the 13-digit number on the receipt.

Postal orders

Postal orders are issued in various amounts up to £20. The sender must complete the name of the payee and the name of the post office of payment (*see* Fig 4.3). A postal order may be crossed to ensure that payment is made only through a bank account. A counterfoil is attached and this should be completed, detached and kept for reference. If the sender has omitted to fill in the name of the payee, this must be done by the payee who must also sign his name on the postal order. Postal orders are valid for a period of six months from the last day of the month of issue. After the expiration of that period the order should be referred to the local Royal Mail Customer Services Centre.

Cash on delivery

By means of the cash on delivery service, invoices up to the value of £500 may be sent to a firm's customer and the goods delivered only on payment for the goods concerned. The amount is collected by the postman and credited directly to the firm's bank account. Sums in excess of £100 (£250 for businesses) must, however, be collected on post office premises. This service is used in conjunction with Registered, Registered Plus or one of the Parcelforce services.

Fig 4.3 Postal order

▶ ALLIANCE & LEICESTER GIRO PAYMENTS

Girobank plc is a subsidiary of the Alliance & Leicester Building Society. A London clearing bank, it offers a wide range of services, including full current account (cheque book) banking, with a cheque guarantee card available to qualifying customers. It operates through the telephone and postal network, holding and processing accounts in one central location, Bootle, Merseyside, and providing cash deposit and withdrawal facilities at around 20,000 post offices throughout the UK. Girobank is a founder member of LINK, the national shared network of ATMs (automated teller machines).

Customers are issued with a Link card for drawing cash from Link cash machines. These cards normally have a £100 withdrawal limit but a £250 limit can be made available on written request.

A Delta card may also be requested as this serves three useful purposes:

1 as a charge card (*see* page 43)
2 as a cheque guarantee card (*see* page 43)
3 as a cash card to withdraw cash from Link machines, as referred to above

Alliance & Leicester Giro cheques are normally provided 'crossed' which means that they must be paid into a bank account.

When paying someone who has another bank account, a crossed cheque should be made out and provided direct to the payee who will then deposit it in his or her own bank account. Keyway, an interest paying current account, offers customers a combined £100 cheque/Visa card which will guarantee cheques or transfers up to £100. Current account holders can apply for a £50 cheque card or a combined £50 cheque/Visa card. Either will guarantee cheques or transfers up to £50, but will allow the customer to draw up to £100 at a nominated post office or up to £50 at other offices. The cheque will travel through the bankers' clearing system, to be returned to Girobank who will then debit the payer's account.

When paying someone with an Alliance & Leicester Giro account, the payment may be made by cheque, as above, but a particularly efficient method is to pay by Girobank transfer, which is a free service to customers.

Because all Alliance & Leicester Giro accounts are centrally held and processed on the same computers, it is easy to debit one account and credit another in the same process. The transfer/deposit slip already mentioned also serves as the transfer instruction document. The slip is simply completed with the number of the account being paid, the amount in figures and words, and the date. A message or other appropriate information may be written on the back of the slip which, after being signed, is sent to the bank in one of the pre-addressed postage paid envelopes supplied.

After the payee account has been credited, the slip is sent on to the account holder, together with a statement of account.

Transcash

This is a service enabling anybody to pay cash into an Alliance & Leicester Giro account at almost any UK post office. A small service charge is usually levied on the payer at the post office. Standard Transcash payment slips (*see* Fig 4.4), which must be completed by the payer and handed in with the payment, are provided at post offices. A message or other required information may be written on the back of the slip. After the money has been credited to the payee's account, the Transcash slips are forwarded daily to the account holder together with a statement of account listing the payments.

Business account holders may produce their own personalised payment slips which may be pre-printed with desired account number and referencing information. Account holders producing their own slips may pay the service fees centrally, thus enabling them to offer a free payment service to those from whom they are receiving payment. The Girobank payment slips attached to public services bills, such as electricity and gas, are examples of personalised Transcash slips. Space should be provided on the slips to allow Alliance & Leicester Giro account holders to add their own account number so that they may make payment through the Girobank free transfer service.

Transcash is widely used by the public utili-

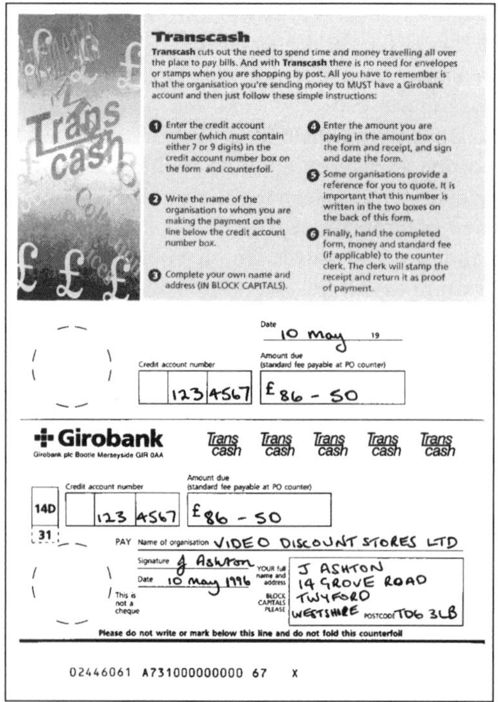

Transcash

Transcash cuts out the need to spend time and money travelling all over the place to pay bills. And with **Transcash** there is no need for envelopes or stamps when you are shopping by post. All you have to remember is that the organisation you're sending money to MUST have a Girobank account and then just follow these simple instructions:

1. Enter the credit account number (which must contain either 7 or 9 digits) in the credit account number box on the form and counterfoil.
2. Write the name of the organisation to whom you are making the payment on the line below the credit account number box.
3. Complete your own name and address (IN BLOCK CAPITALS).
4. Enter the amount you are paying in the amount box on the form and receipt, and sign and date the form.
5. Some organisations provide a reference for you to quote. It is important that this number is written in the two boxes on the back of this form.
6. Finally, hand the completed form, money and standard fee (if applicable) to the counter clerk. The clerk will stamp the receipt and return it as proof of payment.

Date 10 May 19

Credit account number 123 4567

Amount due (standard fee payable at PO counter) £86 - 50

Girobank

Girobank plc Bootle Merseyside GIR 0AA

Transcash Transcash Transcash Transcash Transcash

14D

31

Credit account number 123 4567

Amount due (standard fee payable at PO counter) £86 - 50

PAY Name of organisation VIDEO DISCOUNT STORES LTD

Signature J Ashton

Date 10 May 1996

This is not a cheque

YOUR full name and address BLOCK CAPITALS PLEASE
J ASHTON
14 GROVE ROAD
TWYFORD
WESTSHIRE POSTCODE TD6 3LB

Please do not write or mark below this line and do not fold this counterfoil

02446061 A731000000000 67 X

Front

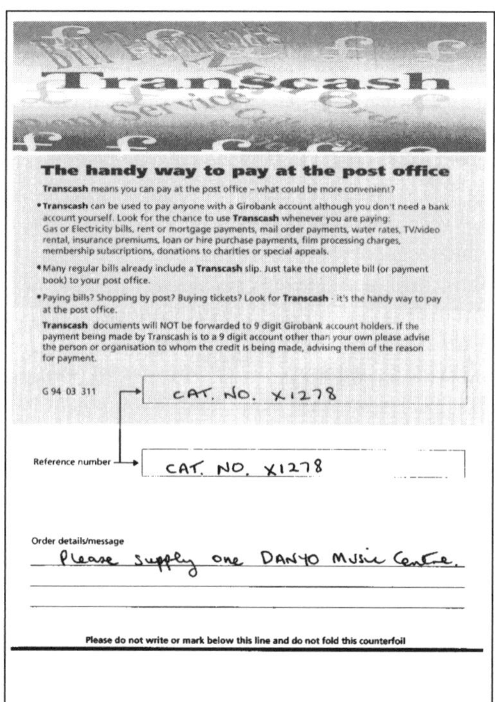

Transcash

The handy way to pay at the post office

Transcash means you can pay at the post office – what could be more convenient?

- **Transcash** can be used to pay anyone with a Girobank account although you don't need a bank account yourself. Look for the chance to use **Transcash** whenever you are paying:
Gas or Electricity bills, rent or mortgage payments, mail order payments, water rates, TV/video rental, insurance premiums, loan or hire purchase payments, film processing charges, membership subscriptions, donations to charities or special appeals.
- Many regular bills already include a **Transcash** slip. Just take the complete bill (or payment book) to your post office.
- Paying bills? Shopping by post? Buying tickets? Look for **Transcash** - it's the handy way to pay at the post office.

Transcash documents will NOT be forwarded to 9 digit Girobank account holders. If the payment being made by Transcash is to a 9 digit account other than your own please advise the person or organisation to whom the credit is being made, advising them of the reason for payment.

G 94 03 311 CAT. NO. X1278

Reference number CAT. NO. X1278

Order details/message

Please supply one DANYO Music Centre.

Please do not write or mark below this line and do not fold this counterfoil

Back

Fig 4.4 Girobank Transcash form

ties for the collection of their bill payments. It is also increasingly used by mail order companies for receiving orders and payments, especially from people without bank accounts. Orders for goods may be written on the back of Transcash slips, or companies may produce their own slips, pre-printed with order details.

Organisations collecting periodic payments from customers or members who are unable to pay by standing order or direct debit may, by arrangement with the Alliance & Leicester Girobank, produce books of personalised Transcash slips, pre-printed with appropriate information including the date payment is due. Customers may then make payment at the post office, using the relevant payment slip.

▶ BANK PAYMENTS

Current account

This is the usual account which a person has with a bank when they wish to have the use of a cheque book and other bank facilities. Money is paid into a current account by the use of a paying-in book or by credit transfers and withdrawals are made by cheque, standing orders or direct debits.

Linked current and savings accounts

A number of accounts and services may be packaged together, as in the case of Midland's Orchard. This provides a current account (with interest on sums which are in credit); a savings account (with higher rates of interest); and 'automatic sweep' from the current account to the savings account, giving automatic transfer when the current account funds reach a predetermined level.

First Direct

First Direct is a telephone operated account

with the normal range of bank services such as current accounts, overdrafts, loans and savings accounts. Its advantage is that it is open for telephoned transactions 24 hours a day every day of the year.

Cheques

Cheques are a very common means of settling accounts because they are efficient, easy to prepare and safe to use. There are three persons involved when a cheque is made out:

1 the drawer: the person who signs the cheque and whose account will be debited (ie reduced by the amount of the cheque)
2 the drawee: the bank on which the cheque is drawn, ie the drawer's bank
3 the payee: the person to whom the cheque is made payable

The three parties concerned are shown on the cheque illustrated in Fig 4.5 which is being used by OP Electronic Services to pay the amount owing on a statement issued by Systems Furniture plc.

Two parallel lines across the face of a cheque with or without the words '& Co' provide an instruction to the banker to pay the amount through a bank only. A crossed cheque cannot be paid to anyone except a banker, ie the payee must pay the cheque into their bank account and their banker must collect the amount from the drawee banker and place it to the credit of the payee. This type of crossing is called a 'general crossing'.

The words 'Account Payee' are normally printed between the lines of the crossing to ensure that the cheque may only be paid into the account of the person to whom it is made out, as in Fig 4.5.

If you require cash for a crossed cheque made payable to you, it is necessary to pay it into your account and make out your own cheque made payable to 'cash'.

If the payee of a cheque without the special crossing wishes someone else to receive the money he or she can endorse the cheque, ie sign their name on the back of it. Thus if Mr X pays into his account a cheque made payable to Mr Y it must have been endorsed by Mr Y.

It is not necessary to endorse cheques which are paid into a bank for the credit of the payee's account, ie when Mr X pays into his bank a cheque made payable to him. The payee's endorsement is required on cheques cashed across the counter of a bank.

The bank statement

Periodically the bank supplies a statement which contains a record of all the transactions which have taken place between the customer and itself involving the receipt and payment of money. A specimen is illustrated in Fig 4.6.

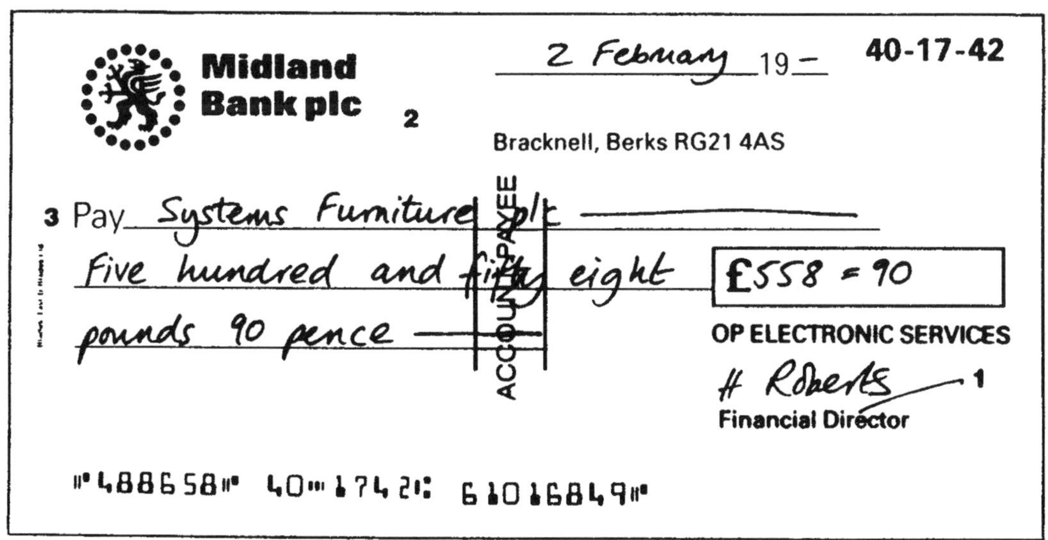

Fig 4.5 Cheque

A statement is a copy of the customer's account with the bank and it shows:

- balance of the account at the end of the previous statement
- credits for money paid into the account debits for money paid out by cheques and other means
- debits for bank charges
- balance of the account at the end of this statement

Advice for bank current account holders:

1 Keep your cheque book in a safe place. If it is lost or stolen advise the bank and the police immediately. It is advisable to keep a separate record of your account number.

2 When making out a cheque
  - **a** always use a pen
  - **b** write the payee's name exactly as described in the invoice or notice to pay, eg Systems Furniture plc
  - **c** write the amount of pounds in words as well as figures
  - **d** begin writing as far to the left as possible and do not leave spaces for other words or figures to be added; draw a line to close up all blank spaces
  - **e** the date must contain the day, month and year
  - **f** sign the cheque with your normal signature as supplied to the bank
  - **g** write the words 'A/C Payee' in the crossing if not pre-printed
  - **h** keep a record of the date, payee's name and amount on the counterfoil

3 If you have a cheque card keep it separately from your cheque book for security reasons.

4 When transferring amounts from your account to another bank account you will need to quote your bank, branch and account numbers. On other occasions you may need to refer to the cheque serial number, located on the specimen cheque (Fig 4.5) as follows:
  - **a** bank and branch number eg 40-17-42
  - **b** account number eg 61016849
  - **c** cheque serial number eg 488658

Credit transfers

A credit transfer system can be used for the payment of several creditors without the drawer having to prepare cheques for each amount. A list containing the names and the amounts is sent to the bank (*see* Fig 4.7) together with one cheque for the total amount. The bank then arranges for credit slips to be sent out to the creditors through their banks. The creditor must in the first place give written authority for payment to be made by credit transfer.

This system is also suitable for individuals who wish to transfer money from a bank to a bank account of a person or business whom they wish to pay. If the remitter does not have a bank account the amount to be paid is handed over the counter of a bank together with a completed credit transfer form and a small fee. The bank clerk will initial and stamp the counterfoil and return it to the remitter as a receipt for the money.

The bankers automated clearing service (BACS) is a fully computerised bank giro credit system in which the funds are paid into the payee's account the same day that the bank's account is debited, providing an even faster means of transferring credit from one account to another.

A comparison of cheques and credit transfers

Cheque	**Credit transfer**
• sent direct to payee by drawer and is more personal	• sent to drawer's bank who send it via clearing house to payee's bank
• arrives next day by post	• takes longer to reach payee
• a separate cheque is required for each creditor	• one cheque is used for several creditors – saving expense in envelopes and postage
• payee must pay cheque into bank	• this is already in the bank and payee does not have to take any action – a safer method of payment

SYSTEMS FURNITURE plc		**Midland Bank plc** TWYFORD, WESTSHIRE TD2 5HD Statement of Account		
19–	Sheet 113 Account No. 21357603	DEBIT	CREDIT	BALANCE Credit C Debit D
MAR 14	BALANCE BROUGHT FORWARD			505.52 C
MAR 16	654627	17.04		
MAR 16	831023	60.00		428.48 C
MAR 17	524776	6.39		422.09 C
MAR 21	524777	35.38		386.71 C
MAR 22	831022	27.30		359.41 C
MAR 24	831026	50.00		309.41 C
MAR 25	359731	6.40		
MAR 25	359732	18.20		
MAR 25	831024	73.63		211.18 C
MAR 29	359733	48.13		163.05 C
MAR 30	831025	9.99		153.06 C
MAR 31	831029	60.00		
MAR 31	100239 CC		861.22	954.28 C
APR 6	359735	6.78		
APR 6	831027	94.35		853.15 C
APR 7	359734	10.95		
APR 7	359737	12.99		
APR 7	831028	19.60		
APR 7	831030	46.75		
APR 7	831032	26.30		736.56 C
APR 8	831033	100.00		
APR 8	PER D/A		350	986.56 C
APR 11	359736	7.79		
APR 11	359738	8.12		
APR 11	TVI LEASING DD	21.25		949.40 C
APR 13	359740	16.48		932.92 C
APR 15	831031	125.18		
APR 15	831035	132.43		
APR 15	831038	50.00		625.31 C
APR 15	BALANCE CARRIED FORWARD			625.31 C

Fig 4.6 Bank statement

• drawer must have a bank account but payee need not	• drawer need not have a bank account but payee must

Standing orders

If a payment has to be made regularly for items such as insurance premiums or hire purchase repayments the bank can be asked to make it from a current account and the customer does not have the trouble of remembering the dates and writing and posting the cheques. The instructions for this service, known as a standing order, must be given to the banker in writing, as must the request to cease such payments.

Direct debiting

Direct debiting is another method of arranging for a bank to make periodic payments on behalf of its customers. When the standing order method is used the drawer initiates the instruction to make payment but in the case of direct debiting it is the payee who requests the bank to collect an amount from the drawer's account. This method can be used for fixed amounts at fixed dates or for varying amounts

TO **Midland Bank plc**

bank giro credit summary form

Branch TWYFORD

Date 1 April 19-

Please distribute the bank giro credits attached as arranged with the recipients.

Number of items 8

Our cheque for £ 4810.56 is enclosed.

Customer SYSTEMS FURNITURE plc

Address BROOKFIELD INDUSTRIAL ESTATE, TWYFORD, WESTSHIRE TD3 2BS

Signature/s *P. T Watkins*

Bank code number	For account of and account number		Amount		Total amount for each bank	
20-19-89	Western Environmental Systems Ltd	19673041	82	00		
20-21-55	T R Hammond & Son Ltd	89472310	132	50		
20-76-14	Quality Sales and Service Ltd	23961045	14	95		
20-83-91	Maystone Car Sales Ltd	11553492	3000	00		
					3229	45
30-99-26	Town & Country Catering	23459847	245	86		
30-17-44	Technical Design Service	94763022	50	00		
					295	86
40-50-34	Customs and Excise	12348832	1045	25		
40-69-91	Westshire County Council	99436814	240	00		
					1285	25
	Totals carried forward £				4810	56

2121

Fig 4.7 Bank giro credit summary form

at irregular intervals.

The payee may send the drawer an invoice and after an agreed interval arrange for the bank to automatically transfer the appropriate amount of credit. By this process the drawer is given an opportunity to check the amount concerned. The payee must, in all cases, have written authority from the drawer in order to arrange for direct debiting to take place.

▶ BANK CARDS

Cheque card

This is a card of authority which makes the cheque more acceptable as a method of payment when goods or services are supplied. A cheque up to the value of £50/£100 accompanied by a cheque card will normally be accepted by traders as they are assured that such a cheque will be honoured by the bank on which it is drawn. Cheque card holders are also entitled to cash cheques up to £50/£100 at any branch of the bank without prior arrangements or any additional charge being incurred.

Some banks issue autocheque cards which are dual-purpose in providing a cheque guarantee card as well as a cash card for drawing cash from an autobank and obtaining a bank statement (see below).

Credit card

A credit card enables a person to purchase goods on credit at shops or other establishments which have agreed to participate in the scheme. It may also be used for withdrawing cash up to the card holder's credit limit, without prior notice, from any branch of the bank. Individuals are notified of their credit limit, which is the maximum amount that they can owe to the bank at any time. The Credit Card Centre issues each card holder with a monthly statement of the amount owing and, provided the card holder makes a payment not later than 25 days after the date on the statement, no charge is incurred.

Charge card

On payment of an annual membership subscription a charge card such as American Express or Diners, may be used to borrow money for the payment of goods and services. With these cards there is usually no credit limit placed on the holder and no interest is charged. Accounts are paid monthly by cheque or direct debit.

Self-service cash card

Bank customers can use a self-service cash card to withdraw cash from autobank cash machines (Fig 4.8) at any time of the day or evening. When customers apply for a self-service card, the bank advises them of their personal identity number (PIN). They have to remember this as it is not recorded on their card nor on any document, for security reasons. If the card is lost or stolen it cannot be used for withdrawing cash unless the personal number is known. To obtain cash the card has to be inserted in the autobank equipment, the personal number keyed in and buttons pressed to select the service and amount required. Step-by-step directions are displayed on a screen to guide the user in operating the machine. The customer is allocated a daily cash withdrawal limit by the bank which remains the same from week to week.

With some machines customers can check their current account balance by having it displayed on the autobank screen. It is also possible to request that a more detailed statement is sent to the customer's address. The most recent machines provide for customers to see details of their last 10 debits or credits, have a printout of their statement showing the last 30 transactions and transfer funds between current and savings accounts.

Advice from the banks for self-service cash card holders:

- keep your cheque book and card separately
- never leave your card in public places or in your car
- keep your card away from any magnetic card used for opening security doors
- do not tell your PIN to anyone

Fig 4.8 An auto bank cash machine

- do not record your PIN in a way that allows another person to discover it
- do not keep a record of your PIN with your card
- never quote your PIN in correspondence or over the telephone
- if you think that someone has discovered your PIN, inform your bank immediately
- if your card is lost or stolen, inform your bank immediately

Computerised banking services

Cheques are now automatically sorted and recorded by computer using magnetic ink character recognition (MICR). You can see the magnetic ink numbers printed at the bottom of the cheque in Fig 4.5. It is expected that computer terminals will soon allow bank customers to carry out more of their transactions in their own offices, homes or even while they are shopping. For example, in the Switch Connect system the sales assistant passes your Switch card through an electronic device that 'reads' the card and produces a voucher for you to sign. In this case, no cheque is used, but the process is similar, as the amount payable is debited to your account and included on your statement within 2 or 3 days. As well as using the card to pay for goods, cash up to £50 can be obtained at the same time from the sales assistant, and this is added to the sales voucher. This process, which uses electronic funds transfer (EFT), eliminates the need for a cheque or for paperwork.

► PROCESSING EXPENSES CLAIMS FOR PAYMENT

Expense claim forms (see Fig 4.9) completed by members of staff must be checked for:

- Accuracy: the arithmetic checked (usually with a calculator)
- Validity: the reason for the claim and the method used checked to ensure that they comply with the company's code of practice
- Authorisation: to ensure that the claim has been approved by an authorised person

Any discrepancies must be singled out and brought to the attention of the supervisor who will be responsible for resolving them with the applicants.

The expenses may have to be coded to particular departmental expense accounts for processing by computer against budgets and any payments involving VAT identified and coded in a VAT outgoing column for eventual inclusion in the VAT return sent to Customs and Excise. Mileage for car travel may also need to be checked against the approved distances for the journeys made. Only authorised and correctly completed expenses claims should be passed forward for payment.

► PROGRESS CHECK

Multiple choice questions

1 The amount to be paid to Mr P Ridley on the employee expenses claim form (Fig 4.9) is:
a £222.26
b £244.66
c £199.86
d £176.90

2 The girobank transcash form (in Fig 4.4) should be
a taken to the post office
b sent to the Girobank Centre
c sent by post to the payee
d taken to the remitter's bank

EMPLOYEE EXPENSES CLAIM

Name: P. Ridley Employee No. 0046 Departmental Code: 08

Bank Code: 302469 Bank account No. 28778135

Date 19–	Particulars	Car Mileage	Public Transport	Car Hire	Hotel accommodation	Meals	Sundries	Total	VAT Recoverable
3 Jan	Visited T.R. Hammond	252				21 15	2 00	23 15	3 15
	and Son Ltd. Birmingham								
	(Parking £2)								
15/16 "	Management Conference		24 50		94 00	35 25		153 75	19 25
	LONDON								
	Hotel: Cumberland								
	Total Mileage	252					Mileage Amount	45 36	
							TOTAL AMOUNT DUE	222 26	22 40

These expenses have been wholly, exclusively and necessarily incurred on authorised business

Signed P. Ridley

Authorised P. Grey Date 2 February 199-

Fig 4.9 Expenses claim form

3 A letter containing a £20 note should be sent:
- **a** recorded delivery
- **b** registered post
- **c** self-service cash card
- **d** cash on delivery

4 Cash and cheques are paid into a bank current account by means of:
- **a** cash and cheque cards
- **b** direct debit
- **c** paying-in book
- **d** cash dispenser

5 A mistake on a cheque can only be corrected by the:
- **a** payee
- **b** payee's bank
- **c** drawer
- **d** drawer's bank

6 In the bank credit transfer system the payee receives the amount by:
- **a** direct payment into his bank account
- **b** cheque posted from the drawer
- **c** credit note posted from the drawer
- **d** cheque posted from the drawer's bank

7 The drawer of the cheque in Fig 4.5 is:
- **a** Midland Bank plc
- **b** OP Electronic Services
- **c** not stated
- **d** Systems Furniture plc

8 The drawer's account no in Fig 4.5 is:
- **a** 401742
- **b** 488658
- **c** 61016849
- **d** not stated

9 A self-service cash card is used to:
- **a** gain entry to the office safe
- **b** make a First Direct telephone call
- **c** obtain credit for the payment of goods
- **d** withdraw cash from autobank cash machines

10 Pair the two lists of words (note that there is a surplus item in the second column):

Expense	**Method of payment**
a suppliers whose accounts are paid monthly	**a** postal order
b hire purchase repayments	**b** credit transfer
c mail order purchase	**c** standing order
d booklet costing 50p	**d** credit card
	e Girobank Transcash

Short answer questions

State the missing words or phrases:

11 When goods are paid for in cash a .... is always issued.

12 A postal order is crossed to ensure that payment is made only through a ....

13 The form used to pay cash into a Girobank account at a post office is ....

14 The computerised bank giro credit system for paying funds into a payee's account is called ....

15 Bank customers must memorise their .... numbers in order to withdraw cash from an autobank cash machine.

Supply brief answers to the following questions:

16 For what purposes would you use each of the following bank cards?

a cheque card...
b credit card...
c self-service cash card...........................

17 State three Royal Mail services which may be used for the payment of money:

a ....
b ....
c ....

18 Name and explain the three parties to a cheque:

a ....
b ....
c ....

19 Give three precautionary measures which should be taken when making out a cheque:

a ....
b ....
c ....

20 List three advantages of using credit transfers:

a ....
b ....
c ....

Unit 5
Petty cash

Competences developed in this unit:

- Check and process routine numerical information (NVQ1)
- Process claims for payment (NVQ2)

Whenever you make a purchase and pay cash on behalf of your firm you are expected to obtain a receipt from the suppliers and complete a petty cash voucher. The voucher is completed with details of the purchase and your signature (*see* Fig 5.1). A supervisor's signature is necessary to give approval for the expenditure. Cash is then paid out from a petty cash box in return for the voucher and receipt.

Petty cash purchases are recorded in a petty cash account (Fig 5.2). An agreed sum of money is allocated to the clerk responsible for petty cash from which the various payments are made. At the end of a month or other period of time the amount spent is refunded by the cashier to the clerk, thus restoring the allocation to the original amount. This method is known as the 'imprest system' with the agreed sum being referred to as the 'imprest' or 'float'. The three stages in the imprest system are:

1 A sum of money (the imprest), eg £100, is allocated to the petty cash account.
2 During the course of the month this money is used to pay for small items of expenditure, eg £75.05.
3 At the end of the month the money spent, eg £75.05, is paid into the petty cash account to restore it to the original amount, ie £100.

Petty Cash Voucher

Folio 20
Date 2 May 19-

For what required	AMOUNT £	p
Ball point pen refills	4	00
plus VAT	-	70
	4	70

Signature L. McCabe

Passed by P Green

Fig 5.1 Petty cash voucher

At any time in the period:

cash held +	current month's vouchers =	imprest
£24.95	**£75.05**	**£100**

Guidelines for the security of petty cash:

- Check sums of money carefully before handing them over.
- Lock the cash in a cash box and keep it in a locked safe.
- Locate the keys to the cash box and safe in a secure place which is only accessible to the petty cashier and supervisor.
- Do not leave your office unattended with the cash box unlocked. Ensure that every payment of cash is supported by an authorised petty cash voucher.
- Make regular checks of the petty cash account and cash to ensure that the petty cash vouchers received + cash held in the box = the imprest.

Key factors in compiling the petty cash account (Fig 5.2) are:

- At the beginning of the month the imprest, ie the balance of cash from the previous month (£17.42) plus cash received (£82.58), is entered on the Dr side of the account. The folio number (CB2) is entered alongside the cash received entry to indicate the cash book page number.
- Every item of expenditure is entered twice

on the Cr side: in the total column and in the appropriate analysis column, eg for the taxi fare £4 is entered in the total column and £4 in the travelling column.

- If the expenditure includes VAT the amount is entered in the VAT column and subtracted from the amount of the purchase in the other analysis column, eg the £4.70 paid for ballpoint pen refills is entered as £4.00 in the stationery column, 70p in the VAT column and £4.70 in the total column.
- The petty cash vouchers are numbered as they are received and filed numerically; the voucher numbers being entered in the petty cash account to facilitate reference to the documents, eg voucher number 20 is entered for the ball point pen refills.
- When totalling the columns at the end of the month the total of all the analysis columns including VAT (£75.05) should be equal to the total payments column (£75.05).
- The total cash paid (£75.05) is subtracted from the imprest (£100) and entered as the balance (£24.95) which is carried down to the Dr side to begin the next month.
- The amount of cash spent (£75.05) is drawn from the cashier and entered on the Dr side in readiness for next month's payments.
- Each of the analysis columns represents an account in the ledger and at the end of the month the total amount is transferred to the ledger account, eg £16.85 in the travelling column is transferred to the Travelling Expenses Ledger Account (L3).

▶ PROGRESS CHECK

Multiple choice questions

1 Imprest is:

- **a** a method of rectifying mistakes in a petty cash account
- **b** a means of topping up the petty cash account
- **c** a form used for claiming petty cash expenses
- **d** a rubber stamp for stamping authorisation marks on petty cash vouchers

Dr — PETTY CASH ACCOUNT — Cr

Received	Date 19–	Details	Fo	V No	Total paid out	Stationery	Office expenses	Travelling	Postage	VAT
17 42	May 1	Balance b/f								
82 58	" 1	Cash received	CB2							
	" 2	Ball point pen refills		20	4 70	4 00				- 70
	" 3	First aid Equipment		21	7 05		6 00			1 05
	" 4	Taxi fare		22	4 00			4 00		
	" 4	Aerogrammes		23	3 98				3 98	
	" 5	Flowers for foyer		24	8 50		8 50			
	" 8	Pkt of envelopes (C4)		25	7 52	6 40				1 12
	" 12	Jar of coffee		26	2 20		2 20			
	" 15	Travelling expenses		27	12 85			12 85		
	" 22	Reg letter envelopes		28	13 75				13 75	
	" 29	Window cleaning		29	10 50		10 50			
					75 05	10 40	27 20	16 85	17 73	2 87
	" 31	Balance c/f			24 95	L1	L2	L3	L4	L5
100 00					100 00					
24 95	June 1	Balance b/f								
75 05	" 1	Cash received	CB3							

Fig 5.2 Petty cash account

2 Petty cash is normally used in an office for the purpose of:
- **a** paying invoices for goods supplied
- **b** drawing cheques under £20
- **c** local cash purchases
- **d** paying for goods purchased on a cash with order basis

3 The main reason for using a petty cash account in an office is:
- **a** to avoid entering small amounts in the cash book
- **b** for security reasons
- **c** to provide new entrants to the office with first-hand experience of controlling cash
- **d** to record invoices received for purchasing petty items of expenditure

4 Payments are entered twice in a petty cash account, once in the total column and again in another column in order to:
- **a** provide confirmation of the amount in the total column
- **b** give an analysis of expenditure
- **c** calculate the total expenditure
- **d** calculate the balance of cash in hand

5 In the petty cash account extract in Fig 5.3 the amount of the imprest is:
- **a** £25.60
- **b** £50.00
- **c** £28.24
- **d** £24.40

6 In Fig 5.3 the total of the postage analysis column at 5 April would be:
- **a** £6.00
- **b** £28.24
- **c** £8.99
- **d** £7.99

7 If the imprest in Fig 5.3 was restored after the transactions on 5 April the petty cash clerk should receive:
- **a** £24.40
- **b** £28.24
- **c** £50.00
- **d** £25.60

8 The 'Fo' column in a petty cash account is used for entering:
- **a** folio numbers of the expenditure accounts in the ledger
- **b** receipt form numbers for cash received by the petty cashier
- **c** code numbers used by the cashier to identify petty cash payments
- **d** folio numbers of the pages of the cash book where petty cash payments are made

9 A petty cash voucher should be countersigned by the:
- **a** petty cashier
- **b** recipient's supervisor
- **c** seller
- **d** recipient of the cash

10 Pair the two lists of words (note that there is a surplus item in the second column):

Expenditure	**Analysis column heading**
a window cleaning	**a** VAT
b VAT for cleaning windows	**b** stationery
c printer ribbons	**c** sundry office expenses
d registered envelopes	**d** cleaning
	e postage

Short answer questions

State the missing words or phrases:

11 .... is normally used in an office for small local purchases.

12 The Fo column in a petty cash account is used for ....

13 A signed .... should be produced when claiming money from the petty cash for office expenditure.

14 The descriptive columns which appear on the credit side of a petty cash book are known as .... columns.

Dr						PETTY CASH ACCOUNT												Cr
Received		Date 19–	Particulars	Fo	V No	Total paid out		Postage		Travelling		Cleaning		Sundry expenses		VAT		
		19--																
25	60	Apr 1	Balance b/f															
24	40	" 1	Cash received	CB8														
		" 2	Postage stamps		20	6	00											
		" 3	Bus fares		21	2	40											
		" 4	Cleaning materials		22	12	50											
		" 5	Tea and sugar		23	5	35											
		" 5	Aerogrammes		24	1	99											

Fig 5.3 Petty cash account

15 In a petty cash system cash held + current month's vouchers = ...

Supply brief answers to the following questions:

16 Give three items that would appear on a petty cash voucher:

a ....

b ....

c ....

17 State the three stages in the imprest system:

a ....

b ....

c ....

18 Suggest the analysis column in which each of the following should be entered:

a floppy disks ....

b postal orders ....

c taxi fare ....

19 State the name of the three columns of a petty cash account in which the purchase of a cash book (costing £6.80+VAT) would be entered and give the amounts entered in each:

a column 1 ....
....

b column 2 ....
....

c column 3 ....

20 Why would you expect to find two signatures on a completed petty cash voucher?

a ....

b ....

Unit 6
Wages and salaries

Competence developed in this unit:
- Prepare a variety of documents

(NVQ2)

Everyone, whether they work part time as a cashier at the local supermarket or full time as an office worker, will be interested to know how their pay is calculated and how and why deductions are made from gross pay. Different methods are used for calculating pay depending on the nature of the work, as will be seen from the following:

1 Flat rate
The term used when an employee is paid an agreed amount for a week (usually for a specified number of hours), a month or a year. The amount, known as basic, remains the same for each pay day until the rate is changed.

2 Overtime
If employees are required to work extra hours they may be entitled to additional pay known as overtime. This is calculated at an agreed rate which may be:
a standard rate which is the same as their normal hourly rate, eg £5.00 per hour
b time and a half which is the normal hourly rate plus half again, eg
£5.00 + £2.50 = £7.50 per hour
c double time which is twice the normal hourly rate, eg £5.00 × 2 = £10.00 per hour

3 Hourly rate
Used for employees whose hours of work vary considerably and especially for part time workers. Time is recorded on a time or clock card and the employee is paid for the number of hours worked in a week or month.

4 Piecework
Commonly used for factory workers to record the time spent on each job, the employee being paid for the number of jobs completed.

5 Commission
Based on performance and paid as an incentive to sales staff.

▶ TIME RECORDING

Where wages are paid on a time basis or the employees work on a flexitime basis, there must be some form of written record of the time worked. If, however, the wages or salaries are calculated on a weekly or monthly 'flat rate' basis the same degree of checking is not essential, but clocking-in cards may still be used to encourage punctuality. This is a simple method of checking the regular attendance of staff because all late or irregular times are highlighted on the cards.

Some recording systems not only record the time staff arrive and leave work but, with the aid of computers, automatically calculate their wages. Each employee is issued with a small personalised plastic card which, when inserted in the timing device (Fig 6.1), registers the attendance time and feeds it into the computer. The employee also sees on a visual display unit the number of hours worked at any time during the working week or month. The terminals are linked to a computer system which can produce a printout giving up to date information on attendance and lateness or overtime worked by staff.

Time recording clocks register the time the employees start work and the time they leave. In many of the systems in use today the employee is given a time or clock card (Fig 6.2) which is used to record the time worked during the course of a week. As the employees enter their place of employment they take their cards

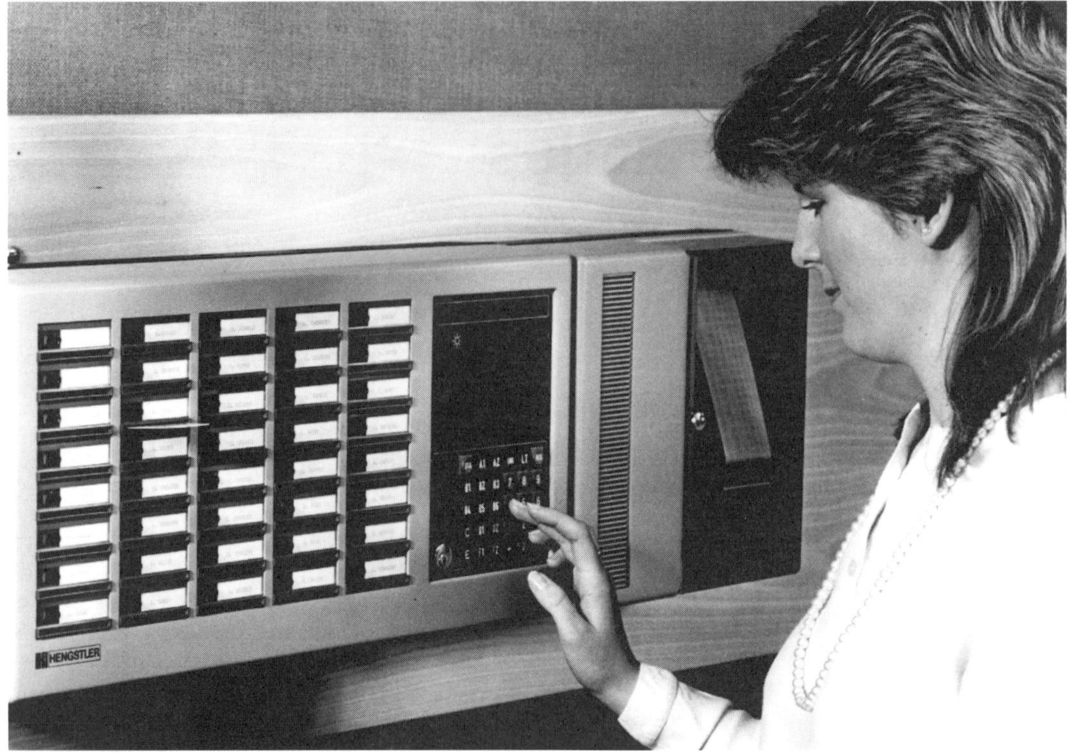

Fig 6.1 Time recording system

out of a rack and insert them in the machine which prints an impression of the time in the appropriate space. The cards are arranged in racks so that the top edges of the cards are visible showing the works numbers or names of the employees.

At the end of the week the completed cards are collected by the wages clerks and form the basis for calculating the gross pay. The total hours worked will be added up and multiplied by the rate of pay per hour. The wages clerk is then ready to calculate the amount of deductions in order to arrive at a net wage.

Deductions

When you receive your pay packet you are given a pay advice slip which states the amount of gross pay, the various deductions which have been made from it and the net pay, ie the amount of money you are actually being paid. The pay slip (Fig 6.3) is explained in more detail below:

1 Basic pay

In this case the basic pay is set at a flat rate or ordinary time of £190.00 for a 38 hour week as stated on the clock card in Fig 6.2. You will see that Michael Brown's total hours are calculated to the nearest quarter of an hour and that is why the extra 7 minutes do not count for pay purposes.

2 Overtime

When this employee works more than 38 hours in a week he is paid double time for his overtime, ie £5.00 × 2 = £10.00 as shown on the clock card.

3 Gross pay

Basic pay + overtime = gross pay,
ie £190.00 + £10.00 = £200.00

This is the figure on which National Insurance contributions are based.

CLOCK CARD					
No 94			Name: Michael BROWN		
Week ending: 19 April 19-			Week No 2		
Day	In	Out	In	Out	TOTAL HOURS
M	0801	1202	1300	1701	8.02
Tu	0758	1200	1301	1702	8.03
W	0802	1202	1301	1659	7.58
Th	0810	1209	1259	1700	8.00
F	0801	1203	1258	1600	7.04
TOTAL					39.07
					£
Ordinary time.....38.. hrs @ £ 5.00 (up to 38 hours)					190.00
Overtime.............1..... hrs @ £ 10.00					10.00
TOTAL GROSS WAGES					200.00

Fig 6.2 Clock card

4 Pension/Superannuation contributions
In a pension or superannuation scheme the employee makes provision for an additional pension to the one provided by the National Insurance contributions. Contributions to a pension scheme may be deducted from gross pay before income tax is calculated if authorised by the Pension Scheme Office.

5 Income tax
This is a statutory deduction, ie the employer is required by law to deduct income tax from the pay of employees to provide a source of income for government expenditure for such services as defence, foreign aid, roads, etc. A pay as you earn (PAYE) method is used to collect this tax with employees paying income tax as they earn their money. The weekly or monthly deduction is related to their actual earnings, eg if the employee receives less pay one week a smaller amount of income tax is paid. The amount of income tax to be deducted by the employer each payday depends upon:

- The employee's code number, eg 350L, as stated on the deductions working sheet. It represents income tax personal allowances and indicates the amount of free pay that the employee can receive without paying tax.
- Total gross pay since the beginning of the tax year.
- The total amount of tax deducted on previous paydays in the current tax year – which runs from 6 April to 5 April.

The three items above are recorded on a P45 form when a new employee joins the firm.

The numbers in the tax code are the first three digits of a person's income tax allowances, eg a single person with a personal allowance of £3500 would have a code number of 350. The letter following the number refers to the type of allowances received. The 'L' in the above example indicates that the employee is in receipt of the single person's allowance. The letter 'H' is used for an employee receiving a married couple's allowance.

The amount of tax to be deducted from an

	PAY ADVICE			
	Name MICHAEL BROWN			Works No 94
	Week No 2	Date 19.04.-		Code No 350L
				£
①	Earnings: basic			190.00
②	overtime			10.00
	bonus			–
	back pay			–
	other			–
③	Total Gross Pay			200.00
④	Less pension			10.00
	Gross pay for tax purposes			190.00
	Less deductions:		£	
⑤	Income tax		27.42	
⑥	National Ins.		15.41	
⑦	Savings		5.00	
	Social club		1.00	
⑧	Total deductions			48.83
⑨	**NET PAYMENT**			141.17

Fig 6.3 Pay advice slip

employee's pay is calculated on a deductions working sheet (Fig 6.4) which is completed as shown on page 56.

Form P45

Parts 2 and 3 of form P45 must be handed to employees when they leave, and Part 1 must be sent to the tax office immediately.

The employee should not separate the two parts. As soon as they begin their next employment they must give both parts of the form to their new employer so that the correct deductions of tax may be continued. The new employer should keep Part 2 and detach Part 3 and send it to the tax office.

6 National Insurance

This is also a statutory deduction which provides cash benefits in return for regular weekly or monthly contributions for unemployment; sickness, attendance allowance and invalidity; National Health Service benefits; industrial injuries disablement; maternity; children; guardian allowances; family credit and income support; one-parent benefits; widowhood; housing and council tax benefits; and retirement.

Employees who pay into occupational pension or superannuation schemes which meet specific requirements can be 'contracted out' and pay lower contributions. The amount of contribution you pay is related to the amount of gross pay you receive and is collected by your employer with income tax and entered on the deductions working sheet (Form P11) as shown on page 56.

Employees who are aged 16 or over and under pension age (65 for men and 60 for women) pay standard rate NI contributions if their gross pay is in excess of the lower earnings limit. This amount may vary from year to year and can be seen in the National Insurance contribution tables. Where earnings do not reach the lower limit there is no liability for contributions from either employee or employer. There is liability for contributions on any payment of earnings made to employees from the date on which they reach the minimum school-leaving age, even though they may be still attending school. Reduced rate contributions are payable by married women and widows authorised to pay contributions at the lower rates.

Your national insurance number is very important. It is used to record the contributions you pay and your benefits depend on these. It is usually given to you on a numbered card when you leave school and remains the same all your working life. You are required to give it to an employer when you start working for them. If you cannot provide this number or if you give them the wrong one and your contributions are not recorded in your account you will lose benefit. You must also state your number on any forms when you claim a benefit so it is important to keep the number carefully for future reference. Any person who has not been given a number must, when he or she first becomes liable for National Insurance contributions, apply to the Department of Social Security or to the local careers office, if they are under 18.

Statutory sick pay scheme

Employers are responsible for paying statutory sick pay (SSP) to their employees for up to 28 weeks of sickness absence. All employees are covered by the scheme if they are sick for four or more consecutive days and are not disqualified for payment, due to being over minimum state pension age; having a contract of employment which is for a period of less than three months; or earning less than the lower weekly earnings limit for National Insurance contribution liability. Employees can normally claim the state sickness benefit if they are not eligible for SSP. Employees may be required to produce evidence in support of their entitlement, eg a self-certificate for four to seven days or a doctor's statement for an absence in excess of seven days. The amount of SSP paid is recorded in column 1f on the deductions working sheet.

Statutory maternity pay scheme

Employers are responsible for paying statutory maternity pay (SMP) for up to 18 weeks to

Procedure for recording national insurance contributions on Form P11 (*see* Fig 6.4)

	Example for Week No. 2
1 Enter the total amount of gross pay in column 1a	£200
2 Refer to the National Insurance contribution tables (Fig 6.7) to find the total of employee's and employer's contributions and the employee's contribution payable on the amount of gross pay and enter them in columns 1b and 1c.	£200 = £29.44 (1b) = £15.41 (1c)
3 Columns 1d and 1e are completed for 'contracted out' employees only (*see* page 54)	
4 Enter statutory sick pay in column 1f	
5 Enter statutory maternity pay in column 1g	

Procedure for calculating and recording income tax on Form P11 (*see* Fig 6.4)

	Example for Week No. 2
1 Calculate the total amount of gross pay due to the employee less pension/superannuation contributions on which there is tax relief and enter it in column 2	£200.00 – £10.00 = £190.00
2 Add the amount in column 2 to the total of all previous payments made to the employee since 6 April and enter the new total in column 3	£180.50 + £190.00 = £370.50
3 Refer to Tax Table A (pay adjustment) (Fig 6.5) to find the amount of free pay to which the employee is entitled according to his code number and enter it in column 4	Code No. 250 £134.98
4 Subtract the 'free pay' in column 4 from the total pay to date in column 3 to arrive at the amount of taxable pay, which is entered in column 5	£370.50 – £134.98 = £235.52
5 Calculate the total tax due by referring to the amount of 'taxable pay' in Tax Table B (Fig 6.6) and enter this sum in column 6. Remember to subtract the Lower Rate Relief given in the Subtraction Tables.	£235 = £52.59
6 Subtract the amount of tax already deducted from the total tax due to date in column 6 giving the amount to be deducted from the employee's pay and entered in column 7.	£52.59 – £25.17 =£27.42

Sometimes, for example if the employee has worked a short week, the figure of total tax shown by the tax tables may be less than the tax already deducted; in that case the wages clerk must refund the difference to the employee instead of making a deduction and must enter the amount of refund in column 7 with the initial 'R'.

Note: The K code columns are used for employees who have K codes, usually to account for benefits in kind such as a company car

Deductions Working Sheet P11 Year to 5 April 19

Employer's name: SYSTEMS FURNITURE PLC

Tax District and reference: TWYFORD 878 AB 300B

Complete only for occupational pension schemes newly contracted-out since 1 January 1986.
Scheme contracted-out number: S 4

Employee's surname *in CAPITALS*: BROWN | First two forenames: MICHAEL

National Insurance no.: LM 48 37 66 B | Date of birth *in figures*: Day 04 Month 12 Year 75 | Works no. etc: 94 | Date of leaving *in figures*: Day Month Year

Tax code †: 350L | Amended code † | Wk/Mth in which applied

National Insurance contributions* | **PAYE Income Tax**

For employer's use	Earnings on which employee's contributions payable 1a	Total of employee's and employer's contributions payable 1b	Employee's contributions payable 1c	Earnings on which employee's contributions at contracted-out rate payable included in column 1a 1d	Employee's contributions at contracted-out rate included in column 1c 1e	Statutory Sick Pay in the week or month included in column 2 1f	Statutory Maternity Pay in the week or month included in column 2 1g	Statutory Maternity Pay recovered 1h	Month no	Week no	Pay in the week or month including Statutory Sick Pay/Statutory Maternity Pay 2	Total pay to date 3	Total free pay to date (Table A) 4a	K codes only: Total 'additional pay' to date (Table A) 4b	Total taxable pay to date i.e. column 3 minus column 4a or column 3 plus column 4b 5	Total tax due to date as shown by Taxable Pay Tables 6	K codes only: Tax due at end of current period Mark refunds 'R' 6a	K codes only: Regulatory limit i.e. 50% of column 2 entry 6b	Tax deducted or refunded in the week or month. Mark refunds 'R' 7	K codes only: Tax not deducted owing to the Regulatory limit 8	For employer's use
	£	£	£	£	£	£	£	£			£	£	£	£	£	£	£	£	£	£	
	190 00	27 74	14 41							1	180 50	180 50	67 49		113 01	25 17			25 17		
	200 00	29 44	15 41							2	190 00	370 50	134 98		235 52	52 59			27 42		
										3											
									1	4											
										5											
										6											
										7											
									2	8											
										9											
										10											
										11											
										12											
									3	13											
										14											
										15											
										16											
									4	17											
										18											
										19											
										20											
									5	21											
										22											
										23											
										24											
										25											
									6	26											
										27											
										28											
										29											
									7	30											
	Total c/fwd	Total c/fwd	Total c/fwd	Total c/fwd	Total c/fwd	Total c/fwd	Total c/fwd	Total c/fwd													

SPECIMEN

* You must enter the NI contribution table letter overleaf beside the NI totals box - *see the note shown there.*

† If amended cross out previous code.

⊘ If any week/month the amount in column 4a is more than the amount in column 3, leave column 5 blank.

P11(1995)

Fig 6.4 Specimen deductions working sheet (P11) (Crown copyright)

Week 2
Apr 13 to Apr 19

TABLE A - PAY ADJUSTMENT

Code	Total pay adjustment to date	Code	Total pay adjustment to date	Code	Total pay adjustment to date	Code	Total pay adjustment to date	Code	Total pay adjustment to date	Code	Total pay adjustment to date	Code	Total pay adjustment to date	Code	Total pay adjustment to date	Code	Total pay adjustment to date
	£		£		£		£		£		£		£		£		£
0	NIL																
1	0.74	**61**	23.82	**121**	46.90	**181**	69.98	**241**	93.04	**301**	116.12	**351**	135.36	**401**	154.58	**451**	173.82
2	1.12	**62**	24.20	**122**	47.28	**182**	70.36	**242**	93.44	**302**	116.50	**352**	135.74	**402**	154.98	**452**	174.20
3	1.50	**63**	24.58	**123**	47.66	**183**	70.74	**243**	93.82	**303**	116.90	**353**	136.12	**403**	155.36	**453**	174.58
4	1.90	**64**	24.98	**124**	48.04	**184**	71.12	**244**	94.20	**304**	117.28	**354**	136.50	**404**	155.74	**454**	174.98
5	2.28	**65**	25.36	**125**	48.44	**185**	71.50	**245**	94.58	**305**	117.66	**355**	136.90	**405**	156.12	**455**	175.36
6	2.66	**66**	25.74	**126**	48.82	**186**	71.90	**246**	94.98	**306**	118.04	**356**	137.28	**406**	156.50	**456**	175.74
7	3.04	**67**	26.12	**127**	49.20	**187**	72.28	**247**	95.36	**307**	118.44	**357**	137.66	**407**	156.90	**457**	176.12
8	3.44	**68**	26.50	**128**	49.58	**188**	72.66	**248**	95.74	**308**	118.82	**358**	138.04	**408**	157.28	**458**	176.50
9	3.82	**69**	26.90	**129**	49.98	**189**	73.04	**249**	96.12	**309**	119.20	**359**	138.44	**409**	157.66	**459**	176.90
10	4.20	**70**	27.28	**130**	50.36	**190**	73.44	**250**	96.50	**310**	119.58	**360**	138.82	**410**	158.04	**460**	177.28
11	4.58	**71**	27.66	**131**	50.74	**191**	73.82	**251**	96.90	**311**	119.98	**361**	139.20	**411**	158.44	**461**	177.66
12	4.98	**72**	28.04	**132**	51.12	**192**	74.20	**252**	97.28	**312**	120.36	**362**	139.58	**412**	158.82	**462**	178.04
13	5.36	**73**	28.44	**133**	51.50	**193**	74.58	**253**	97.66	**313**	120.74	**363**	139.98	**413**	159.20	**463**	178.44
14	5.74	**74**	28.82	**134**	51.90	**194**	74.98	**254**	98.04	**314**	121.12	**364**	140.36	**414**	159.58	**464**	178.82
15	6.12	**75**	29.20	**135**	52.28	**195**	75.36	**255**	98.44	**315**	121.50	**365**	140.74	**415**	159.98	**465**	179.20
16	6.50	**76**	29.58	**136**	52.66	**196**	75.74	**256**	98.82	**316**	121.90	**366**	141.12	**416**	160.36	**466**	179.58
17	6.90	**77**	29.98	**137**	53.04	**197**	76.12	**257**	99.20	**317**	122.28	**367**	141.50	**417**	160.74	**467**	179.98
18	7.28	**78**	30.36	**138**	53.44	**198**	76.50	**258**	99.58	**318**	122.66	**368**	141.90	**418**	161.12	**468**	180.36
19	7.66	**79**	30.74	**139**	53.82	**199**	76.90	**259**	99.98	**319**	123.04	**369**	142.28	**419**	161.50	**469**	180.74
20	8.04	**80**	31.12	**140**	54.20	**200**	77.28	**260**	100.36	**320**	123.44	**370**	142.66	**420**	161.90	**470**	181.12
21	8.44	**81**	31.50	**141**	54.58	**201**	77.66	**261**	100.74	**321**	123.82	**371**	143.04	**421**	162.28	**471**	181.50
22	8.82	**82**	31.90	**142**	54.98	**202**	78.04	**262**	101.12	**322**	124.20	**372**	143.44	**422**	162.66	**472**	181.90
23	9.20	**83**	32.28	**143**	55.36	**203**	78.44	**263**	101.50	**323**	124.58	**373**	143.82	**423**	163.04	**473**	182.28
24	9.58	**84**	32.66	**144**	55.74	**204**	78.82	**264**	101.90	**324**	124.98	**374**	144.20	**424**	163.44	**474**	182.66
25	9.98	**85**	33.04	**145**	56.12	**205**	79.20	**265**	102.28	**325**	125.36	**375**	144.58	**425**	163.82	**475**	183.04
26	10.36	**86**	33.44	**146**	56.50	**206**	79.58	**266**	102.66	**326**	125.74	**376**	144.98	**426**	164.20	**476**	183.44
27	10.74	**87**	33.82	**147**	56.90	**207**	79.98	**267**	103.04	**327**	126.12	**377**	145.36	**427**	164.58	**477**	183.82
28	11.12	**88**	34.20	**148**	57.28	**208**	80.36	**268**	103.44	**328**	126.50	**378**	145.74	**428**	164.98	**478**	184.20
29	11.50	**89**	34.58	**149**	57.66	**209**	80.74	**269**	103.82	**329**	126.90	**379**	146.12	**429**	165.36	**479**	184.58
30	11.90	**90**	34.98	**150**	58.04	**210**	81.12	**270**	104.20	**330**	127.28	**380**	146.50	**430**	165.74	**480**	184.98
31	12.28	**91**	35.36	**151**	58.44	**211**	81.50	**271**	104.58	**331**	127.66	**381**	146.90	**431**	166.12	**481**	185.36
32	12.66	**92**	35.74	**152**	58.82	**212**	81.90	**272**	104.98	**332**	128.04	**382**	147.28	**432**	166.50	**482**	185.74
33	13.04	**93**	36.12	**153**	59.20	**213**	82.28	**273**	105.36	**333**	128.44	**383**	147.66	**433**	166.90	**483**	186.12
34	13.44	**94**	36.50	**154**	59.58	**214**	82.66	**274**	105.74	**334**	128.82	**384**	148.04	**434**	167.28	**484**	186.50
35	13.82	**95**	36.90	**155**	59.98	**215**	83.04	**275**	106.12	**335**	129.20	**385**	148.44	**435**	167.66	**485**	186.90
36	14.20	**96**	37.28	**156**	60.36	**216**	83.44	**276**	106.50	**336**	129.58	**386**	148.82	**436**	168.04	**486**	187.28
37	14.58	**97**	37.66	**157**	60.74	**217**	83.82	**277**	106.90	**337**	129.98	**387**	149.20	**437**	168.44	**487**	187.66
38	14.98	**98**	38.04	**158**	61.12	**218**	84.20	**278**	107.28	**338**	130.36	**388**	149.58	**438**	168.82	**488**	188.04
39	15.36	**99**	38.44	**159**	61.50	**219**	84.58	**279**	107.66	**339**	130.74	**389**	149.98	**439**	169.20	**489**	188.44
40	15.74	**100**	38.82	**160**	61.90	**220**	84.98	**280**	108.04	**340**	131.12	**390**	150.36	**440**	169.58	**490**	188.82
41	16.12	**101**	39.20	**161**	62.28	**221**	85.36	**281**	108.44	**341**	131.50	**391**	150.74	**441**	169.98	**491**	189.20
42	16.50	**102**	39.58	**162**	62.66	**222**	85.74	**282**	108.82	**342**	131.90	**392**	151.12	**442**	170.36	**492**	189.58
43	16.90	**103**	39.98	**163**	63.04	**223**	86.12	**283**	109.20	**343**	132.28	**393**	151.50	**443**	170.74	**493**	189.98
44	17.28	**104**	40.36	**164**	63.44	**224**	86.50	**284**	109.58	**344**	132.66	**394**	151.90	**444**	171.12	**494**	190.36
45	17.66	**105**	40.74	**165**	63.82	**225**	86.90	**285**	109.98	**345**	133.04	**395**	152.28	**445**	171.50	**495**	190.74
46	18.04	**106**	41.12	**166**	64.20	**226**	87.28	**286**	110.36	**346**	133.44	**396**	152.66	**446**	171.90	**496**	191.12
47	18.44	**107**	41.50	**167**	64.58	**227**	87.66	**287**	110.74	**347**	133.82	**397**	153.04	**447**	172.28	**497**	191.50
48	18.82	**108**	41.90	**168**	64.98	**228**	88.04	**288**	111.12	**348**	134.20	**398**	153.44	**448**	172.66	**498**	191.90
49	19.20	**109**	42.28	**169**	65.36	**229**	88.44	**289**	111.50	**349**	134.58	**399**	153.82	**449**	173.04	**499**	192.28
50	19.58	**110**	42.66	**170**	65.74	**230**	88.82	**290**	111.90	**350**	134.98	**400**	154.20	**450**	173.44	**500**	192.66
51	19.98	**111**	43.04	**171**	66.12	**231**	89.20	**291**	112.28								
52	20.36	**112**	43.44	**172**	66.50	**232**	89.58	**292**	112.66								
53	20.74	**113**	43.82	**173**	66.90	**233**	89.98	**293**	113.04								
54	21.12	**114**	44.20	**174**	67.28	**234**	90.36	**294**	113.44								
55	21.50	**115**	44.58	**175**	67.66	**235**	90.74	**295**	113.82								
56	21.90	**116**	44.98	**176**	68.04	**236**	91.12	**296**	114.20								
57	22.28	**117**	45.36	**177**	68.44	**237**	91.50	**297**	114.58								
58	22.66	**118**	45.74	**178**	68.82	**238**	91.90	**298**	114.98								
59	23.04	**119**	46.12	**179**	69.20	**239**	92.28	**299**	115.36								
60	23.44	**120**	46.50	**180**	69.58	**240**	92.66	**300**	115.74								

Pay adjustment where code exceeds 500

1. Where the code is in the range **501** to **1000** inclusive proceed as follows:
   - **a.** Subtract **500** from the code and use the balance of the code to obtain a pay adjustment figure from the table above.
   - **b.** Add this pay adjustment figure to the figure given in the box alongside to obtain the figure of total pay adjustment to date * **£192.32**
2. Where the code **exceeds 1000** follow the instructions on **page 2.**

4

Fig 6.5 Income tax table A – Pay adjustment (Crown copyright)

Pages 2 and 3 tell you when to use these tables

Table B
(Tax at 25%)

Remember to use the Subtraction Tables on Page 7

Tax Due on Taxable Pay from £1 to £99

Total TAXABLE PAY to date	Total TAX DUE to date	Total TAXABLE PAY to date	Total TAX DUE to date
£	£	£	£
1	0.25	61	15.25
2	0.50	62	15.50
3	0.75	63	15.75
4	1.00	64	16.00
5	1.25	65	16.25
6	1.50	66	16.50
7	1.75	67	16.75
8	2.00	68	17.00
9	2.25	69	17.25
10	2.50	70	17.50
11	2.75	71	17.75
12	3.00	72	18.00
13	3.25	73	18.25
14	3.50	74	18.50
15	3.75	75	18.75
16	4.00	76	19.00
17	4.25	77	19.25
18	4.50	78	19.50
19	4.75	79	19.75
20	5.00	80	20.00
21	5.25	81	20.25
22	5.50	82	20.50
23	5.75	83	20.75
24	6.00	84	21.00
25	6.25	85	21.25
26	6.50	86	21.50
27	6.75	87	21.75
28	7.00	88	22.00
29	7.25	89	22.25
30	7.50	90	22.50
31	7.75	91	22.75
32	8.00	92	23.00
33	8.25	93	23.25
34	8.50	94	23.50
35	8.75	95	23.75
36	9.00	96	24.00
37	9.25	97	24.25
38	9.50	98	24.50
39	9.75	99	24.75
40	10.00		
41	10.25		
42	10.50		
43	10.75		
44	11.00		
45	11.25		
46	11.50		
47	11.75		
48	12.00		
49	12.25		
50	12.50		
51	12.75		
52	13.00		
53	13.25		
54	13.50		
55	13.75		
56	14.00		
57	14.25		
58	14.50		
59	14.75		
60	15.00		

Remember to use the Subtraction Tables on Page 7

Tax Due on Taxable Pay from £100 to £24,300

Total TAXABLE PAY to date	Total TAX DUE to date	Total TAXABLE PAY to date	Total TAX DUE to date	Total TAXABLE PAY to date	Total TAX DUE to date	Total TAXABLE PAY to date	Total TAX DUE to date
£	£	£	£	£	£	£	£
100	25.00	6100	1525.00	12100	3025.00	18100	4525.00
200	50.00	6200	1550.00	12200	3050.00	18200	4550.00
300	75.00	6300	1575.00	12300	3075.00	18300	4575.00
400	100.00	6400	1600.00	12400	3100.00	18400	4600.00
500	125.00	6500	1625.00	12500	3125.00	18500	4625.00
600	150.00	6600	1650.00	12600	3150.00	18600	4650.00
700	175.00	6700	1675.00	12700	3175.00	18700	4675.00
800	200.00	6800	1700.00	12800	3200.00	18800	4700.00
900	225.00	6900	1725.00	12900	3225.00	18900	4725.00
1000	250.00	7000	1750.00	13000	3250.00	19000	4750.00
1100	275.00	7100	1775.00	13100	3275.00	19100	4775.00
1200	300.00	7200	1800.00	13200	3300.00	19200	4800.00
1300	325.00	7300	1825.00	13300	3325.00	19300	4825.00
1400	350.00	7400	1850.00	13400	3350.00	19400	4850.00
1500	375.00	7500	1875.00	13500	3375.00	19500	4875.00
1600	400.00	7600	1900.00	13600	3400.00	19600	4900.00
1700	425.00	7700	1925.00	13700	3425.00	19700	4925.00
1800	450.00	7800	1950.00	13800	3450.00	19800	4950.00
1900	475.00	7900	1975.00	13900	3475.00	19900	4975.00
2000	500.00	8000	2000.00	14000	3500.00	20000	5000.00
2100	525.00	8100	2025.00	14100	3525.00	20100	5025.00
2200	550.00	8200	2050.00	14200	3550.00	20200	5050.00
2300	575.00	8300	2075.00	14300	3575.00	20300	5075.00
2400	600.00	8400	2100.00	14400	3600.00	20400	5100.00
2500	625.00	8500	2125.00	14500	3625.00	20500	5125.00
2600	650.00	8600	2150.00	14600	3650.00	20600	5150.00
2700	675.00	8700	2175.00	14700	3675.00	20700	5175.00
2800	700.00	8800	2200.00	14800	3700.00	20800	5200.00
2900	725.00	8900	2225.00	14900	3725.00	20900	5225.00
3000	750.00	9000	2250.00	15000	3750.00	21000	5250.00
3100	775.00	9100	2275.00	15100	3775.00	21100	5275.00
3200	800.00	9200	2300.00	15200	3800.00	21200	5300.00
3300	825.00	9300	2325.00	15300	3825.00	21300	5325.00
3400	850.00	9400	2350.00	15400	3850.00	21400	5350.00
3500	875.00	9500	2375.00	15500	3875.00	21500	5375.00
3600	900.00	9600	2400.00	15600	3900.00	21600	5400.00
3700	925.00	9700	2425.00	15700	3925.00	21700	5425.00
3800	950.00	9800	2450.00	15800	3950.00	21800	5450.00
3900	975.00	9900	2475.00	15900	3975.00	21900	5475.00
4000	1000.00	10000	2500.00	16000	4000.00	22000	5500.00
4100	1025.00	10100	2525.00	16100	4025.00	22100	5525.00
4200	1050.00	10200	2550.00	16200	4050.00	22200	5550.00
4300	1075.00	10300	2575.00	16300	4075.00	22300	5575.00
4400	1100.00	10400	2600.00	16400	4100.00	22400	5600.00
4500	1125.00	10500	2625.00	16500	4125.00	22500	5625.00
4600	1150.00	10600	2650.00	16600	4150.00	22600	5650.00
4700	1175.00	10700	2675.00	16700	4175.00	22700	5675.00
4800	1200.00	10800	2700.00	16800	4200.00	22800	5700.00
4900	1225.00	10900	2725.00	16900	4225.00	22900	5725.00
5000	1250.00	11000	2750.00	17000	4250.00	23000	5750.00
5100	1275.00	11100	2775.00	17100	4275.00	23100	5775.00
5200	1300.00	11200	2800.00	17200	4300.00	23200	5800.00
5300	1325.00	11300	2825.00	17300	4325.00	23300	5825.00
5400	1350.00	11400	2850.00	17400	4350.00	23400	5850.00
5500	1375.00	11500	2875.00	17500	4375.00	23500	5875.00
5600	1400.00	11600	2900.00	17600	4400.00	23600	5900.00
5700	1425.00	11700	2925.00	17700	4425.00	23700	5925.00
5800	1450.00	11800	2950.00	17800	4450.00	23800	5950.00
5900	1475.00	11900	2975.00	17900	4475.00	23900	5975.00
6000	1500.00	12000	3000.00	18000	4500.00	24000	6000.00
						24100	6025.00
						24200	6050.00
						24300	6075.00

Where the exact amount of taxable pay is not shown, add together the figures for two (or more) entries to make up the amount of taxable pay to the nearest £1 below

6

Fig 6.6 Income tax table B – taxable pay (Crown copyright)

Table B Subtraction Tables

(Lower Rate Relief)

Do not use the subtraction tables for code BR

For all ordinary suffix codes and prefix K codes - When you have used the table on Page 6 to work out the tax at 25% refer to the tables below to give the benefit of the lower rate band. Find the week or month in which the pay day falls. (it is the same week or month you have used in Tables A) and **subtract** the amount shown to arrive at the tax due.

There is an example below and further examples on Page 8

Employee paid at Weekly rates

Week No.	Amount to subtract £
1	3.08
2	6.16
3	9.24
4	12.31
5	15.39
6	18.47
7	21.54
8	24.62
9	27.70
10	30.77
11	33.85
12	36.93
13	40.00
14	43.08
15	46.16
16	49.24
17	52.31
18	55.39
19	58.47
20	61.54
21	64.62
22	67.70
23	70.77
24	73.85
25	76.93
26	80.00
27	83.08
28	86.16
29	89.24
30	92.31
31	95.39
32	98.47
33	101.54
34	104.62
35	107.70
36	110.77
37	113.85
38	116.93
39	120.00
40	123.08
41	126.16
42	129.24
43	132.31
44	135.39
45	138.47
46	141.54
47	144.62
48	147.70
49	150.77
50	153.85
51	156.93
52	160.00

Employee paid at Monthly rates

Month No.	Amount to subtract
1	13.34
2	26.67
3	40.00
4	53.34
5	66.67
6	80.00
7	93.34
8	106.67
9	120.00
10	133.34
11	146.67
12	160.00

Use of Table B *Example 1*

Employee's code is **352L**
The payment is made in **Week 7**

Pay in the week	£ 200	
Previous pay to date	£1200	
Total pay to date	£1400	
Less free pay in Week 7 (from Table A)	£ 475.09	
Total taxable pay to date	**£ 924.91**	

The tax is worked out by first looking in Table B on Page 6 for the nearest round figure below £924

		Tax due
It is	£900	£225.00
Look in the shaded columns for the remainder	£ 24	£ 6.00
Totals	£924	£231.00
Then give the Lower Rate Relief by looking in the table on this page for Week 7 and subtract the amount from the tax due. It is		£ 21.54
Total tax due to date		**£209.46**

7

6 April 1995 to 5 April 1996 A

Weekly table for not contracted-out standard rate contributions

Use this table for:

- employees who are over age 16 and under pension age
- employees who have an Appropriate Personal Pension

Do not use this table for:

- married women and widows who pay reduced rate National Insurance contributions
- employees who are over pension age
- employees for whom you hold form RD950

Completing form P11:

- enter 'A' in the space provided on the Deductions Working Sheet P11 or substitute
- copy the figures in columns 1a, 1b and 1c to columns 1a, 1b and 1c of form P11

If the exact gross pay is not shown in the table, use the next smaller figure shown.

Earnings on which employee's contributions payable 1a	Total of employee's and employer's contributions payable 1b	Employee's contributions payable 1c	Employer's contributions*
£	£	£	£
58	2.90	1.16	1.74
59	3.09	1.31	1.78
60	3.22	1.41	1.81
61	3.35	1.51	1.84
62	3.48	1.61	1.87
63	3.61	1.71	1.90
64	3.74	1.81	1.93
65	3.87	1.91	1.96
66	4.00	2.01	1.99
67	4.13	2.11	2.02
68	4.26	2.21	2.05
69	4.39	2.31	2.08
70	4.52	2.41	2.11
71	4.65	2.51	2.14
72	4.78	2.61	2.17
73	4.91	2.71	2.20
74	5.04	2.81	2.23
75	5.17	2.91	2.26
76	5.30	3.01	2.29
77	5.43	3.11	2.32
78	5.56	3.21	2.35
79	5.69	3.31	2.38
80	5.82	3.41	2.41
81	5.95	3.51	2.44
82	6.08	3.61	2.47
83	6.21	3.71	2.50
84	6.34	3.81	2.53
85	6.47	3.91	2.56
86	6.60	4.01	2.59
87	6.73	4.11	2.62
88	6.86	4.21	2.65
89	6.99	4.31	2.68
90	7.12	4.41	2.71
91	7.25	4.51	2.74
92	7.38	4.61	2.77
93	7.51	4.71	2.80
94	7.64	4.81	2.83
95	7.77	4.91	2.86
96	7.90	5.01	2.89
97	8.03	5.11	2.92

Earnings on which employee's contributions payable 1a	Total of employee's and employer's contributions payable 1b	Employee's contributions payable 1c	Employer's contributions*
£	£	£	£
98	8.16	5.21	2.95
99	8.29	5.31	2.98
100	8.42	5.41	3.01
101	8.55	5.51	3.04
102	8.68	5.61	3.07
103	8.81	5.71	3.10
104	8.94	5.81	3.13
105	11.18	5.91	5.27
106	11.33	6.01	5.32
107	11.48	6.11	5.37
108	11.63	6.21	5.42
109	11.78	6.31	5.47
110	11.93	6.41	5.52
111	12.08	6.51	5.57
112	12.23	6.61	5.62
113	12.38	6.71	5.67
114	12.53	6.81	5.72
115	12.68	6.91	5.77
116	12.83	7.01	5.82
117	12.98	7.11	5.87
118	13.13	7.21	5.92
119	13.28	7.31	5.97
120	13.43	7.41	6.02
121	13.58	7.51	6.07
122	13.73	7.61	6.12
123	13.88	7.71	6.17
124	14.03	7.81	6.22
125	14.18	7.91	6.27
126	14.33	8.01	6.32
127	14.48	8.11	6.37
128	14.63	8.21	6.42
129	14.78	8.31	6.47
130	14.93	8.41	6.52
131	15.08	8.51	6.57
132	15.23	8.61	6.62
133	15.38	8.71	6.67
134	15.53	8.81	6.72
135	15.68	8.91	6.77
136	15.83	9.01	6.82
137	15.98	9.11	6.87

* for information only - do not enter on P11

Page 11

Fig 6.7 Extract from national insurance contribution tables (Crown copyright)

A

6 April 1995 to 5 April 1996

Weekly table for not contracted-out standard rate contributions

Earnings on which employee's contributions payable 1a	Total of employee's and employer's contributions payable 1b	Employee's contributions payable 1c	Employer's contributions*
£	£	£	£
138	16.13	9.21	6.92
139	16.28	9.31	6.97
140	16.43	9.41	7.02
141	16.58	9.51	7.07
142	16.73	9.61	7.12
143	16.88	9.71	7.17
144	17.03	9.81	7.22
145	17.18	9.91	7.27
146	17.33	10.01	7.32
147	17.48	10.11	7.37
148	17.63	10.21	7.42
149	17.78	10.31	7.47
150	20.94	10.41	10.53
151	21.11	10.51	10.60
152	21.28	10.61	10.67
153	21.45	10.71	10.74
154	21.62	10.81	10.81
155	21.79	10.91	10.88
156	21.96	11.01	10.95
157	22.13	11.11	11.02
158	22.30	11.21	11.09
159	22.47	11.31	11.16
160	22.64	11.41	11.23
161	22.81	11.51	11.30
162	22.98	11.61	11.37
163	23.15	11.71	11.44
164	23.32	11.81	11.51
165	23.49	11.91	11.58
166	23.66	12.01	11.65
167	23.83	12.11	11.72
168	24.00	12.21	11.79
169	24.17	12.31	11.86
170	24.34	12.41	11.93
171	24.51	12.51	12.00
172	24.68	12.61	12.07
173	24.85	12.71	12.14
174	25.02	12.81	12.21
175	25.19	12.91	12.28
176	25.36	13.01	12.35
177	25.53	13.11	12.42
178	25.70	13.21	12.49
179	25.87	13.31	12.56
180	26.04	13.41	12.63
181	26.21	13.51	12.70
182	26.38	13.61	12.77
183	26.55	13.71	12.84
184	26.72	13.81	12.91
185	26.89	13.91	12.98
186	27.06	14.01	13.05
187	27.23	14.11	13.12
188	27.40	14.21	13.19
189	27.57	14.31	13.26
190	27.74	14.41	13.33
191	27.91	14.51	13.40
192	28.08	14.61	13.47
193	28.25	14.71	13.54
194	28.42	14.81	13.61
195	28.59	14.91	13.68
196	28.76	15.01	13.75
197	28.93	15.11	13.82

Earnings on which employee's contributions payable 1a	Total of employee's and employer's contributions payable 1b	Employee's contributions payable 1c	Employer's contributions*
£	£	£	£
198	29.10	15.21	13.89
199	29.27	15.31	13.96
200	29.44	15.41	14.03
201	29.61	15.51	14.10
202	29.78	15.61	14.17
203	29.95	15.71	14.24
204	30.12	15.81	14.31
205	36.87	15.91	20.96
206	37.07	16.01	21.06
207	37.27	16.11	21.16
208	37.48	16.21	21.27
209	37.68	16.31	21.37
210	37.88	16.41	21.47
211	38.08	16.51	21.57
212	38.28	16.61	21.67
213	38.49	16.71	21.78
214	38.69	16.81	21.88
215	38.89	16.91	21.98
216	39.09	17.01	22.08
217	39.29	17.11	22.18
218	39.50	17.21	22.29
219	39.70	17.31	22.39
220	39.90	17.41	22.49
221	40.10	17.51	22.59
222	40.30	17.61	22.69
223	40.51	17.71	22.80
224	40.71	17.81	22.90
225	40.91	17.91	23.00
226	41.11	18.01	23.10
227	41.31	18.11	23.20
228	41.52	18.21	23.31
229	41.72	18.31	23.41
230	41.92	18.41	23.51
231	42.12	18.51	23.61
232	42.32	18.61	23.71
233	42.53	18.71	23.82
234	42.73	18.81	23.92
235	42.93	18.91	24.02
236	43.13	19.01	24.12
237	43.33	19.11	24.22
238	43.54	19.21	24.33
239	43.74	19.31	24.43
240	43.94	19.41	24.53
241	44.14	19.51	24.63
242	44.34	19.61	24.73
243	44.55	19.71	24.84
244	44.75	19.81	24.94
245	44.95	19.91	25.04
246	45.15	20.01	25.14
247	45.35	20.11	25.24
248	45.56	20.21	25.35
249	45.76	20.31	25.45
250	45.96	20.41	25.55
251	46.16	20.51	25.65
252	46.36	20.61	25.75
253	46.57	20.71	25.86
254	46.77	20.81	25.96
255	46.97	20.91	26.06
256	47.17	21.01	26.16
257	47.37	21.11	26.26

* for information only - do not enter on P11

Page 12

employees whom they have employed for at least six months into the qualifying week, ie 15 weeks before the week in which the baby is due, and who pay National Insurance contributions. SMP will usually be paid at the same time as the normal payment of wages and it is entered in column 1 g on the deductions working sheet.

Once a month the employer must send a cheque to the Collector of Taxes for income tax and national insurance less any sums paid for statutory sick pay and statutory maternity pay.

7 Other deductions
These are voluntary deductions made only with the consent of the employee and may relate to union subscriptions, social club contributions or savings schemes.

8 Total deductions
In the example this is £48.83 which is the total of income tax, national insurance, savings and social club contributions and is the amount subtracted from gross pay to arrive at net pay or 'take home' pay.

9 Net pay
Gross pay – total deductions = net pay
ie £190.00 – £48.83 = £141.17. The procedure we have followed to calculate pay is illustrated in Fig 6.8.

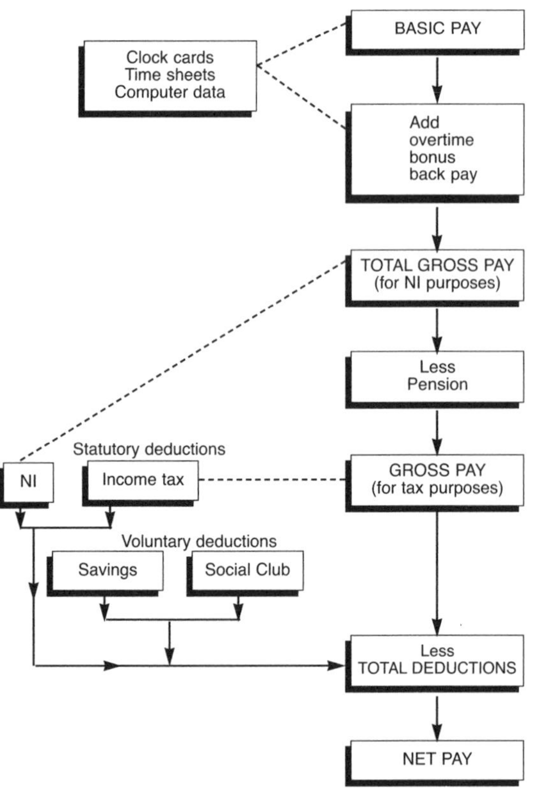

Fig 6.8 Procedure for calculating pay

▶ PAYROLL

The gross pay, total deductions and net pay are entered on a payroll which contains a list of all employees. Computers may be used to prepare pay records which will include the payroll, individual employee earnings record sheets and pay advice slips.

When a computer is used to calculate and prepare wages the employees' pay record sheets are stored on disk and updated each week or month. The income tax deductions and national insurance contributions are extracted from the computer 'memory' and the payroll and pay advice slips printed together with a cash analysis to indicate the number of notes and coins required from the bank. The input to the computer can either be keyed in on a terminal or provided automatically by a time recording system, as mentioned on page 51.

▶ METHODS OF PAYMENT FOR WAGES

Figure 6.10 compares the office procedures involved in paying wages by cash, cheque and credit transfer.

▶ COINING ANALYSIS

When wages are paid in cash the number of coins and notes required for each employee has to be calculated and totalled, an exercise known as 'coining'. Figure 6.9 shows a coining analysis and cash summary for five employees. The cash summary indicates the number of different coins and notes required to make up the pay packets when cashing the wages cheque at the bank.

COINING ANALYSIS

Net payments £	£20	£10	£5	£1	50p	20p	10p	5p	2p	1p
140.83	7				1	1	1		1	1
101.57	5			1	1			1	1	
118.38	5	1	1	3		1	1	1	1	1
76.87	3	1	1	1	1	1	1	1	1	
136.21	6	1	1	1		1				1
573.86	26	3	3	6	3	4	3	3	4	3

CASH SUMMARY

NOTES:		£
26 @ £20	=	520.00
3 @ £10	=	30.00
3 @ £5	=	15.00
Coins:		
6 @ £1	=	6.00
3 @ 50p	=	1.50
4 @ 20p	=	0.80
3 @ 10p	=	0.30
3 @ 5p	=	0.15
4 @ 2p	=	0.08
3 @ 1p	=	0.03
		573.86

Fig 6.9 Coining analysis

▶ PROGRESS CHECK

Multiple choice questions

1 Which of the following is a statutory deduction from an employee's wages?
- **a** national savings
- **b** national insurance
- **c** life assurance
- **d** union subscription

2 The income tax code number is arrived at by assessing the employee's:
- **a** gross pay
- **b** age
- **c** personal allowances
- **d** total deductions

3 Free pay is the term used to denote:
- **a** gross pay
- **b** bonus pay
- **c** net pay
- **d** untaxed pay

4 The National Insurance Contribution is calculated on an employee's:
- **a** age
- **b** gross pay
- **c** income tax deduction
- **d** net pay

5 A code number is necessary to calculate an employee's:
- **a** National Insurance Contributions
- **b** tax free pay
- **c** taxable pay
- **d** overtime pay

6 The basic 'ordinary time' pay Joan Barry will receive from the clock card in Fig 6.11 is:
- **a** £228
- **b** £224
- **c** £232
- **d** £240

7 The total gross wages Joan Barry will receive from the clock card (Fig 6.11) is:
- **a** £256
- **b** £252
- **c** £248
- **d** £246

8 Jane Travers' tax deduction for week 2 based on the information given in the tax deductions working sheet in Fig 6.12 and the tax tables in Figs 6.5 and 6.6 is:
- **a** £36.59
- **b** £19.67
- **c** £16.92
- **d** £33.84

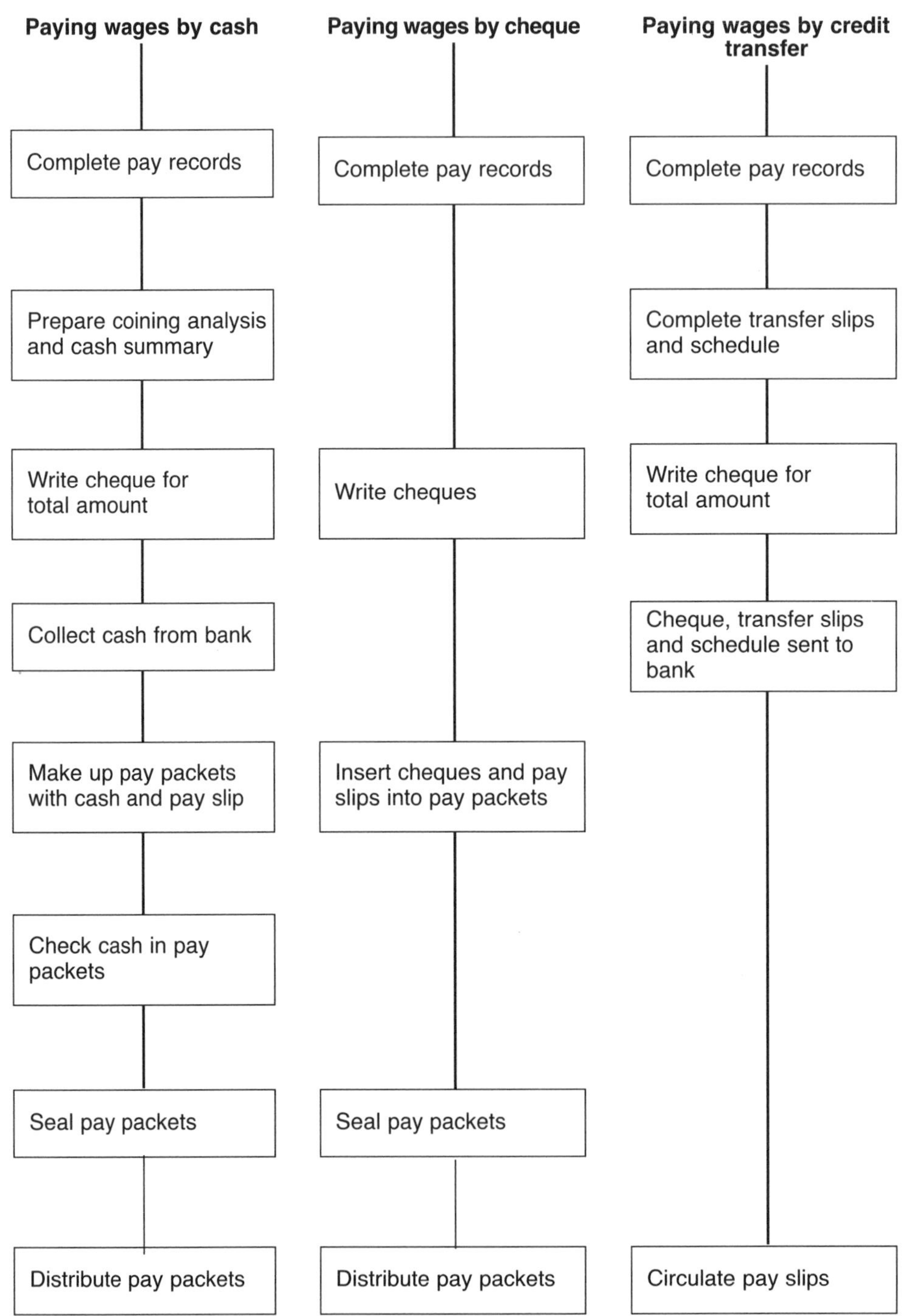

Fig 6.10 Office procedures for the payment of wages using different methods of payment

9 Jane Travers' National Insurance Contribution for week 2 based on the information given in her tax deductions working sheet (Fig 6.12) and the NI table in Fig 6.7 is:
a £11.23
b £11.41
c £22.64
d £10.41

10 The net pay which Christine Clarke should receive with the pay slip in Fig 6.13 is:
a £96.67
b £106.67
c £101.67
d £99.67

CLOCK CARD					
No 98			Name: Joan BARRY		
Week ending: 19 April 19-			Week No 2		
Day	In	Out	In	Out	TOTAL HOURS
M	0801	1203	1301	1800	
Tu	0800	1202	1300	1701	
W	0802	1159	1302	1702	
Th	0756	1158	1300	1658	
F	0800	1202	1301	1602	
TOTAL					
					£
Ordinary time.......... hrs @ £ 6.00 (up to 38 hours)					
Overtime.................. hrs @ £ 12.00					
TOTAL GROSS WAGES					

Fig 6.11 Clock card

Short answer questions

State the missing words or phrases:

11 The term used for paying workers on the basis of the number of jobs completed is ....

12 Clock cards are used to register the time employees start work and the ....

13 The letters PAYE stand for ....

14 Income tax is calculated and recorded on form ....

15 Gross pay – total deductions = ...

Supply brief answers to the following questions:

16 List three cash benefits of National Insurance:
a ....
b ....
c ....

17 Give three voluntary deductions which may be made from wages:
a ....
b ....
c ....

18 State what happens to the three parts of Form P45:
Part 1 ....
Part 2 ....
Part 3 ....

Name	Basic pay £	Over-time £	Gross pay £	Deductions: Income tax £	NI £	SAVINGS £	Social fund £	Total deductions £	NET PAY £
C CLARKE	125.00	5.00		12.92	8.41	5.00	2.00		

Fig 6.13 Pay slip

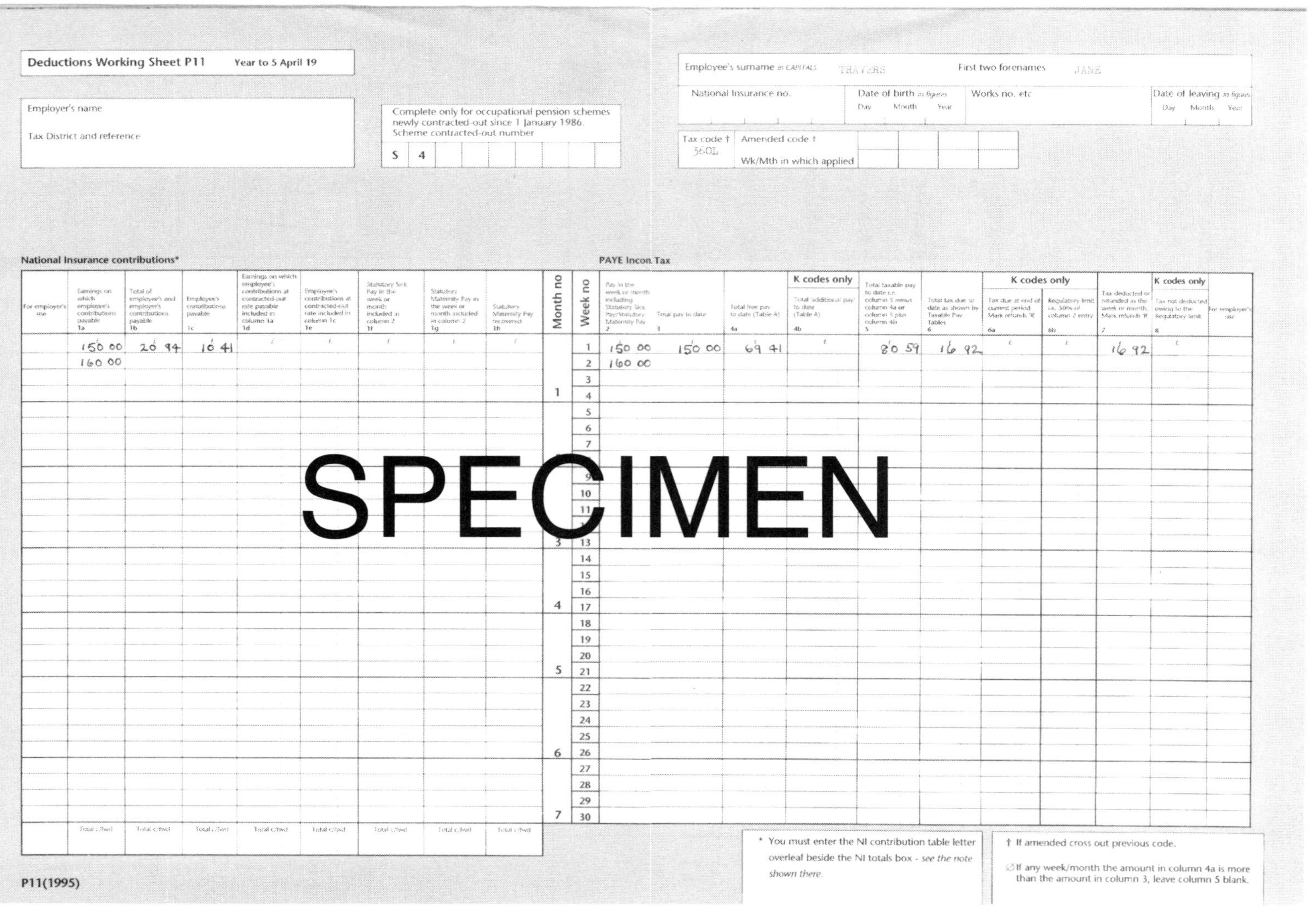

Deductions Working Sheet P11 Year to 5 April 19

Employer's name

Tax District and reference

Complete only for occupational pension schemes newly contracted-out since 1 January 1986.
Scheme contracted-out number

S 4

Employee's surname *in CAPITALS* TRAVERS First two forenames JANE

National Insurance no. | Date of birth *in figures* Day Month Year | Works no. etc | Date of leaving *in figures* Day Month Year

Tax code † 360L | Amended code † | Wk/Mth in which applied

National Insurance contributions* **PAYE Incon Tax**

For employer's use	Earnings on which employee's contributions payable 1a	Total of employee's and employer's contributions payable 1b	Employee's contributions payable 1c	Earnings on which employee's contributions at contracted-out rate payable included in column 1a 1d	Employee's contributions at contracted-out rate included in column 1c 1e	Statutory Sick Pay in the week or month included in column 2 1f	Statutory Maternity Pay in the week or month included in column 2 1g	Statutory Maternity Pay recovered 1h	Month no	Week no	Pay in the week or month including Statutory Sick Pay/Statutory Maternity Pay 2	Total pay to date 3	Total free pay to date (Table A) 4a	K codes only: Total 'additional pay' to date (Table A) 4b	Total taxable pay to date i.e. column 3 minus column 4a or column 3 plus column 4b 5	Total tax due to date as shown by Taxable Pay Tables 6	K codes only: Tax due at end of current period Mark refunds 'R' 6a	K codes only: Regulatory limit i.e. 50% of column 2 entry 6b	Tax deducted or refunded in the week or month. Mark refunds 'R' 7	K codes only: Tax not deducted owing to the Regulatory limit 8	For employer's use
	£ 150 00	£ 20 94	£ 10 41	£	£	£	£	£		1	£ 150 00	£ 150 00	£ 69 41	£	£ 80 59	16 92	£	£	16 92	£	
	160 00									2	160 00										
										3											
									1	4											
										5											
										6											
										7											
										[illegible]											
										9											
										10											
										11											
										[illegible]											
									3	13											
										14											
										15											
										16											
									4	17											
										18											
										19											
										20											
									5	21											
										22											
										23											
										24											
										25											
									6	26											
										27											
										28											
										29											
									7	30											
	Total c/fwd	Total c/fwd	Total c/fwd	Total c/fwd	Total c/fwd	Total c/fwd	Total c/fwd	Total c/fwd													

SPECIMEN

P11(1995)

* You must enter the NI contribution table letter overleaf beside the NI totals box - *see the note shown there.*

† If amended cross out previous code.

∅ If any week/month the amount in column 4a is more than the amount in column 3, leave column 5 blank.

Fig 6.12 Tax deductions working sheet (Crown copyright)

19 Name the source of reference for each of the following:

a Free pay ....

b Taxable pay ....

c National Insurance Contributions ....

20 Under the PAYE system, on what does the amount of tax to be deducted depend?

a ....

b ....

c ....

Unit 7 Filing

Competences developed in this unit:

- Maintain an established storage system
- supply information for a specific purpose

(NVQ2)

Office forms and correspondence are filed not only to keep them clean and tidy but to ensure that information contained in them is available for quick reference. Requirements for filing differ: the firm with few correspondents does not require the elaborate system of the firm with many. The large variety of filing equipment which may be used includes vertical suspension cabinets, lateral installations, microfilm processes, computer assisted retrieval systems, computer data storage etc, but whichever method is selected it is important that the system used has the following essential qualities:

- It must be quick and simple to operate.
- The equipment must be compact and should not take up too much office space.
- The system must be capable of expansion or contraction.
- The cabinets must be conveniently situated in the office and the information within them easy to locate.
- The most suitable form of classification must be used to cater for the size, volume and nature of the correspondence to be filed.
- Only 'live' correspondence should be held in the cabinet and 'dead' files, ie files no longer required, should be removed or transferred to another cabinet which need not be kept in the office.
- It should be capable of safeguarding documents and, in particular, confidential information.

► METHODS OF CLASSIFICATION

The principal methods of classification are the following:

1 alphabetical: correspondents' names
geographical
subject
2 numerical
3 combined alphabetical and numerical
4 chronological

Alphabetical

In the alphabetical method each folder is given the name of a correspondent and the folders are arranged in strict alphabetical order. Guide cards, miscellaneous suspension files or individual letter bars are used to divide different letters. The first letters of the surname determine the position of the file in the drawer. Fig 7.1 illustrates this arrangement.

Miscellaneous files are used for holding small amounts of correspondence when individual files are not needed. The front cover of a miscellaneous file should contain an index of the names of the correspondents enclosed. Alphabetical classification is suitable for correspondence with customers or clients in a small to medium-sized organisation.

Hill, P L & Co	
Heath, W K	
Harrod's Television Service Co	
Hammond, K	
H	**MISCELLANEOUS**
Griffith & Barrett	
Green, F J & Son	
Godfrey, M	
Gilbert, Smith & Sons	
Garner, Smith & Sons	
G	**MISCELLANEOUS**
Freeman Bros	

Fig 7.1 Alphabetical method of filing

Geographical

In the geographical method the correspondence is classified according to the location of each of the correspondents, ie country, county, town, etc. The principle is identical to that of the alphabetical method, except that papers are filed by alphabetically arranged places instead of correspondents' names. The correspondents' files are, however, arranged after the appropriate place file (see Fig 7.2). The geographical method can be used for correspondence with agents or representatives from different locations.

Spencer, T	
Liverpool	
Partridge & Dove	
Lincoln	
Johnson Bros	
Leicester	
Pollock & Sons	
Leeds	
Watts, F G	
Browning & Sons	
Lancaster	
L	**MISCELLANEOUS**

Fig 7.2 Geographical method of filing

Subject

In this method papers are filed under the heading of subject matter. This system is used for filing general correspondence which is not concerned with specific individuals such as that relating to the activities of a company, advertising, shipping, management, etc where it is convenient to have all the relevant data and correspondence concerned with any one topic grouped together for easy reference.

Primary guides in subject filing give the main headings of the subjects. In Fig 7.3 the subject primary guides are staff, stationery and text processing equipment.

Record cards	
Maintenance contract	
TEXT PROCESSING EQUIPMENT	
T	**MISCELLANEOUS**
Quotations	
Orders	
STATIONERY	General
Salaries	
Outings	
Holidays	
Establishments	
STAFF	General

Fig 7.3 Subject method of filing

Numerical

Files are arranged numerically, each correspondent being allotted a number. Index cards or strips are required to connect the numbers with the names. Each index card contains the name of the correspondent and their allotted file number and is arranged in alphabetical order in an index card drawer. When a file is required a number must first be obtained from the index card and then the appropriate file can be found in the filing cabinet. This method would be used for correspondence with a large number of clients or customers or for account records, particularly if coded and prepared by computer. It is capable of indefinite expansion as new files are placed at the back of existing ones. The number of the file is useful as a reference to be used on all relevant correspondence and the index card or strip is useful for maintaining an address record or for making notes, eg when someone borrows a file. Fig 7.4 illustrates this system.

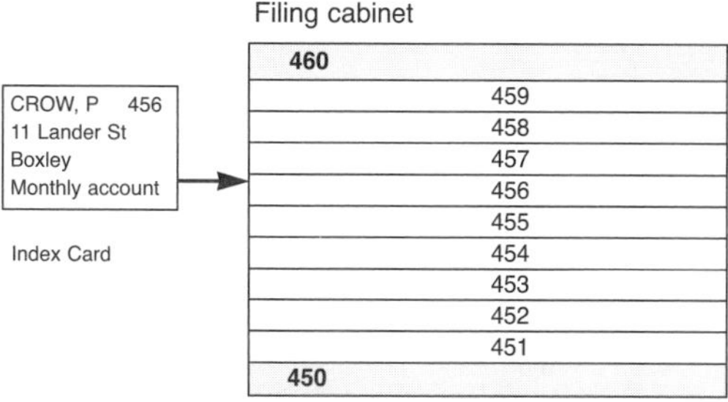

Fig 7.4 Numerical filing system

Combined alphabetical and numerical

The alphabetical system referred to on page 68 may also incorporate reference numbers as illustrated in Fig 7.5. Each letter or part of a letter is given a number and a further number is allocated to each file as it is made, eg if letter B

C	MISCELLANEOUS 3
Burgess, J	2/8
Bryant & Miller Ltd	2/3
Brown, G T	2/5
British Motor Accessories plc	2/9
Booth & Sons Ltd	2/1
Black, A I	2/10
Bishops & Spears	2/2
Bennet, P L	2/6
Beard Bros	2/7
Baxter Stores plc	2/11
Barber, P	2/4
B	MISCELLANEOUS 2
Avon Manufacturing Co	1/6

Fig 7.5 Alphabetical-numerical method of filing

is numbered 2 and there are twelve files in the B section, the last file to be opened is numbered 2/12. It should be noted that the files are arranged alphabetically, and the numerical aspect is secondary and is used as a reference number for correspondence.

Chronological

This is the name of the method used for filing documents according to their dates in numerical order. Chronological filing is not often used as a basic system but it is the normal method of filing papers within files.

▶ FILING EQUIPMENT

Lateral filing cabinet

The files are stored side by side in a lateral filing cabinet and the titles are placed vertically along the front of the files (see Fig 7.6). Space does not have to be allowed for the opening of drawers and the cabinets can be built up as high as the ceiling will allow. A large number of files can be on view at the same time but because of the large opening they may attract dust. A disadvantage of this method is the difficulty experienced in reading the titles arranged vertically but this can be overcome by using a numerical system.

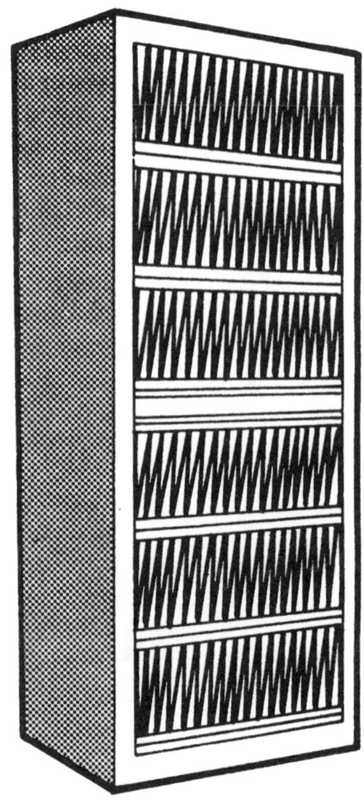

Fig 7.6 Lateral filing cabinet

Vertical filing cabinet

In this method the files are arranged vertically (upright) and papers can be inserted or replaced without removing the file (*see* Fig 7.7). The titles appear on the top edges and can be

Fig 7.7 Vertical filing cabinet

read easily. The files may be suspended vertically from metal runners fitted inside the cabinet drawers which protect them from wear and tear. A disadvantage of using this method is the amount of space required not only for the cabinet itself but for opening the drawers.

Plan filing

Plans, drawings, maps and other large documents may be stored horizontally in large flat drawers, as in Fig 7.8, or vertically in storage cabinets where the documents are arranged in an upright position. Suspended plan filing cabinets provide a high density and fast retrieval system for the storage of large documents up to a sheet size of 1520 × 1020mm. Each item is individually filed using a perforated suspension tape or a plastic suspension wallet. Each compartment can have its own indexing signal device so that the documents can be easily identified and extracted.

Fig 7.8 Horizontal plan chest

Electronic filing system

Figure 7.9 illustrates a computerised document management system which automatically retrieves and returns files at the touch of keyboard keys. When a file is required, the operator keys in its index number into a PC and the computer automatically locates the file. The PC activates the rotation of the shelves, bringing the required shelf to operator height. A light then indicates the precise location of the file on the shelf.

Fig 7.9 Computerised document management system

Once the desired information has been extracted from the file, the keyboard is again operated to restore the file automatically to its storage location.

The index number and the location of every file in the system is first entered into the computer either by keying them manually using a PC keyboard or automatically using a swipe of a barcode scanner if identifying barcodes have been attached to the files. Each time a file is retrieved and returned, the date and name of user are keyed into the PC which provides:

- a means of monitoring the file when it is taken away
- a 'history' of the file
- a means of tracking the file as it goes from being:
  - active
  - suitable for archiving
  - ready for destruction

This system can also be used for locating records kept on microfilm or computer discs.

Microfilming

This is a method used to reduce the space occupied by business documents and correspondence. The papers are filmed to reduce them in size for storage and quick retrieval and when reference is required the film is fitted into a viewer where the documents can be seen in enlarged form.

Microfilm can be stored as follows:

- roll film usually held in cassettes or cartridges
- acetate jackets which can store up to 60 frames of film – used in situations where it is necessary to update individual files
- microfiche, ie single sheets of film with the capacity to hold between 98 and 420 A4 size documents (*see* Fig 7.10)
- COM, ie computer output microfilm or computer-originated microfilm – data from a computer recorded directly on to roll film or microfiche. When documents are required for reference they are either viewed on a reader or a hard copy produced by a reader/printer

These methods of microfilm can be reproduced from paper or computer output.

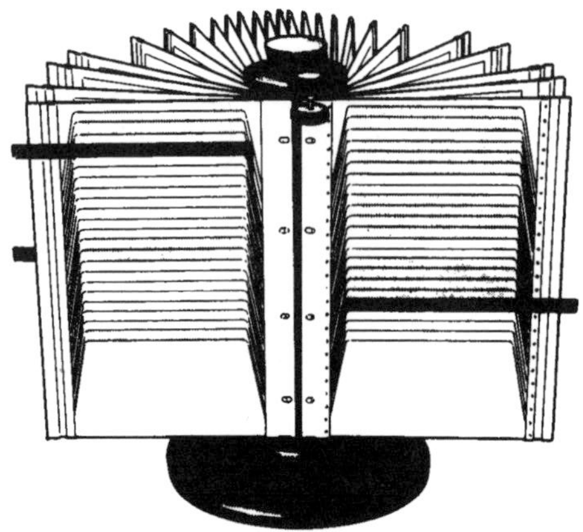

Fig 7.10 Stand for storing and displaying microfiche

Microfilm must be viewed from a reader and some (such as the one illustrated in Fig 7.11) have a dual role of reader and printer providing the facility to reproduce copies when required. Recent developments in microfilm technology make it possible for microfilm images, both text and graphics, to be scanned

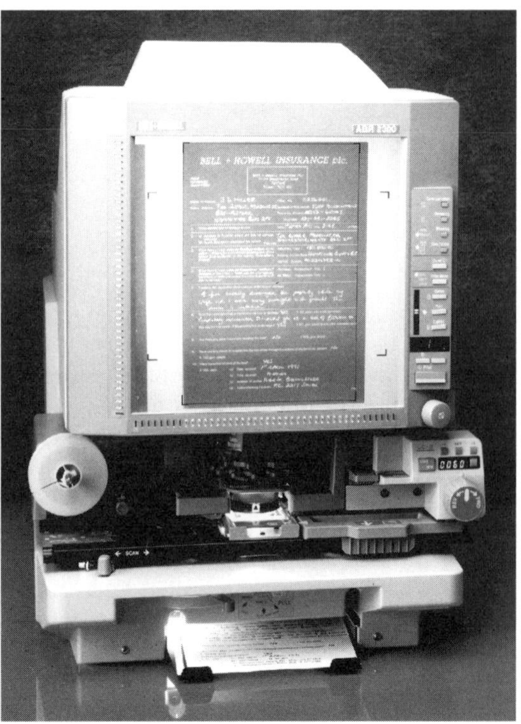

Fig 7.11 Microfilm reader-printer

into digital form so that they can be transmitted by telephone line. The images can also be edited, if required, and integrated into a computer generated file, allowing them to be stored on an optical disk for immediate access from computer terminals.

Microfilm can be used for business documents, legal documents, drawings, parts manuals, journals and newspapers by reducing them in size for storage and quick retrieval. For example, 120,000 A4 pages can be stored on microfilm in a single loose-leaf binder.

Computer-assisted retrieval of microfilm

This involves the use of a micro-processor for quick retrieval of microfilm. VDU terminals are used to communicate directly with a computer which is able to locate a document filed on microfilm. The computer advances the film to the correct frame, stops the film and displays the image of the required document on the screen, thus providing immediate access by

VDU of information stored on a computer as well as a means of gaining access to original source documents stored on microfilm.

Computer data storage and retrieval methods

The computer can be used to store vast quantities of data in its storage devices which comprise main storage and subsidiary storage. Main storage holds the program and data for the transaction currently in hand, but regular back-up copies of data are taken and transferred to subsidiary storage which may be:

- floppy disks, usually 3½ inch disks capable of storing the text for 400 A4 pages
- magnetic tape, cassette or cartridge

It is expected that CD disks will eventually be used for this purpose.

▶ FILING CHECKLIST

The efficiency of a filing system depends not only upon use of the most suitable equipment and method but on the ability and reliability of the staff responsible for filing. The following checklist is necessary to ensure complete accuracy, and easy and quick access to all papers filed.

Check that:

- the papers have been passed for filing, ie they have been marked to indicate that they are ready for filing
- you sort and group the papers before filing
- you have removed paper clips from correspondence
- you are placing the correspondence in the correct file
- the papers are placed squarely in the file so that the edges are straight and neat
- the correspondence is arranged in chronological order with the most recent on top
- a record is made if:
  a a document has to be removed from a file
  b a file has to be removed from a cabinet (see the absent file record in Fig 7.12)
- you follow up all overdue files and papers, as recorded above
- your files are up to date by filing daily
- you use a cross reference when a file is known by more than one name, ie a reference to the correct location is made in places where the file is not held (*see* Fig 7.13)
- you are aware of your company's file retention policy so that files are thinned out regularly and correspondence is not kept in the current system longer than is necessary (see below)
- you seek guidance when in doubt concerning the filing of non-classified papers and any which are unclear
- you always close filing cabinet drawers after use
- you lock filing cabinets before leaving the office at night or for any length of time
- you seek to maintain the efficiency of the system and recommend modifications/ improvements to it as appropriate

File retention policy

If correspondence is retained unnecessarily,

FILE ABSENT CARD

File no/Name: 2.10

Borrowed by	Department	Date borrowed	Date returned
K Ash	Buying	3-11-19-	

Fig 7.12 File absent card

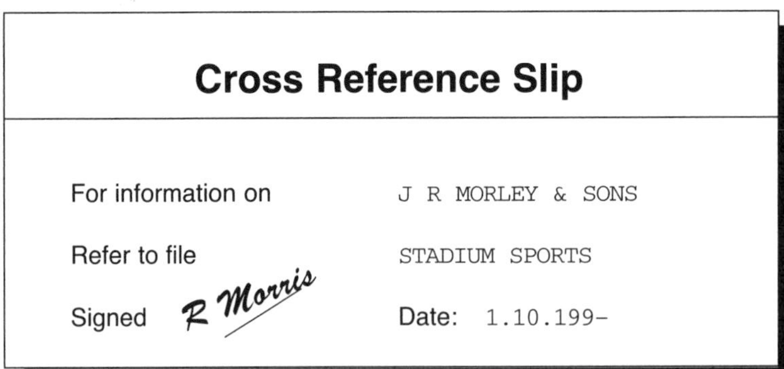
Cross Reference Slip

For information on J R MORLEY & SONS

Refer to file STADIUM SPORTS

Signed R Morris Date: 1.10.199-

Fig 7.13 Cross reference slip

files become bulky, occupy valuable space in cabinets and make the retrieval of documents more difficult. For this reason it is necessary for a file retention policy to be agreed by the organisation and to take account of:

- any legal requirements for the documents to be retained
- the need to retain documents for auditing purposes
- the possible need for documents to be produced in their original form as evidence in a court of law
- records which may be duplicated elsewhere in the organisation – both copies need not be kept
- whether the organisation would be at a disadvantage if the records could not be produced on a future date

Absent files

One of the most frequent sources of delay and annoyance in filing is to find that a folder has been removed from its place in the cabinet and a lengthy, irritating search all over the office is necessary to trace it. This can be avoided by monitoring the movement of files on absent cards, as illustrated in Fig 7.12.

Cross reference slips

These are used whenever a file may be known by more than one title. A cross reference slip, as in Fig 7.13, is placed in the section of the cabinet for the secondary title, stating the name or position in the cabinet where the file can be found, eg Stadium Sports (formerly known as J R Morley & Sons) is filed under 'S' and a cross reference slip filed under 'M' to indicate that the file can be found in the position for Stadium Sports.

Visible card systems

Visible cards and strip indexing systems can be employed for a large number of office and shop record purposes such as staff records, sales records, accounts, mailing lists, current retail prices, stock records, etc. The information in the records can be seen at a glance as the cards or strips are arranged so that the titles are all visible. In addition to their titles, the exposed portions carry various control features which summarise essential details contained in entries on the records. Colour markers or indicators can be clipped to the cards for identification purposes. Transparent plastic shields are generally fitted over the exposed portions of the cards to protect them from dirt and to provide a suitable carrier for the coloured markers. An illustration of a visible card system is given in Fig 7.14. In a system of strip indexing each item of information is recorded on a separate strip and these are then built up, one above the other, in suitable carrying devices so that all the information contained in them is exposed to view. Additions, amendments and deletions can

Fig 7.14 Visible card record system

be made without affecting the continuity of the records. The strips may be housed in panels, wall fitments, books, stands, revolving units or cabinets. Individual references to addresses, telephone numbers, prices, quantities or measurements – each on its own strip – can be made easily and information pinpointed quickly.

Rules for indexing

When arranging files or index cards in alphabetical order the filing clerk should observe the following rules:

	Examples
• The surname is placed before the forenames or other names and if the surnames are the same the first forename determines the position	Grant Paul Grant Roy
• If the forenames and surname are contained in the name of a firm, the surname is written first followed by the forenames and finally by the remainder of the firm's name.	Jackson, John plc
• If a firm has several names the first is taken as the surname for indexing purposes.	Collins, Rushton & Brown
• The first name is taken in hyphenated names.	Davis R Ewing-Davies R
• For impersonal names such as county councils use the name that distinguishes it from the others for indexing purposes.	Westshire County Council
• Names beginning with Mac, Mc or M' are treated as if they were spelt 'Mac'.	M'Bride G R McBride P T MacBride W G
• Names beginning with St are treated as if they were spelt 'Saint'.	St John Courtney Salon
• Nothing comes before something, ie a name without an initial precedes a name with one.	Thomas Thomason Thomason P Thomason P P
• Names which consist of initials separated by spaces or full stops are placed before full names. Those which are not separated are treated as words and are placed in the usual alphabetical position.	M.F.I. Furniture Centre Maffey I MFD Product Design
• Names which begin with a number should either be listed before the alphabetical names in numerical order or converted to words and placed in the appropriate alphabetical position, depending on the rules of the organisation.	3M United Kingdom plc file as 'Three M'

▶ PROGRESS CHECK

Multiple choice questions

1 If documents are filed in chronological order they are arranged according to:
a reference number
b subject
c date
d geographical location

2 Back-up storage consists of:
a floppy disks or tapes
b filing cabinet specially designed for computer accessories
c a storeroom for computer supplies
d computer printout

3 Which method of filing is capable of indefinite expansion by placing new files at the back of existing files?
a geographical
b alphabetical by name
c subject
d numerical

4 Which of the following would you use to indicate that a document in a file also referred to correspondence in another file?
a a cross reference
b an out guide
c a microfilm cartridge
d a signalling device

5 A file retention policy ensures that documents are:
a retained permanently
b retrieved by computer
c thinned out regularly
d retained pending action

6 In a visible card system:
a the cards have a magnetic strip
b overlapping cards are used
c a viewer is used to enlarge the data
d each item is recorded in strip form

7 The index numbers and locations for files in a computerised document management system may be entered into the system by:
a barcode scanners
b visible record cards
c reader printers
d datapost

8 The name to be indexed first in an alphabetical method would be:
a Smith P P
b Smith P
c Smithers Hardware Ltd
d Smith T

9 Re-arrange the following names in the correct order for alphabetical indexing:
a John Harris & Sons Ltd
b Grand Hotel (Bournemouth) Ltd
c The British Nylon Company
d Department of the Environment

10 Pair the two lists of words (note that there is a surplus item in the second column):

Documents to be filed	Most suitable filing method
a petty cash vouchers	**a** chronological
b export correspondence	**b** alphabetical
c personnel records	**c** subject
d paying-in slips	**d** numerical
	e geographical

Short answer questions

State the missing words or phrases:

11 The filing classification system which requires a separate index is ....

12 Nothing comes before .... when arranging names in alphabetical order.

13 Files are arranged .... in a vertical filing cabinet.

14 Documents which have no specific file are placed in a .... file.

15 Overlapping cards are used in a .... system of indexing.

Supply brief answers to the following questions:

16 List three checks you should make when filing a document:

a ....

b ....

c ....

17 Describe and/or draw a cross reference slip/card.

18 Place each list of cities in order appropriate to an alphabetical filing system by writing 1, 2 or 3 against each city:

a Budapest ....
Berlin ....
Basle ....

b London ....
Londonderry ....
Lisbon ....

c Seville ....
St Albans ....
Shanghai ....

19 Describe three items of information needed as part of any system designed to locate files not in the filing system:

a ....

b ....

c ....

20 Give three advantages of microfilm as a form of storage of documents:

a ....

b ....

c ....

Unit 8
Incoming and outgoing mail

Competences developed in this unit:

- Receive and send mail (NVQ2)
  (in conjunction with Unit 16 Mail Services)

▶ OPENING AND DISTRIBUTING THE INCOMING MAIL

The work of opening and distributing the incoming post should be organised in such a way that the correspondence is on the desks of the staff when they arrive at the office in the morning. A delay in distributing the morning's post can seriously affect the day's work, so a highly organised and efficient system is necessary. The first task is to sort and arrange the mail into the following categories:

	Action required
• registered mail	• signed for upon receipt, opened separately and any remittances recorded (Fig 8.1)
• mail marked PRIVATE PERSONAL or CONFIDENTIAL	• delivered unopened to the persons concerned
• mail marked URGENT	• opened separately and delivered immediately
• mail not addressed to the firm	• reposted unopened
• all other mail addressed to the firm	• opened as illustrated in Fig 8.2

REMITTANCES BOOK						
Date	Remitter's name	Method of payment	Account No	Amount £		Signature
19–						
Jan 1	Garfield, G	Chq	R1162	11	00	T. Jones
" 1	Palmer	Chq	T490	12	50	
" 1	Shell Garage	P.O.	R1169		65	
" 1	Cox	Chq	T499	52	00	
" 1	Lamb Engineering	Chq	P1119	14	48	
" 1	Sanderson	Cash	P1231	1	00	
" 1	Donald	Chq	T515	20	50	

Fig 8.1 Remittances book

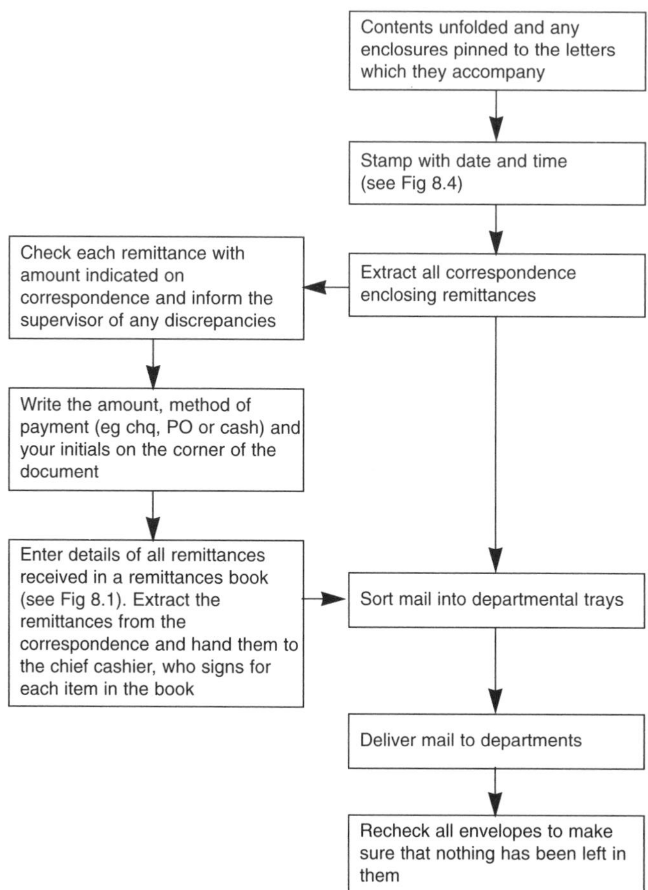

Fig 8.2 Procedure for incoming mail

Note:
When signing for parcels, recorded delivery and registered mail check that you receive the correct packages and that they are not damaged in any way.

▶ LETTER OPENING MACHINE

A letter opening machine may be used for cutting open the envelopes received in the incoming mail (*see* Fig 8.3). These machines are normally electrically operated and by a rotary blade cut a strip off the edge of the envelope. Any size of envelope can be accommodated up to a thickness of approximately 12.7 mm (½ inch). These machines are quick and efficient and because only a very narrow strip is cut from the envelopes the contents are unlikely to be damaged.

▶ SUSPICIOUS POSTAL PACKETS

All packages received in the post should be inspected carefully for any suspicious signs of a letter bomb, eg look out for packages:

- of an unusual shape or size
- with wires attached

Fig 8.3 Letter-opening machine

- with oil or grease marks on the cover
- of a heavier weight than the size suggests
- having a smell of almonds
- with a pin hole in the wrapping

If you discover a suspicious package which complies with any of the above descriptions:

- do not open it or allow anyone else to touch it
- handle the package gently, placing it on a flat surface above floor level and away from a corner of the office
- leave the office as soon as possible, lock the door and hold on to the key for use by the police when they arrive
- inform your security/safety officer who will inform the police (dial 999) immediately
- keep the entrance to the office clear of people

▶ ELECTRONIC TIMESTAMP MACHINE

An electronic timestamping machine may be used for stamping incoming mail or any other documents which require a printed record of the exact time and date of receipt. The Super Facile 40 Timestamp in Fig 8.4 prints the company's name or departmental code; day, month, year and time; and the serial number of the impression. The print impression can be placed at the top of the document or in any other predetermined position.

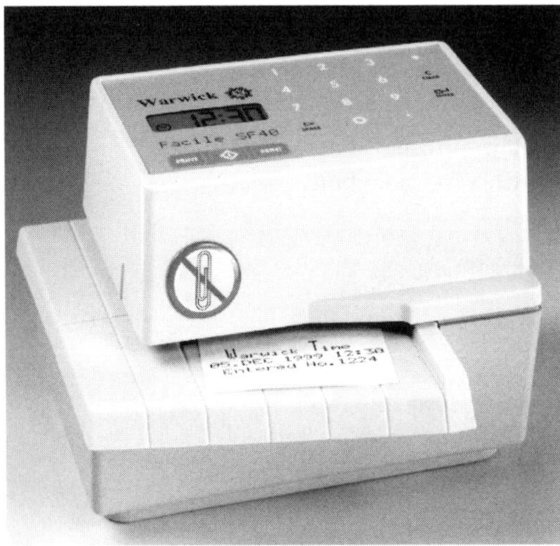

Fig 8.4 Electronic timestamp machine

▶ CIRCULATION OF DOCUMENTS

If a document requires the attention of more than one person it can be copied on an office copier and copies sent to each person or a circulation slip (*see* Fig 8.5) can be attached to the original document detailing each person concerned. As it is received, each person initials and dates the slip after taking the necessary action and passes the document on to the next person named.

CIRCULATION SLIP		
Name	Initials	Date
1 Mr T A Dent	T.A.D.	1.3.-
2 Mr R Fergus	RF	3.3.-
3 Mr P Bell		
4 Mrs G Clifton		
5 Mr S Waller		
6		
Please circulate the attached document quickly		

Fig 8.5 Circulation slip

▶ PREPARING OUTGOING MAIL FOR THE POST

All outgoing post passes through the stages outlined in Fig. 8.6.

▶ ADDRESSING MAIL

The Royal Mail advises its customers that high-speed postal deliveries depend on correct addressing, according to the following guidelines:

- the address should normally comprise:
  1 name of addressee
  2 house number (or name) and street
  3 locality name, where necessary
  4 post town
  5 county name, where required
  6 postcode
- begin each item of the address on a separate line
- allow sufficient space at the top of the envelope for the postage stamps or franking impression and postmarks

- use block capitals for the post town
- normally include the name of the county
- type the postcode at the bottom of the address in block capitals with a space between the two parts
- place any special directions, such as 'Private', 'Confidential' or 'For the attention of . . .', clear of the address – usually two spaces above the addressee's name (*see* Fig 8.7, for example)

Letter is checked to see that it is signed and enclosures are, where necessary, attached

↓

Address on the envelope is checked with the address on the letter. If there is a discrepancy both the letter and the envelope should be returned to the typist for verification and retyping

↓

Letter is folded, care being taken not to fold it more than is necessary to fit into its envelope

↓

Letter is placed in the envelope which is sealed securely

↓

Envelope is weighed and stamped or franked by machine

↓

Details from the envelope may be entered in a postage account

↓

First class letters are separated from second class letters

↓

The envelopes are tied in bundles or placed in franking machine pouches with all the addresses facing in one direction

↓

Special items of mail, such as registered, recorded delivery, airmail, etc which require labels or forms or have to be handed over the counter of the post office are kept apart from the remainder of the post

↓

The postal clerk arranges for the mail to be delivered to the post office, completes any necessary forms and collects the receipts

Fig 8.6 Procedure for outgoing mail

```
For the attention of Mr W Morris
Systems Furniture plc
Brookfield Industrial Estate
TWYFORD
Westshire
TD3 2BS
```

Fig 8.7 Addressed envelope

▶ WRAPPING UP PARCELS

Parecelforce gives the following advice on wrapping up parcels to ensure their safe and speedy delivery:

- except for soft and unbreakable items it is advisable to use a strong box large enough to allow you to pack plenty of cushioning material round the contents on all sides
- for many small items such as books and leaflets use a padded bag
- where it is not necessary or practicable to use a box or padded bag, wrap the article in corrugated paper followed by strong brown paper
- each article should be surrounded by cushioning material and always ensure that the box is filled to prevent the contents moving about inside
- boxes should be firmly sealed along all flaps and edges with 38 mm or 50 mm plastic or re-inforced carton sealing tape
- where a box is not used, it is advisable, in addition to sealing with tape, to tie string firmly around the parcel in at least two directions, knotting tightly where the string crosses
- if staples are used ensure that they are applied firmly and exposed ends are covered with strips of tape to guard against possible injury to persons handling the package
- follow the guidelines given above for addressing the parcel
- where it is necessary to use a tie-on label, make sure that it is securely tied and will not come off in the post
- include the sender's address on the outer cover, at right angles to the destination address, so that if for any reason Parcelforce cannot deliver the parcel it can be returned to the sender
- a separate label showing both the sender's and the addressee's address should be attached to the article inside the parcel

▶ FRANKING MACHINES

The franking machine is the postal machine most commonly found in offices and is used to print postal impressions on envelopes and parcels. Use of the franking machine saves the clerk the unpleasant and unhygienic task of sticking stamps to the packages. All types of mail can be franked including ordinary letter post, registered letters, overseas mail and parcels.

Franking machines are either leased, rented or purchased from the manufacturers but before they can be used a licence must be obtained from Royal Mail. The user must pay in advance for the postage units and most machines have to be presented at a specified post office for meter setting or registering.

Keys are operated for the required postal value and when the envelope is passed through the machine an impression is made giving the date, postal district, value and, if desired, an advertisement or the user's name and address (*see* Fig 8.8). Every time the machine prints an impression the number of units is registered on the meter and the value of the units in hand is reduced accordingly. Both amounts are shown on the dials on the machine, the units normally being 1p.

Fig 8.8 Franking impression

If a package is too thick to pass through the machine a strip of gummed label can be franked and fixed to the package.

The mailing clerk is responsible for changing the date on the machine, cleaning the type and replenishing the supply of red ink as required.

When all the post has been franked it must be separated into first and second class packages and placed into the relevant pouches (red for first class and green for second class), with the names and addresses all facing the same way. The pouches may be collected by the post office or taken to a specified post office. If the post office is closed the franked mail may be posted in a posting box provided that it is placed in a special envelope for the purpose.

Any envelope franked in error should be retained and submitted to Royal Mail which will issue a refund for the value of the impressions less a charge of 5%.

Electronic mailing systems, as in Fig 8.9, have push-button controls for selecting postage values. The amounts keyed in are displayed in a digital display panel. A built-in memory reveals how much credit is left, how much postage has been used and how many items have been franked. The electronic franking machine, when interfaced with electronic scales, automatically combines the weighing, postage calculation and franking operations.

When electronic scales are used, there is no need to refer to postal rates as these are programmed into its memory. To obtain the correct amount of postage for a packet, you place it on the scales and press the appropriate key for the service required, eg first class, and the rate appears instantly in a digital display panel. It also reveals the exact weight, which is useful for recording on customs declaration forms.

A remote meter-resetting system using a special telephone data pad may be used for purchasing additional units and for resetting your franking machine by telephone instead of having to deliver the machine to the specified post office.

An alternative system for resetting the franking machine is the use of a credipac module, which is sent with a cheque to Royal Mail in a special reply-paid pouch. The module registers the units used and the amount of credit in hand and, after resetting by the post office, it is returned to the user within 72 hours. The franking machine remains with the user during resetting and continues to be used without a break.

Modern franking machines can include such features as:

- a date-change control which flashes 'set date' immediately after switching on the machine to alert the operator to set the new date
- a warning light when the credit begins to run low
- a safeguard in printing high values, as a signal flashes when amounts in excess of £1 are set

Fig 8.9 A mailing system with electronic scales

- a credit management control system which provides a printout of usage by individual departments

▶ POSTAGE ACCOUNT

After the letters have been stamped, particulars may be entered in a postage account which serves as:

- a check on the number of stamps used and
- a record of all letters posted

The postal clerk brings down the balance in the postage book every morning, showing the difference between the amount of stamps purchased and the amount used; the value of any remaining stamps must agree with the balance shown in the book.

Postage books are rarely kept in offices today, largely because of the time taken to maintain them and the popular use of franking machines which automatically register the amount of postage used. Where postage stamps are still in use and details of correspondents are not required, the postal clerk may simply keep a record of the total number of stamps used each day (*see* Fig 8.10).

▶ COLLECTION OF MAIL BY THE POST OFFICE

Instead of the mailroom staff having to deliver large quantities of mail to the post office, arrangements can be made through Royal Mail for a postman to collect it from the company. A free collection of letters is available on request if you are posting 500 or more items.

Charges for collecting parcels vary depending on collection patterns and on the number of parcels involved. A parcel contract can be arranged with Parcelforce for regular large postings of parcels and this includes free delivery of parcels to the post office, with the exception of Parcelforce Standard where a collection fee may be payable.

▶ MAILING EQUIPMENT

Mailroom operations can be carried out more efficiently and faster with the aid of appropriate equipment, eg:

Applications	**Machines**
• stamping the date and time on incoming mail	• date and time stamp
• automatic folding of documents	• folding machine (*see* Fig 8.11)
• printing postal impressions on mail	• franking machine
• mechanising the following procedures: collating; opening envelope flap; sealing envelope; franking postage impression; counting items and stacking envelopes	• inserting and mailing machine
• slitting envelopes received in the mail	• letter opening machine
• tying string/tape round parcels	• package tying machine
• preparing newspapers, magazines, etc for posting	• rolling and wrapping machine
• shredding documents	• shredder
• moistening and sealing flaps of envelopes	• sealing machine (*see* Fig 8.11)
• moistening stamps and envelopes	• sponge/roller moistener
• fixing wire staples into documents	• stapler
• preparing documents for posting without envelopes	• tucking and folding machine
• weighing packets for calculation of postage	• weighing machine

▶ FOLDING AND INSERTING SYSTEM

The equipment illustrated in Fig 8.11 is capable of automating the process of collating, folding and inserting documents into envelopes at a rate of 2700 per hour. It monitors the contents of the filled envelopes, ensuring that only the correct number of items are enclosed. Any envelope containing more than the memorised number of items causes the machine to stop and alerts the operator A built-in resettable counter allows the operator to monitor the number of items processed and the diagnostic display highlights any matters requiring attention such as when the envelope hopper needs re-filling.

Stamps bought £		Stamps used		Total £	
		Number	Denomination		
30	00		1 January 19- Balance b/f		
		15	20p	3	00
		20	22p	4	40
		16	24p	3	84
		18	26p	4	68
		6	30p	1	80
				17	72
			Balance c/f	12	28
30	00			30	00
12	28		2 January 19- Balance b/f		

Fig 8.10 Daily stamp record

▶ PROGRESS CHECK

Multiple choice questions

1 A date stamp is used in a mailroom to provide a record of when letters are:

a checked
b typed
c received
d despatched

Fig 8.11 Folding and inserting machine

2 Remittances received in the post should be:
- **a** signed for on delivery
- **b** checked and entered in a remittances book
- **c** checked and entered in a paying-in book
- **d** date stamped and delivered to the department concerned

3 A letter received in the post marked Private and confidential should be:
- **a** opened carefully by the mail clerk in the presence of a supervisor
- **b** opened by the mail clerk and delivered immediately to the addressee
- **c** opened only by the mailroom supervisor
- **d** delivered unopened to the addressee

4 An application form for an audio/wp operator vacancy received in the morning's post would be delivered to the:
- **a** chief accountant
- **b** personnel manager
- **c** secretary to the managing director
- **d** company secretary

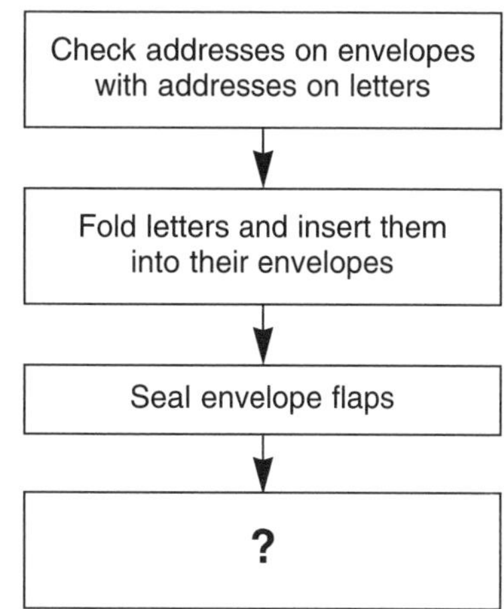

Fig 8.12 Letter mail procedure

5 In which of the following departmental mail boxes would you place an invoice received for goods ordered for stock?
- **a** accounts
- **b** buying
- **c** stores
- **d** sales

6 Before franking the envelopes in the procedure shown in Fig 8.12 you would:
- **a** place envelopes in appropriate pouches
- **b** enter the envelopes in the postage account
- **c** check that the enclosures were correct
- **d** weigh the envelopes

7 Using the letter post rates in Fig 8.13 a first class letter weighing 480 g should contain postage stamps to the value of:
- **a** £0.98
- **b** £1.13
- **c** £1.25
- **d** £1.55

8 If you franked an envelope with an excessive amount of postage what would you do?
- **a** destroy it and enter a credit entry for the incorrect amount
- **b** amend the amount with a pen and sign your name
- **c** record the error on the postage account
- **d** retain the envelope and frank another one with the correct amount of postage

9 Pair the two lists of words (note that there is a surplus item in the second column):

Mailroom tasks	**Mailroom equipment**
a incoming post	**a** stapler
b outgoing post	**b** letter opening machine
c incoming cheques	**c** franking machine
d document for several departments	**d** remittances book
	e circulation slip

10 Pair the two lists of words (note that there is a surplus item in the second column):

Item received in post	**Sorted in mail box**
a letter requesting a catalogue	**a** goods received section
b statement from a supplier	**b** despatch section
c price list from a supplier	**c** accounts department
d advice note from a supplier	**d** buying department
	e sales department

Rates for letters

Weight not over	First Class	Second Class	Weight not over	First Class	Second Class
60g	26p	20p	500g	£1.30	£1.05
100g	39p	31p	600g	£1.60	£1.25
150g	49p	38p	700g	£2.00	£1.45
200g	60p	45p	750g	£2.15	£1.55
250g	70p	55p	800g	£2.30	Not admissible over 750g
300g	80p	64p	900g	£2.55	
350g	92p	73p	1000g	£2.75	
400g	£1.04	83p	Each extra 250g or part thereof 65p		
450g	£1.17	93p			

Fig 8.13 Letter postage rates

Short answer questions

State the missing words or phrases:

11 Cheques received in the incoming mail should be logged in a/an ....

12 When processing incoming mail................. .... are often attached to magazines and other items which may be of interest to more than one person.

13 An envelope marked .... should not be opened in the mailroom.

14 When all the post has been franked it must be separated into .... packages.

15 Confidential documents no longer required may be destroyed by using a/an ....

Supply brief answers to the following questions:

16 Some documents have to be seen by more than one person. How can this be done? Describe three ways:
- **a** ....
- **b** ....
- **c** ....

17 What should a mail-clerk check before he or she seals a letter?

a ....
b ....
c ....

18 Describe three of the signs that could suggest a parcel might contain an explosive device:

a ....
b ....
c ....

19 Give three advantages of using a franking machine in the mailroom:

a ....
b ....
c ....

20 Name three items of equipment which could be used to help process outgoing mail:

a ....
b ....
c ....

Unit 9
Work planning and scheduling

Competences developed in this unit:

- Identify and agree own development needs
- Prepare and agree a plan of action to develop self
- Implement and review a personal development plan
- Plan and organise own work schedule
- Obtain and organise information in support of own work activities

(NVQ2)

▶ PERSONAL DEVELOPMENT

It is important for you to identify your specific role in your organisation and to demonstrate your keenness to develop it to the fullest extent. By doing this both you and your employer benefit in the following ways:

- you establish your unique place within the organisation
- you are seen to be taking positive steps to fulfil your potential
- you gain greater job satisfaction and interest from taking an active part in your own personal development
- you are laying the foundations for your career development and promotion
- you are helping the organisation to be successful in achieving its objectives

The steps which you will need to take to prepare and agree a plan of action for your personal development include:

1 Identifying and understanding your role, usually as laid down in your job description
2 identifying your personal development objectives in order to undertake your role in (1)
3 drawing up an action plan to show the steps you intend to take to achieve the objectives in (2). This may entail on-the-job training and/or part-time attendance at a college to gain qualifications. Your immediate objectives may be to achieve the qualifications given in the assessment chart (page xi) such as NVQs or the PQ Office Procedures examinations
4 agreeing your personal development plan with your supervisor/manager
5 maintaining regular progress in accordance with your personal development plan
6 reviewing the agreed objectives with your Assessor/Supervisor/Manager to determine your achievement of them

To succeed in your career you have to take responsibility for your own learning and personal development and so ensure a successful outcome of your personal action plan. You need to recognise your strengths and weaknesses in all aspects of your work. Honesty in self-appraisal and objective-setting and getting are important elements in the process of developing your role or niche in the organisation as well as achieving professional and personal fulfilment.

A checklist with key questions to ask yourself about your personal performance at work:

- Do you always carry out your work in a helpful and willing manner?
- What are your strengths? Are they being utilised to their full potential?
- What are your weaknesses? What action are you taking to overcome them and improve your performance?
- What kind of image do you project in the workplace? Does this do you credit?
- Who do you admire at work and why? What qualities make that person a success?
- How could your relationship with your supervisor and your colleagues be improved?

- Do you seek information and advice from your supervisor as and when required?
- How do you react under pressure? In what ways could your job be made less stressful?
- How could you improve your existing office systems/methods? If you were absent from work tomorrow, could someone else pick up your systems/methods and work efficiently without any input from you?
- How does your present job differ from the role you would like to see yourself fulfilling? Have you discussed this with your supervisor or personnel officer?
- How would you like to see your career develop in the next few years?

▶ WORK PLANNING AND SCHEDULING

It will already be obvious to you that careful planning of office procedures and tasks is essential to ensure that deadlines are met, the workload is spread and controlled, and priorities are established. Looking back over our work to date, considerable planning was needed to achieve a successful outcome as in the following examples:

- **Buying:** To select and order goods of the right type from the most suitable firms supplying them at a price which is acceptable and in the time required.
- **Sales:** To ensure that goods are delivered to customers on time and that the invoices, statements, etc are sent at appropriate times to ensure prompt settlement of accounts.
- **Stock control:** To control stock levels so that materials/goods are always available on the premises for production/sales.
- **Wages:** To make-up wages on a regular date for issuing to staff.

▶ HOW TO PLAN

1 Begin by preparing a checklist of all the activities involved in a task and arrange them in the order in which they should be carried out, noting especially any deadlines for completing parts of a task as well as the date when the total task should be completed. Figure 18.1 is a checklist for making travel arrangements and Fig 19.1 a checklist for arranging a meeting.

2 Forward planning is essential: plan well ahead to allow adequate time for each stage of the work schedule. Reminders of work to be done at different stages can be entered in an office diary (*see* Fig 9.1).

3 Plan each day's work and assess your priorities as follows:
   - i urgent – top priority – must be done today
   - ii not so urgent but important – so try to do it today
   - iii not urgent and less important – low priority – could wait for another day if time does not permit for it to be done today.

4 Prioritise unexpected tasks according to the needs of the organisation.

5 Report any anticipated difficulties in meeting deadlines to the appropriate person.

6 Make use of planning aids such as diaries, computerised desk diary planners, year planner charts, follow-up systems, control boards, etc.

▶ DESK DIARIES

A desk diary can be used as a reminder of:

- work deadlines
- appointments and meetings
- files to be followed up
- staff absences – holidays, etc.
- social engagements

Key factors in using the desk diary

- Be systematic –
  At the beginning of the day: refer to the diary and take the necessary action on all entries, eg prepare the papers and files for appointments, meetings and correspondence (follow-up).
  During the course of the day: keep in mind and prepare for the various activities – make amendments, additions and deletions to the diary as required;
  At the end of the day: ensure that all items have been dealt with or, if necessary, transferred to a future date.
- Write entries clearly and concisely with a pen, including essential details of appoint-

DIARY

7 APRIL 19-- | ROSEMARY FISH, Secretarial Services Supervisor

WEDNESDAY

0900		
1000	Meeting with Mr K Pratt re purchase of new word processor	Room C10
1100	Appointment: R L Jones, British Telecom	Reception Office
1200		
1300–1400	Lunch with Mr P S Adams, Employment and Training Manager	Staff Restaurant
1500–1600	Training session for clerical staff - new fax system	Training Room
1700		
1800		
1900	'South Pacific' with Brenda and Paul	Twyford Theatre
2000		

Notes: Draft minutes of SSP Group Meeting
Prepare job specification for new secretarial post
T. A. Green attending Time Management Course
Follow up files: 21 346
26 789

Fig 9.1 Office diary

ments, time and place.

- Enter provisional appointments in pencil and ink them in when they are confirmed.
- Appointments for each day should be entered in the correct time sequence.

▶ COMPUTERISED DESK DIARY PLANNERS

A desk diary can be kept on a computer so that the entries can be seen on a VDU and a print-out made when required. An entry is made by keying in the date, time and brief details of the appointments, and if it has to be cancelled or changed to another time or date it can be removed from the 'memory' and re-entered on another date or time, as necessary. The computer can be programmed to reject any entries at certain times of the day or even whole days when appointments cannot be held. An appointment which occurs several times during the year at regular intervals can be entered once with the relevant dates and it is automatically entered on each of the dates. Each day's entries can be viewed at the beginning of the day and, for planning purposes, it is possible to view a month's entries. All forthcoming events, reminders and 'unavailable' days can be displayed up to a maximum of 30 days.

A computerised system, such as this, is particularly good for following up correspondence and for reminders of work to be done on particular dates, such as the preparation of an agenda for a meeting. Computerised diary programs can be used to co-ordinate dates for meetings if all staff keep their diaries on the computer. When it is necessary to call a meeting, the convenor can call up the program on a workstation and enter the likely duration of the meeting. The computer searches the diaries of each of the participants and gives a choice of times and dates when all are free to attend. The convenor can select one of the options and the diaries are automatically updated with the selected meeting date and time.

▶ PLASTIC YEAR PLANNERS

These are large plastic calendars with spaces for every day of the year on which information can be written with wipe-off pens. They can be used for planning appointments, meetings, holidays, etc. You can see at a glance a year's activities and plan future events methodically on one single sheet.

▶ PLANNING CONTROL BOARDS

Project planning, progress of work and trends can be monitored and easily controlled by visual planning boards. The magnetic planning board illustrated in Fig 9.2 has a modular format which caters for all display sizes and applications such as staff control, sales planning and performance, stock control, production control, etc. It is easy to read and quick to update, showing changes as they occur. By simply sliding a planned display of coloured signals along a modular panel, a programme can be updated easily in seconds without affecting a sequence of events.

▶ FOLLOW-UP SYSTEM

A follow-up system (Fig 9.3) is used to ensure that a matter is not overlooked, especially when action is required following the writing of a letter. If, for example, a letter is written on the 7th of the month, the writer may wish to send a further letter on the 17th if a reply has not been received. When the writer signs the letter on the 7th he or she completes a memo form, attaches it to the copy of the letter in question, enters on it the date when the file is next wanted, and places it in the filing tray. The filing clerk fills in the name of the correspondent and, if necessary, the subject matter, and detaches the form, which is filed in the appropriate monthly pocket of the follow-up filing cabinet. The letter itself is then filed away in its proper file with other correspondence, where it can be found at any time it is required.

The follow-up filing cabinet drawer contains twelve pockets, entitled January to December. Memos are placed in the appropriate monthly

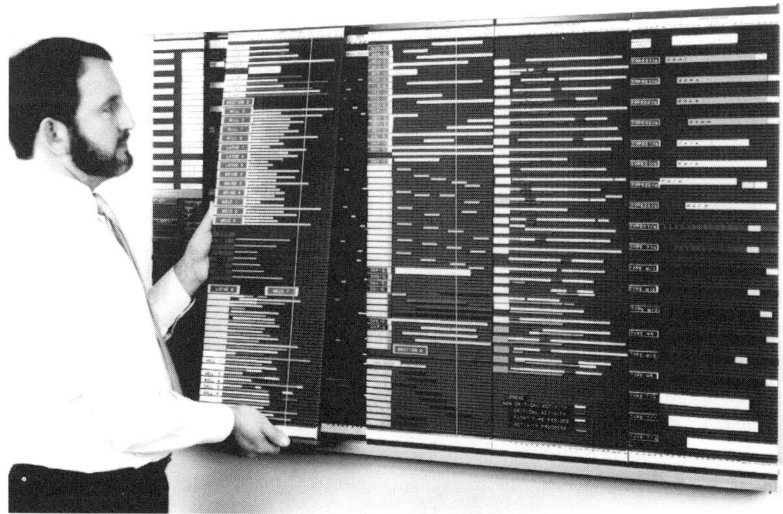

Fig 9.2 Magnetic planning board

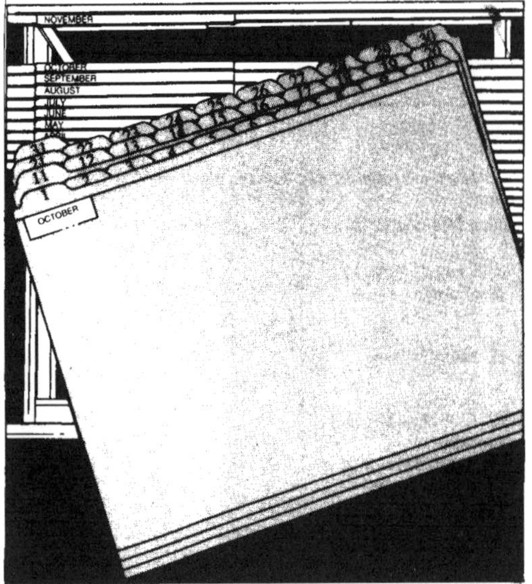

Fig 9.3 Follow-up system

pocket which, when the month becomes current, is sub-divided on a daily basis by daily insert sheets. If the quantity of papers requires it, the system may have a separate pocket for each day of the month.

Each day the filing clerk extracts any memo forms from the current daily pocket, finds the files to which they refer and passes them to the individuals whose initials appear on the forms. After appropriate action, the writer places the form and file back in the filing tray with, if necessary, a further date marked in for follow-up, and the whole process is repeated. Note the information recorded on the memo form and the arrangement of the pockets in the follow-up system illustrated in Figs 9.3 and 9.4.

▶ APPOINTMENTS

When making an appointment:

- record the name of the contact, organisation, time and venue on the relevant day of your diary
- confirm by letter any appointment made by telephone – a letter of confirmation is shown in Fig 9.5
- allow sufficient travelling time between appointments arranged outside the office on the same day
- if a telephone caller requests an appointment and a date and time are agreed, make a note of the caller's name, address and telephone number in case you need to contact them to amend the date or time
- if an appointment has to be cancelled because of illness or other unforeseen circumstances, telephone an apology and arrange another appointment

▶ BOOKING PROCEDURES

The planning of appointments for the services of people or the use of equipment, accommodation, etc must be well co-ordinated and organised. A diary may be used for booking

TICKLER MEMO — DATE 27/1/–

NAME Charles Broad & Co Ltd			PHONE	
ADDRESS			LETTER DATE 26/1/–	
SUBJECT				
REMARKS Renewal of Transport Contract				
RETURN TO R. Johnson	ON 9/2/–	9/3/–	7/4/–	
ON				
ON				

Fig 9.4 Follow-up system memo

SYSTEMS FURNITURE plc

Brookfield Industrial Estate, Twyford, Westshire TD3 2BS

Tel: 0193-384 1923 Telex: 342689
Fax: 0193-2196734

Our ref: RPL/PE
Your ref:

11 March 19--

Mr G R Fullbrook
Manager
Midland Bank plc
14 The Square
Twyford
Westshire
TD9 4LT

Dear Mr Fullbrook

This is to confirm my telephone conversation with you today when you kindly agreed to see Mr R P Lodge, Chief Accountant of this company, at 1400 hrs on Monday 18 March 19-- at your bank. Mr Lodge would like to discuss with you a new scheme which the company has under consideration for the payment of staff salaries.

In the meantime, I shall be grateful if you will please send Mr Lodge a copy of your brochure outlining the new system which your bank offers.

Yours sincerely

Pauline Ellis

Pauline Ellis (Miss)
Secretary to Chief Accountant

Registered office: Brookfield Industrial Estate, Twyford, Westshire
TD3 2BS Registered No. 584305 England

Fig 9.5 Letter of confirmation

appointments or for booking the use of accommodation such as a conference room. A rota, displayed with staff names down the left-hand side and dates along the top, could be used to co-ordinate staff holiday bookings. Where there is just one item of equipment, such as a word processor or dictating machine, to be shared by several members of staff, a booking procedure is necessary to ensure the efficient use of the equipment. In these circumstances the booking procedure should be:

- clearly understood by all users so that they know exactly what they have to do to make a booking
- controlled by one person who should monitor progress on a regular basis
- administered by written bookings on a form held at a central point
- simple to operate with as little inconvenience as possible to users

A booking form for the use of an overhead projector is shown in Fig 9.6.

▶ SOURCES OF INFORMATION IN SUPPORT OF WORK PRACTICES

Unit 20 outlines the principal sources of information for various business purposes and pro-

BOOKING FORM FOR
OVERHEAD PROJECTOR

Week commencing: 1 September 19–

Time	Monday	Tuesday	Wednesday	Thursday	Friday
0900		P S Adams			
1000		↓			
1100	W. Morris	↓			
1200	↓	↓			
1300		↓			
1400		↓			R. Fisher
1500		↓		R. Williams	↓
1600		↓			↓
1700		↓			
1800					
1900					
2000					

Note: Any faults should be reported immediately to PS Adams, Employment and Training Manager on a defect form.

Fig 9.6 Booking form for overhead projector

vides a guide to finding information in reference books. It is essential for you to know:

- where to look for information to support your work tasks, eg in books of reference, videotex, internet, etc
- what information is relevant and sufficient to aid your decision-making
- the importance of checking that the information is up-to-date
- the most suitable form in which to supply the information
- the need to treat information with the appropriate confidentiality

▶ PROGRESS CHECK

Multiple choice questions

1 Staff development should match the employees' achievements against the needs of:
- **a** the nation
- **b** the organisation
- **c** the office
- **d** their home circumstances

2 An employee's role in their organisation is described in:
- **a** an organisation chart
- **b** a staff manual
- **c** a job description
- **d** a personnel record card

3 An employee's personal development plan has to be agreed with his/her:
- **a** supervisor
- **b** training officer
- **c** next of kin
- **d** colleagues

4 The most satisfactory means of recording and displaying a holiday rota would be to use:
- **a** an overhead projector
- **b** a follow-up system
- **c** a desk diary
- **d** a year planner

5 Reminders of work scheduled for future dates would be given in:
- **a** a booking form
- **b** viewdata
- **c** a desk diary
- **d** a gazetteer

6 The memo in Fig 9.4 was first used to follow up the letter of 26 January to Charles Broad & Co Ltd on:
- **a** 27 January
- **b** 9 March
- **c** 9 February
- **d** 7 April

7 Which of the following tasks should be given top priority on arrival at the office first thing in the morning?
- **a** filing yesterday's mail
- **b** checking today's entries in the desk diary
- **c** balancing the petty cash account
- **d** making travel arrangements for a meeting next week

8 The correct order for the pockets in a follow-up cabinet is:
- **a** numerical
- **b** alphabetical
- **c** chronological
- **d** subject

9 A checklist is used:
- **a** to list cheques paid into the bank
- **b** to list the activities involved in a task
- **c** as an inventory for recording equipment and furniture
- **d** to record cheques received in the incoming mail

10 Re-arrange the following tasks relating to the planning of an office party in the correct order of priority, with the first at 'a':
- **a** confirm numbers with caterer
- **b** book venue and caterer
- **c** decide date
- **d** invite staff

Short answer questions

State the missing words or phrases

11 Begin planning by preparing a .... of all the activities involved.

12 Each employee is required to prepare and agree a .... to develop self.

13 A follow-up system is used to ensure that ....

14 Computerised desk diary entries can be seen on a ....

15 When making an appointment, record the name of the contact, their organisation, the venue and .... on the relevant day of your diary.

Supply brief answers to the following questions:

16 State your priorities when planning each day's work for:

a urgent work:

....

b not so urgent but important work

....

c not urgent and less important work

....

17 State three office work planning aids:

a ....

b ....

c ....

18 List three functions of a desk diary:

a ....

b ....

c ....

19 Suggest the initial steps which should be taken to prepare a plan of action for your personal development:

a ....

b ....

c ....

20 When a telephone caller requests an appointment, you should make a record of:

a ....

b ....

c ....

d ....

e ....

f ....

Section C
OFFICE TECHNOLOGY

Unit 10
Computer systems and terminology

This unit provides the essential background knowledge and terms which are associated with acquiring the following data and information processing competences:

- Input data and text into a computer system
- Locate and retrieve data from a computer system
- Print documents using a computer system (NVQ2)

It is now common practice for office workers to use computers for many of the tasks they perform, for example they word process their own letters and messages; use e-mail; send and receive faxes; gain access to data stored on a computer; make calculations using spreadsheets; and update records with new data.

▶ HARDWARE

These are the physical parts of a computer and they include:

- Central Processing Unit and disk storage (CPU) — controls and co-ordinates the operations of the computer, makes calculations and comparisons
- Visual Display Unit (VDU) — input and output devices which display data on a screen
- Keyboard — used to input data into the computer and through which the operator gives instructions to the computer
- Mouse — the meaning of this term is manually operated user signal encoder – another input device. A mouse is a portable instrument with a rolling ball which, when rolled across a flat surface near the computer, moves a pointer on the screen. When the mouse button is pressed, the computer activates the item in the position occupied by the mouse.
- CD-ROM — meaning compact disk with read only memory. Most modern personal computers have CD-ROM drives which provide multi-media facilities (as in Fig 10.1). Books, training programmes, catalogues and newspapers can now be obtained on CD-ROM as an alternative to an on-line service.
- Printer — The output device for printing data (ie hard copy). They may be classified as character, line and page printers as follows:

- Character printers, which print one character at a time similar to a typewriter, include daisy wheel, dot matrix, ink jet and bubble jet printers.
- Line printers, which print a complete line in one operation.
- Page printers, which print a complete page at a time, such as laser printers (as in Fig 10.2), which can produce letter-quality printing.

Fig 10.2 A modern computer with laser jet printer and multi-media capability

Fig 10.1 Loading a compact disk into a CD writer

▶ SOFTWARE

This is the operating system which tells the hardware what to do and is the non-physical or intangible part of the computer system.

Software applications packages are programs which are written for a particular function such as word processing; database (which may include integrated data for sales, purchases, stock and wages systems); spreadsheets (calculations and accounts); or management information systems (including meetings and appointments scheduling); voice recognition which employs a large active vocabulary and sophisticated language models to analyse spoken words and turn them into text on a pc screen.

Software packages are loaded and stored on the hard disk. There are many business software packages on the market which can be bought 'off the shelf'.

All current operating environments use the 'windows' technique which provides a graphic interface for the operator to select commands. Most new computers work with windows-based software.

Spreadsheets

A spreadsheet program, which is in the form of a computerised analysis sheet, can be used to make rapid calculations to help with financial planning and decision-making. A spreadsheet displays a matrix of cells identified by columns and rows. The screen is a window through which any part of the matrix may be viewed. Data and formulae are entered to give a rapid means of forecasting and financial planning. For example, it can reveal the effects of an increase in wages or raw materials on the cost of finished products, profit margins, etc. Hard copy of the spreadsheet figures can be printed out at any stage. Spreadsheets are particularly useful if amendments have to be made quickly or there is a need for columns of figures to be updated regularly, as recalculations can be done automatically. Graphs and charts can also be produced from spreadsheets to present numerical data graphically.

Desktop publishing (DTP)

See page 107.

Disk storage

See page 73.

▶ LAPTOP COMPUTERS

Many business executives now use laptop computers (or notebooks), as illustrated in Fig 10.3, which they carry around with them and use in meetings. This allows them to gain instant access to vast amounts of information, previously transferred from their office computer to the hard disk of their laptop computer. They can also be fitted with a modem to enable them to communicate with a head office network and read their e-mail or access data from different sources, including company databases and the Internet.

Fig 10.3 A laptop computer

A recent development in computing provides a pen computer as an alternative to the portable computers. Users write directly on a notepad – a digitised screen (as in Fig 10.4) with a cordless pen-like stylus to input data, sign their names, print or draw. The system records what is written and computes the data.

Fig 10.4 A pen computer notepad

Salespeople visiting clients could, for example, have all the details of the calls already loaded into the notepad. They could then add any new information and, at the end of each call, the revised information may be loaded back into the company's computer system, providing faster access to data for both representatives and head office staff.

▶ DATA HIERARCHY

database – a collection of information relating to several files so that the records can be sorted and accessed in a variety of ways using different fields, such as invoice numbers, customers' names, regions, products, etc

↑

file – a collection of records/fields relating to a particular topic, such as personnel records, wages, customers' records, etc

↑

record – a collection of fields relating to a specific entity, eg a customer's record

↑

field – a subdivision of an item of infor-

mation, eg a customer's account number, stock number, etc

byte – represents one alphabetical or numerical symbol. (NB: 1000 bytes = 1 kilobyte; 1000 kilobytes = 1 megabyte)

bit – a contracted binary digit representing a zero or one in binary arithmetic. (8 bits = 1 byte)

In ascending order, the above is the structure of the information system data hierarchy.

▶ CONFIGURATION OF COMPUTER SYSTEMS

- **Stand-alone** a single self-contained computer
- **Shared resource** two or more workstations sharing the same printer and possibly storage devices
- **Local area network (LAN)** connects computers, printers and telecommunications within a limited area, usually one building
- **Wide area networks (WAN)**
  - **Company based** links together several branches of a company using discreet phone lines. No other organisation has access to their network
  - **Internet** an international network, such as the Internet, or the Information Super Highway as it is sometimes called. This is a huge on-line computer networking service which is currently linked to over 40 million users from 152 countries. It provides access to databases holding vast sources of information and electronic mail between suppliers and customers. Computer users are able to use the Internet by subscribing to a commercial online service or establishing a link via a local Internet Access Service provider. If a local Internet Access Service is used, eg Net connect, the user accesses the Internet using a local phone call to a Point of Presence (POP) and pays a standard monthly fee. Software for accessing the World Wide Web (WWW) can be used to send e-mail via the Internet to almost any country abroad.

▶ COMPUTER APPLICATIONS

Typical business applications of the computer are:

- customer records and sales ledger
- supplier records and bought ledger
- personnel records and payroll
- stock control
- cash flow
- costing and budgetary control
- production planning
- market research and sales forecasting
- fax
- e-mail
- production of artwork (desktop publishing)
- text processing:
  - reports, letters, minutes, etc
  - standard or form letters merged with a mailing list to provide 'individual' style letters
  - updating price lists, internal telephone directories, mailing lists, parts lists, etc, where amendments are inserted without having to retype all of the material

Text processing common terms:

- **Back up** a duplicate copy of a working disk, kept as a safeguard in the event of loss or damage of the original disk
- **Boiler plating** using a selected group of standard paragraphs and merging them to form one document
- **Character string** a group of identical alphabetical/numeric characters, eg words, date, etc, appearing within a text. A search can be made by comparing a character string with the characters contained in a document
- **Cursor** a device on a screen for positioning the next entry
- **Cut and paste** moving a block of text, eg a paragraph from one position of a document to another. Also referred to as 'block move'
- **Emboldening** a means of producing bolder type
- **Fonts** relates to different type faces and point-sizes
- **Global search and replace** searching for a character string and replacing it with a different one, eg changing all references to 1996 to 1997
- **Headers and footers** headings, page numbering and other information which can be automatically generated at the top or bottom of every or specified pages in a document
- **Icons** pictures depicting actions
- **Interface** a link between a computer and a peripheral such as a modem
- **Justification** a means of producing text with aligned left- and right-hand margins
- **Mail merge** an automatic process for merging a document file, eg a standard letter, with a mailing list containing names, addresses, dates, amounts, etc, to produce personalised letters
- **Menu** a method of making a system 'user friendly': sets of commands are dropped down on the screen so that the operator does not have to refer to a manual for instructions
- **Save** a method of transferring a file from the screen of a word processor to a disk
- **Scrolling** the movement of text vertically or horizontally on a screen
- **Spell check** a means of checking a passage for spelling/keying errors against a program containing a dictionary of standard words. Users can add their own words to meet their individual needs
- **Status line** the line which appears at the top or bottom of a screen giving information about the work situation under review, eg name of file, page no, column no, line no, etc
- **Toolbars** a row of buttons offering a choice of different actions
- **Wraparound** a means of automatically transferring the last word(s) on a line to the next line if it does not fit within the line length

▶ SECURITY OF COMPUTERISED DATA

Special precautions must be taken to safeguard computerised data against loss or corruption and this may entail:

- taking back-up copies daily on a disk or tape streamer
- keeping back-up duplicate copies of disks in a secure place
- arranging for personal passwords to be used by the staff authorised to have access to the

computer, the passwords being changed at regular intervals
- using codes, known only to the users, for document files
- using write-protect tags on program disks to prevent master disks from being corrupted
- controlling entry to the office, eg pass cards, TV cameras, etc

Care of floppy disks

Do
- Keep floppy disks in disk boxes/cabinets, when not in use, to protect them from dust
- Label each disk with a description of its contents
- Insert disks carefully into the disk drive, without forcing them, to avoid damage
- As a safeguard against damage or loss, keep a back-up (duplicate) of any disk containing important data, eg all master program disks should be copied and the masters stored in a secure place
- Use a write protect tag on a system disk to prevent data from being added to it

Do not
- Bend, fold or scratch disks
- Touch the exposed portion of a disk
- Store disks near a hot radiator, fire or heat of the sun
- Remove disks when the drive light is on
- Leave disks around on the top of a screen, printer, telephone and other electronic equipment (sources of magnetism) which could corrupt them
- Use disks which have not been checked for viruses

▶ DATA PROTECTION

The Data Protection Act 1984 establishes rights for individuals to have access to their own personal data held on computer files. The Act contains the following principles which govern the processing of personal data:

1 Data must be obtained fairly and lawfully, ie people must not be misled as to the use to which information they supply about themselves will be put.
2 Data must only be held for registered and lawful purposes. Data users are required to register the personal data they hold with the Data Protection Registrar.
3 Data must only be used and disclosed for the purposes registered.
4 Data must be adequate, relevant and not excessive for its purpose.
5 Data must be accurate and, where necessary, kept up to date.
6 Data must be held for no longer than is necessary.
7 Individuals must be allowed access to data about themselves at reasonable intervals and without undue expense and they must be provided with a copy of it in an intelligible form. Where appropriate, the data must be corrected or erased.
8 Data users must take appropriate security measures to prevent unauthorised access, disclosure, alteration or destruction of personal data and against its accidental loss or destruction.

▶ PROGRESS CHECK

Multiple choice questions

1 A computer program contains:
a the times when the computer has been booked
b the operator's manual
c a list of instructions to the computer
d the 'hard' copy from a computer

2 The Internet is:
a an international network for controlling viruses
b a wide area network
c a shared resource
d a local area network

3 One million bytes of data in a storage system is:
a a megabyte
b a kilobyte
c a bit
d a millibyte

4 Figure 10.5 is an example of:
a MICR
b magnetic tape
c OCR
d bar coding

5 Which of the following is computer hardware?
a a program
b a spreadsheet
c a printer
d a datapost

6 Hard copy produced from a computer is:
a a metal plate
b an operating manual
c a hard disk
d printed paper

7 Which of the following is an output device for a computer?
a printer
b windows
c cursor
d mouse

8 A spreadsheet program takes the form of a:
a dictionary of standard words
b computerised analysis sheet
c system in which several users have access to one processor
d computerised desk diary

9 The Data Protection Act was passed in:
a 1980
b 1984
c 1988
d 1992

Fig 10.5

10 Pair the two lists of words (note that there is a surplus item in the second column):

Term	**Meaning**
a back up	**a** pictures
b emboldening	**b** group of identical alphabetic/numeric characters
c character string	**c** duplicate copy of disk
d icons	**d** moving a block of text
	e bolder type

Short answer questions

State the missing words or phrases:

11 A password keyed into a computer is used to maintain .... of information.

12 An example of a letter quality printer would be a/an .... printer.

13 The letters VDU stand for ....

14 .... bits = 1 byte.

15 Mouse means ....

Supply brief answers to the following questions:

16 State three items of computer hardware:
a ....
b ....
c ....

17 Explain each of the following items of data:
a byte ....
b field ....
c database ....

18 Suggest three precautions which must be taken to safeguard computerised data against loss or corruption:
a ....
b ....
c ....

19 List three computer input devices:

a ....

b ....

c ....

20 State three principles which govern the processing of data in the Data Protection Act:

a ....

b ....

c ....

Unit 11
Reprography

Competences developed in this unit:

- Produce copies using reprographic equipment (NVQ1)
- Follow instructions and operate equipment (NVQ1)
- Keep equipment in a clean and working condition (NVQ1)
- Obtain and maintain physical resources to carry out own work (NVQ2)

▶ REPROGRAPHIC PROCESSES

Reprographic processes include:

- duplicators which produce copies from stencils and masters
- copiers which produce replicas from originals
- computer printers which produce 'original' copies from disks

Duplicators

There are three processes:

1 **Offset litho**	ink is offset from a greasy litho plate dampened with water
2 **Stencil**	ink passes through indentations made into a stencil and on to semi-absorbent paper
2 **Spirit**	aniline dye is transferred from the master to the copy using spirit

Although there are still a few duplicators in use today, most organisations now use copiers for reproducing large or small quantities of copies.

Copiers

There are many different types and sizes of copiers to choose from ranging from small desktop models for personal use to high-capacity laser printing models for large-scale print operations and sophisticated colour reproduction. Different features may include:

- *Document feed:* the originals may be fed into the copier by hand or by semi-automatic or fully automatic devices – a recirculating document feeder allows for copying double-sided originals
- *Paper feed:* magazines, trays or cassettes may be used for feeding the paper into the copier – the quantities ranging from 250 to 4000 sheets. Some machines hold different sizes of paper and make automatic selection of the size of paper required as in the copier illustrated in Fig 11.1. Facilities can also be provided for printing on both sides of the paper.
- *Paper size:* most copiers handle originals and copies of A3–A5 international paper size but the range can extend to A2–A6
- *Speed:* ranges from 20 copies per minute, although colour copiers are much slower
- *Image editing:* this includes mask and trim facilities for cutting out unwanted material; image shift for relocating parts of an original from one position to another; reversing out graphics or text, ie white on black instead of black on white
- *Reduction and enlargement of original:* different ratios of reduction and enlargement may be provided
- *Collation:* bin sorters, ranging from 10 to 40, may be provided for collating the printed copies
- *Finishing functions:* these include collation bins for online sorting (as above); jogging; folding; stitching/ adhesive binding; automatic stapling
- *Memory:* programmed instructions may be stored in a memory so that they can be

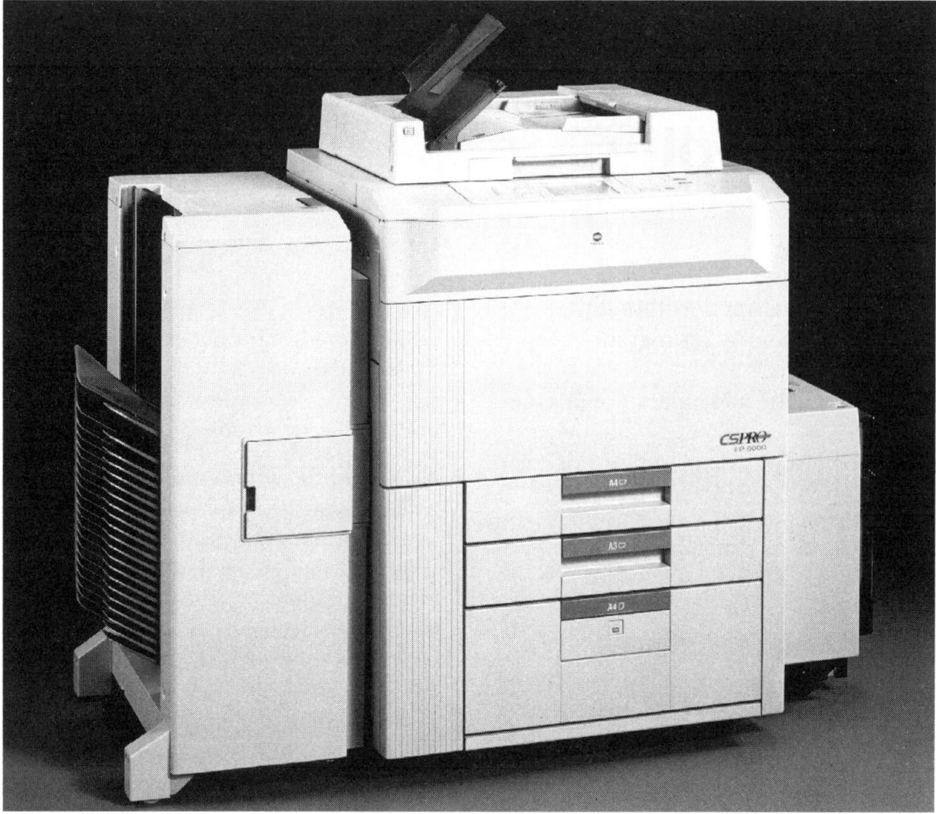

Fig 11.1 Electrostatic copier with automatic paper selection

recalled at a later date by operating a pre-set key or for storing images of originals

- *Colour reproduction:* there are several different processes for reproducing colour, eg electrophotographic, photographic/laser, thermal transfer and encapsulation using light-sensitive paper – the user must consider whether the extra cost of a colour copier is advantageous
- *Control of use:* by issuing users with code numbers or charge cards, which are essential to activate the copier, the machine can record the number of copies made by each user
- *Modular design:* a means of allowing the user to extend the copying facilities if required in the future
- *Multi-functional:* equipment is now available which combine the functions of copying, printing and faxing, as in Fig. 11.3. It has the ability to fax images from books and magazines without copying them first.
- *Uses:* reproducing copies of printed documents, legal documents, insurance policies, statistical returns, diagrams and drawings, extracts from books and magazines, incoming letters required for several departments; making overhead transparencies; preparing offset litho masters.

Laser 'intelligent' copiers

These are advanced copiers capable of handling large quantities and accepting information directly from computers and word processors. The image of the original is converted into a digital electrical signal as the intermediate process instead of using a drum. This signal turns the laser on and off to reproduce the image which can be processed, transmitted to other locations or stored for later recall. The machine is in two parts: a reader and a print unit which work separately from one another,

Fig 11.2 An electronic printing system

allowing one reader to be interfaced with up to three printers to produce copies very quickly. The printer units can be remote from the reader unit to meet the departmental copying needs of a company. Long-life toner is used which produces up to 20,000 copies at one filling. Fig 11.2 illustrates an advanced copying system which prints at speeds of up to 92 pages per minute.

Desktop publishing

This is a means of producing artwork with integrated text and graphics ready for copying or printing. It is a multi-functional process integrating the use of a scanner, a computer (with a hard disk), a laser printer and specially-designed software combining text creation, editing and graphics (*see* Fig 11.4). A scanner is an electronic copying device for transferring images directly from source documents to the computer memory or screen, providing complete accuracy and reliability. These images can be enlarged, reduced or edited before being combined with the text.

Desktop publishing is ideal for producing forms, letter headings, advertising copy, price lists and catalogues, brochures, bulletins, in-house journals, technical manuals, handouts, 35 mm slides and overhead projector transparencies.

The equipment used in desktop publishing is illustrated in Fig 11.5.

▶ FORM AND PAPER HANDLING EQUIPMENT

Form and paper handling equipment ranges from sophisticated automatic electronic high-speed machines to desk-top models, including collators, joggers, folding machines, bursters and decollators.

Collators

The considerable table space normally required for spreading out stacks of paper for collation is saved when a collating machine is

Fig 11.3 A multi-functional copier, fax and printer

used. Most are electrically operated and foot controlled. The stacks of papers are fitted into individual shelves or compartments and the top sheet from each is automatically ejected in readiness for rapid hand collection. The compact arrangement of the shelves eliminates much of the fatigue normally experienced when reaching for papers from stacks spread out over a table. After collation, a set of papers can be placed in a jogger to vibrate them into alignment ready to be bound or stapled.

Binders

These are used for fastening multi-page documents and booklets. Several types are available but the most commonly used are spiral binders and flat comb binders (as in Fig 11.6). In the spiral method the pages are punched and a plastic spiral binder is threaded into the holes to hold the pages together. Flat comb binders are made up of two plastic strips which are placed on either side of the pages and heat-sealed to provide a permanent binding.

Bursters

Much of today's paperwork is produced from a computer in the form of sprocketed continuous stationery. A burster, as illustrated in Fig 11.7, cuts or 'bursts' the continuous stationery at the perforations into single sheets, neatly trimmed and ready for the post. A burster can handle a variety of forms of different sizes and thicknesses and stack them in strict sequential order. The cut offs or trimmings are collected in a waste bin.

Decollators

If the forms are printed in multi-part sets a decollator (*see* Fig 11.8) is used to separate the parts into individual continuous printouts and dispose of the carbons.

▶ GUIDELINES FOR THE CLEANING, CARE AND MAINTENANCE OF EQUIPMENT

Check that:

- Day-to-day maintenance and cleaning procedures are the responsibility of the operator or an appointed person and that they are carried out in accordance with the advice given in operating manuals – kept with the machines for ease of reference.
- Operators do not smoke, drink or eat when using the equipment.
- Regular servicing takes place and, where necessary, a servicing contract is arranged.
- A procedure is laid down for reporting faults and, when necessary, arranging for a mechanic to attend.
- before calling in a mechanic for a breakdown *Check*:
  - ○ that the power supply is on
  - ○ that fuses in the equipment are working but take care when handling electric parts (if the fuse is at fault, the reason for its failure should be investigated by an electrician)
  - ○ there are no faults in the connecting cables and plugs

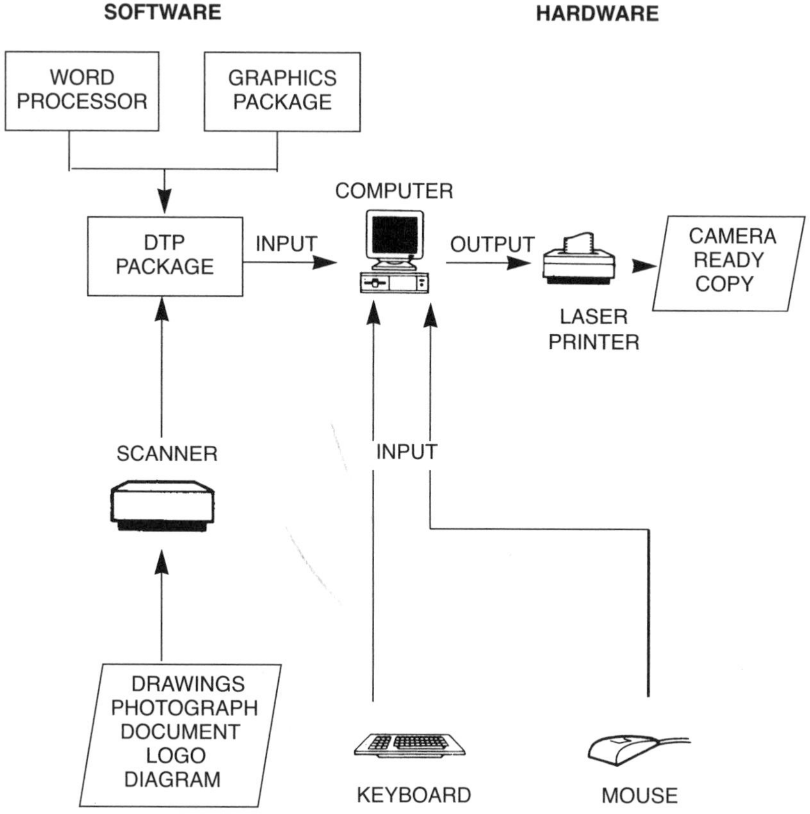

Fig 11.4 Desktop publishing diagram

- ○ the 'trouble shooting' section in the operating manual for useful tips on tracing the fault

If, after taking these steps, there is still a fault with the equipment, call for the services of a maintenance engineer.

- A maintenance log record is kept of any intermittent faults which occur and the dates and times when maintenance engineers call to attend to the equipment.
- Procedures are complied with for dealing with any problems experienced in operating equipment.
- The electrical supply is disconnected if a machine has to be moved.
- All operators are given adequate training and the instructions are understood before any use is made of the equipment.
- Any waste materials are discarded safely and appropriately in accordance with organisational procedures.
- Equipment work areas are left in a clean and tidy condition.
- Appropriate materials for the equipment are obtained and stored safely and securely in adequate quantities. *See* page 30 for the key factors in the efficient organisation of a stationery stock room.
- The attention of all users is drawn to safety procedures and copyright regulations.

▶ ADDRESSING ENVELOPES

Computers and copiers can be used to print out names and addresses and other repetitive data on sheets, with adhesive backing if required, thus providing a rapid and efficient means of supplying address labels for large quantities of envelopes and other mailing applications.

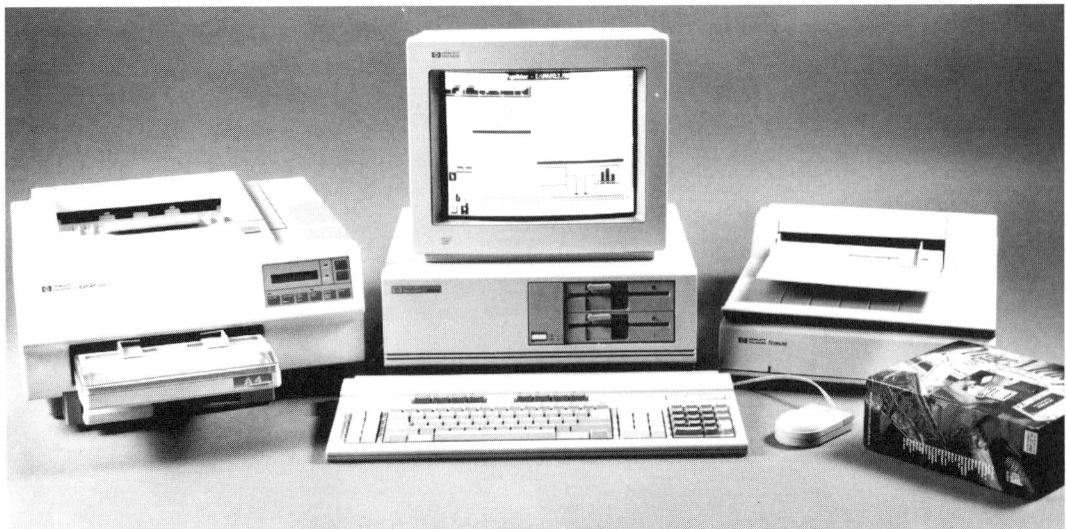

Fig 11.5 Desktop publishing equipment

Database software packages can be supplied for large scale addressing applications. The 'quick address' system, as illustrated in Fig. 11.9, is an on-line rapid addressing system which uses a computer to accept a postcode and automatically reproduce the address to street level and, after entering in the house number, completes the full address. The system also ensures that correctly spelt data is returned even if an error is made during data entry. Files of existing addresses can be verified and any missing or incorrect postcodes inserted.

Fig 11.6 Wire-O desktop electric binding machine (Wire-O is the registered trade mark of James Burn International)

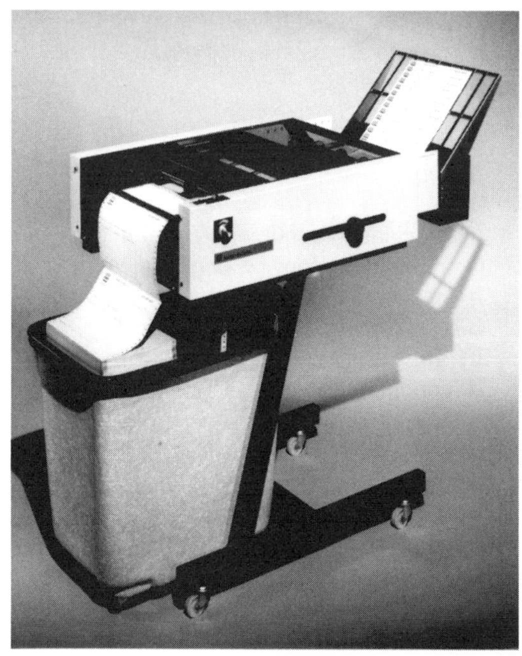

Fig 11.7 A burster

► COPYRIGHT LAW

Under the 'fair dealing' provisions of the Copyright, Designs and Patents Act 1988 you are permitted to make one copy only of an agreed maximum amount of any published material for the purposes of research, private study, criticism, or review, but you are not permitted to copy a substantial part of the work. In addition, for the purposes of review, sufficient acknowledgment must be made. In order to copy a substantial part of a work, ie more than a single chapter or article of a publication, or to copy for any purpose outside the 'fair dealing' provision, it is necessary for you to first obtain the permission of the copyright holder (usually the publisher or author) or you must have taken all reasonable steps to find out the name and address of the copyright holder and have been unsuccessful. You must make at least three attempts at regular (say one monthly) intervals before you can be regarded as having made 'all reasonable attempts' to contact the copyright holder. If you do not succeed, you must indicate this in your publication or review

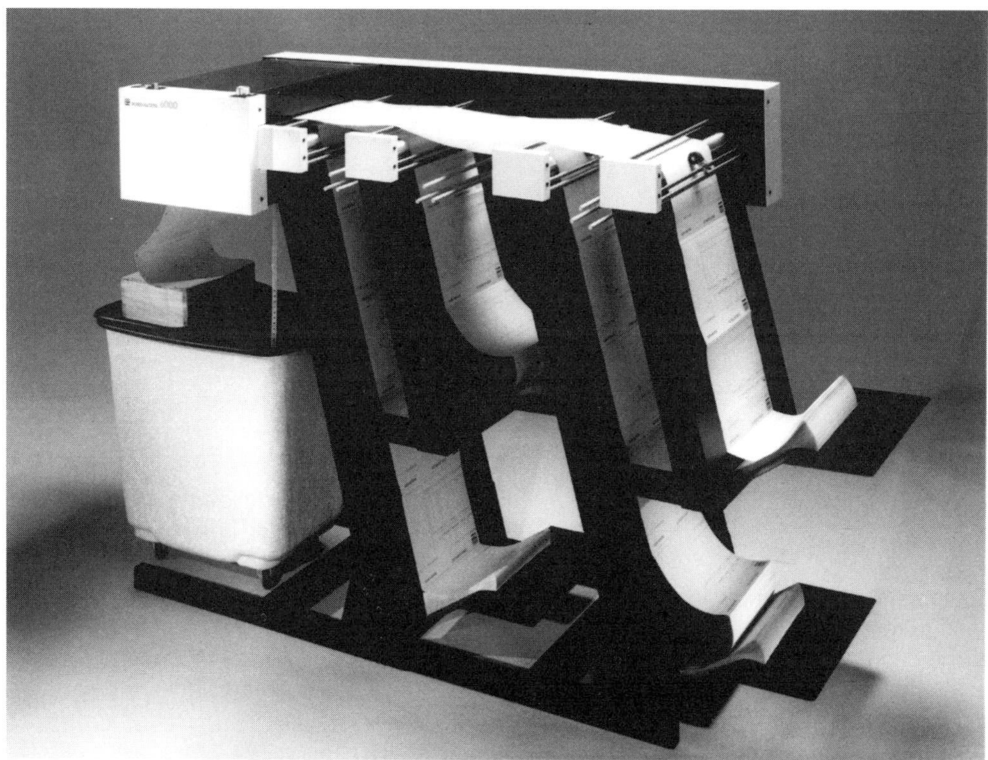

Fig 11.8 A decollator

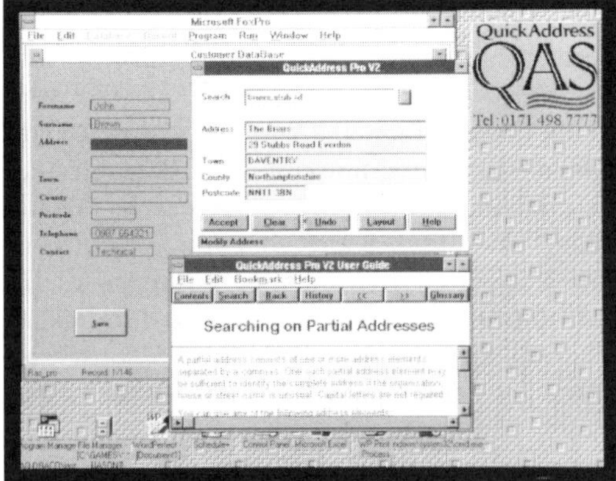

Fig 11.9 A Quick address software package

in the form of an acknowledgment along the following lines:

'Unfortunately, I have been unable to trace the copyright holder(s) of the following material (*list material*) and would welcome any information which would enable me to do so.'

The main provisions of the Act and Regulations should be brought to the notice of staff using copying facilities.

▶ SAFETY CHECKS FOR OPERATING REPROGRAPHIC EQUIPMENT

(See Unit 13)

▶ PROGRESS CHECK

Multiple choice questions

1 The Copyright, Designs and Patents Act was passed in:
- **a** 1984
- **b** 1988
- **c** 1992
- **d** 1996

2 Equipment maintenance log records are used to record:
- **a** the depreciation of equipment
- **b** intermittent faults
- **c** the number of copies made by each user
- **d** operating procedures

3 Which one of the following can be used to reproduce a facsimile copy from a book?
- **a** computer
- **b** telex
- **c** duplicator
- **d** copier

4 A recirculating document feeder in a copier is intended for copying originals which are:
- **a** single-sided
- **b** too large for automatic feeding
- **c** required for repeat printing
- **d** double-sided

5 Desktop publishing is a means of producing:
- **a** artwork
- **b** typescript
- **c** printer's proofs
- **d** author's manuscripts

6 Envelopes for circulars can be addressed by means of:
- **a** a computer
- **b** an offset litho duplicator
- **c** a burster
- **d** a franking machine

7 A machine which assembles pages into the required order is called:
- **a** an assembler
- **b** a jogger
- **c** a collator
- **d** a duplicator

8 Multi-part sets of forms are separated by a:
- **a** collator
- **b** burster
- **c** laminator
- **d** decollator

9 Rearrange the following items of equipment in the order in which they would be used to produce a booklet:
- **a** jogger
- **b** binder
- **c** copier
- **d** collator

10 Pair the two lists of words (note that there is a surplus item in the second column):

Machines	**Materials/ equipment used**
a binder	**a** toner powder
b copier	**b** mouse
c decollator	**c** plastic strips
d desktop publishing	**d** stylus pen
	e multi-part set

Short answer questions

State the missing words or phrases:

11 Copying machines enable .... from original documents to be produced without the preparation of masters.

12 A/an .... is a useful device for ensuring that the edges of papers in multiple copy documents are even prior to binding.

13 A machine which assembles pages into the correct order is called a/an ....

14 A multifunctional copier combines the functions of copying, printing and ....

15 The letters DTP stand for ....

Supply brief answers to the following questions:

16 Apart from the production of an exact copy, list three other functions of a modern copier:

a ....
b ....
c

17 You are producing copies of a document and notice that the copies are too faint to read easily. List three possible actions you could take:

a ....
b ....
c ....

18 List three items of equipment used in desktop publishing:

a ....
b ....
c ....

19 Before calling in a mechanic for a breakdown of a machine check that the power supply is on as well as checking:

a ....
b ....
c ....

20 State what you, as a student, are permitted to copy from published material under the Copyright, Designs and Patents Act:

a ....
b ....
c ....

Unit 12
Calculators

Competence developed in this unit:

- Check and process routine numerical information (NVQ1)

Electronic calculators with printing facilities are commonly used in offices for tasks which involve calculations. The tally roll is useful for providing printed proof of the accuracy of calculations and also for attaching to documents for future reference and checking. Calculators can be used for arithmetical processes such as addition, subtraction, multiplication, division, percentages and square roots. Functions include:

- a decimal point selector (including a floating decimal point)
- sub-total key
- rounding switch rounds up or down when the fixed decimal point is chosen in multiplication and division
- item counter switch providing the total number of items added or subtracted
- non-add key for printing reference numbers which are not to be included in the calculation
- automatic constant feature which enables you to add, subtract, multiply or divide by the same number repeatedly without having to re-enter the number for each new calculation
- memory to provide for the storage of products or quotients during the course of a calculation

Addition

1 Calculate 6.00 + 7.00 + 3.57

	Enter	*Depress*
Ref No	**1**	#
– use the	**6**	+
non-add	**7**	+
key	**3.57**	+
		+

Tally roll

```
          0.00  *

            1.  #
          6.00  +
          7.00  +
          3.57  +
003
         16.57  *
```

Subtraction

2 Calculate 1498.26 – 123.38

Enter	*Depress*
2	#
1498.26	+
123.38	–
	*

Tally roll

```
000
          0.00  *

            2.  #
       1498.26  +
        123.38  –
002
       1374.88  *
```

Addition and subtraction with repeat items

3 Calculate 219 + 187 + 187 + 187 + 187 – 56 – 56

Enter	*Depress*
3	#
219	+
187	++++
56	– –
	*

Tally roll

```
000
          0.00  *

            3.  #
          219.  +
          187.  +
          187.  +
          187.  +
          187.  +
           56.  –
           56.  –
007
          855.  *
```

Multiplication

4 Calculate 234.61 × 381.42

Enter	*Depress*
4	#
234.61	×
381.42	=

Tally roll

```
000
          0.00  *

            4.  #
        234.61  ×
        381.42  =
      89484.95  T
```

Multiplication of constant factors

5 Calculate *248 × 19
*248 × 109
*248 × 219

Enter	*Depress*
5	#
248	×
19	=
109	=
219	=

***constant factors**

Tally roll

```
000
        0.00  *

          5.  #
        248.  ×
         19.  =
     4712.00  T
        109.  =
    27032.00  T
        219.  =
    54312.00  T
```

Division

6 Calculate 789 ÷ 234

Enter	*Depress*
6	#
789	÷
234	=

Tally roll

```
000
        0.00  *

          6.  #
        789.  ÷
        234.  =
        3.37  T
```

Percentages

7 Calculate 25% of £700

Enter	*Depress*
7	#
700	×
25	%

Tally roll

```
000
        0.00  *

          7.  #
        700.  ×
         25.  %
      175.00  T
```

8 Calculate £700 + 25%

Enter	*Depress*
8	#
700	×
25	%
	+

Tally roll

```
000
        0.00  *

          8.  #
        700.  ×
         25.  %
      175.00  T
      175.00  +
      875.00  T
```

9 Calculate £700 – 25%

Enter	*Depress*
9	#
700	×
25	%
	–

Tally roll

```
000
        0.00  *

          9.  #
        700.  ×
         25.  %
      175.00  T
      175.00  -
      525.00  T
```

10 Calculate the invoice net price

Add £14.62
£13.34
£20.92

Sub-total
Deduct 25% trade discount
Add 17½% VAT

Enter	*Depress*
10	#
14.62	+
13.34	+
20.92	+
	◊
	×
25	%
	–
	×
17.5	%
	+

Tally roll

```
000
        0.00  *

         10.  #
       14.62  +
       13.34  +
       20.92  +
003
       48.88  ◊
       48.88  ×
         25.  %
       12.22  T
       12.22  -
       36.66  T
       36.66  ×
        17.5  %
        6.42  T
        6.42  +
       43.08  T
```

Remember always to clear the calculator before each new operation by using the C key or *

▶ EXAMPLES OF THE USE OF A CALCULATOR

Common applications include: calculating and checking time cards and payroll totals, invoice extensions, travelling expenses claims, stock valuations, foreign exchange rates, bills of quantities, sales analysis.

▶ PROGRESS CHECK

Use a calculator to calculate the following:

1 29.23 + 1489.32 + 1.63 + 24 000

2 2189.48 – 341.99

3 387 + 284 + 284 + 284 + 284 – 125 – 125 – 125

4 186.19 × 2348.62

5 **a** 356 × 28
b 356 × 69
c 356 × 196

6 2843 ÷ 186

7 8% of £149

8 £149 + 8%

9 £149 – 8%

10 The net invoice price for the invoice illustrated in Fig 12.1

INVOICE

No A1286

From: SYSTEMS FURNITURE plc
Brookfield Industrial Estate, Twyford, Westshire TD3 2BS

Tel: 0193 3841923
Telex: 342689
Fax: 0193 2196734
VAT Registration No: 3027560 21
Date: 1 March 19--

To: Messrs R N Fothergill & Co
202 High Street
Twyford
Westshire TD1 5AT

Terms: Delivered Twyford
Payment one month after delivery

Completion of Order No AR 1296 dated 26 February 19--

Quantity	Description	Cat No	Price each £	Cost £	VAT rate %	VAT amount %
1	Systems Desk	AS1	300.00	300.00		
1	Systems Desk (split level)	AS4	320.00	320.00		
1	Executive Desk	AE1	400.00	400.00		
	Sub-total			?		
	Less trade discount 10%			?		
				?	$17\frac{1}{2}$	?
	Plus VAT			?		
				?		

Delivered on:
by

Fig 12.1 Invoice

Unit 13
Health and safety

Competence developed in this unit:

- Monitor and maintain health and safety within the workplace (NVQ2)

Safe working in the office situation involves:

- being orderly and tidy to ensure that your office is free from hazards
- recognising and reporting promptly potential hazards
- dealing competently with any hazardous or potentially hazardous situations
- observing laid down safety procedures and practices for dealing with accidents, fires or other emergencies

▶ SAFETY LEGISLATION AND REGULATIONS

The health and safety of office employees is protected by legislation and in particular by the Health and Safety at Work Act 1974 and regulations arising from it which were brought into use in 1993, including:

1 Management of health and safety at work.
2 Workplace health, safety and welfare (relating to many of the provisions of the Offices, Shops and Railway Premises Act 1963).
3 Provision and use of work equipment.
4 Personal protective equipment.
5 Display screen equipment.
6 Manual handling operations.

1 Health and Safety at Work Act 1974

Under this act the employer is required to provide:

- a safe and healthy working environment
- safe equipment (including efficient maintenance)
- safe systems of work
- safe methods of handling, storing and transporting goods
- training in safety practices
- supervision
- consultation for promoting health and safety

It is also the employer's duty to protect persons not in the company's employment, eg the public, customers, visiting workers, delivery men, etc, when they are visiting the premises. The employees have a duty to:

- take reasonable care for the health and safety of themselves and of other persons who may be affected by their acts or omissions at work
- follow safety practices
- co-operate with their employer in promoting and maintaining health and safety
- refrain from interfering with or misusing anything provided for health and safety of themselves or others

2 Workplace (health, safety and welfare) regulations 1992

Under these regulations and related codes of practice the employer must provide:

- **Maintenance of equipment** — Regular maintenance (including, as necessary, inspection, testing, adjustment, lubrication and cleaning) must be carried out at suitable intervals.

  Any potentially dangerous defects must be remedied and access to any defective equipment prevented.

  A suitable record

should be kept to ensure that the system is properly controlled.

- **Ventilation** Effective suitable provision of ventilation must be provided.
- **Temperature** There must be a reasonable temperature in workrooms, ie at least 16 degrees Celsius unless much of the work involves severe physical effort in which case the temperature must be at least 13 degrees Celsius.

  Thermometers should be available at a convenient distance from every part of the workplace to enable temperatures to be measured, but these need not be provided in each workroom.
- **Lighting** There must be suitable and sufficient lighting. This should be sufficient to enable people to work, use facilities and move from place to place safely and without experiencing eyestrain.
- **Cleanliness** Every workplace and the furniture, furnishings and fittings must be kept sufficiently clean. Floors and indoor traffic routes should be cleaned at least once a week.
- **Office space** There must be sufficient floor area, height and unoccupied space for the purposes of health, safety and welfare. In a typical office, where the ceiling is 2.4 m high, a floor area of 4.6 m^2 (for example 2.0 × 2.3 m) will be needed to provide adequate space of 11 m^3. Where the ceiling is at least 3.0 m high the minimum floor area will need to be 3.7 m^2 (for example 2.0 × 1.85 m).

  Offices may need to be larger, or to have fewer people working in them, than indicated above, depending on such factors as the contents and layout of the office and the nature of work undertaken.
- **Seating** A suitable seat must be provided for each person at work in the workplace whose work includes operations of a kind that the work can or must be done sitting. Workstations should be arranged so that each task can be carried out safely and comfortably. Seating in offices should provide adequate support for the lower back and a footrest should be provided for any worker who cannot comfortably place their feet flat on the floor.
- **Sanitary conveniences** Suitable and sufficient sanitary conveniences must be provided at readily accessible places.
- **Washing facilities** Suitable and sufficient washing facilities must be provided at readily accessible places. They should include a supply of clean hot and cold water and showers where appropriate.
- **Drinking water** An adequate supply of wholesome drinking water must be provided for all persons at work in the workplace.
- **Accommodation for clothing** Suitable and sufficient accommodation must be provided for clothing.
- **Facilities for rest and meals** Suitable and sufficient rest facilities and places for employees to eat meals should be made available.

Further details are given in the Approved Code of Practice and Guidance for the Workplace (Health, Safety and Welfare) Regulations 1992 published by HMSO for the Health and Safety Commission.

▶ SAFE WORKING PRACTICES

Premises

	Hazards to look out for
• Plan the layout of the office to reduce the danger of accidents	• Overcrowding • Unsuitable siting of furniture and equipment • Trailing telephone or electric leads
• Situate furniture and equipment in safe positions	• Filing cabinet drawers obstructing passages • Protruding sharp corners of furniture and equipment
• Ensure that corridors, stairs, etc are safe and free from combustible storage materials and other obstructions	• Worn or missing stair treads • Missing or damaged handrail on stairs • Slippery floors • Parcels, luggage, furniture, etc obstructing passages
• Load and position filing cabinets safely	• Cabinets toppling over because of heavy top drawer • Drawers obstructing passages
• Use a step-ladder when reaching files or other objects in a high position	• Standing on a swivel chair
• Make suitable arrangements for heating water and preparing hot drinks, preferably away from the work station	• Boiling water and pouring out hot water in a confined space

Use of equipment

	Hazards to look out for
• Read and comply with operating instructions	• Meddling with equipment and using it without proper training and supervision
• Know how to stop electric supply in an emergency	• Worn or dangerous appliances
• Avoid having a trailing flex from a socket to a machine	• Trailing flex
• Arrange regular care and maintenance of equipment. If a machine does not work properly, do not tamper with electrical parts but call in a mechanic	• Loose and damaged connections • Unearthed equipment • Defective insulation
• Report faulty or damaged equipment without delay	• Overloaded circuits
• Check that dangerous parts of machinery are fitted with guards, especially paper-cutting machines	• Loose or missing safety guard
• Place equipment securely on desks and tables	• Equipment falling off desk

• Use a trolley to move heavy machines and equipment, but do not attempt to lift very heavy weights. When lifting heavy loads from the floor, there is less strain if you bend your knees and keep your back straight	• Lifting heavy weights
• Report accidents promptly on an accident report form (see Fig 13.1)	• Incomplete records for claiming damages

Fire precautions

	Hazards to look out for
• Keep all fire exits clear to ensure that they are immediately available for use in an emergency	• Obstruction of fire exit
• Make sure that all personnel know what to do should a fire break out, ie: – how to raise the fire alarm – how to use fire-fighting equipment if required to do so – where to assemble outside the building – which is the shortest escape route to the assembly point and what other routes might be used if the shortest route is blocked	• Inadequate or missing fire-fighting/evacuation notices • Damaged fire-fighting equipment

See specimen fire instructions notice (Fig 13.2) for fire/evacuation procedure and action to be taken if you discover a fire.

• When dealing with a fire: – If a person's clothing is on fire, wrap a blanket, rug or similar article closely round them and lay them down on the ground to prevent flames from reaching the head – If electrical appliances are on fire, switch off the current before dealing with the fire – Shut the doors and, if possible, the windows of the room in which the fire is discovered	
• Keep fire doors closed – except in situations where the Fire Brigade has given permission for the doors to be held open by an automatic device	• Fire doors locked or propped open
• Do not allow smoking in any part of the building where there is a risk of fire. Ensure that smokers use ash-trays and not the waste-paper bin or the floor	• Use of wicker waste-paper baskets as ash-trays
• Make sure that bulk quantities or large cans of highly flammable correcting and cleaning fluids are locked away in a well ventilated store room or metal cabinet when not in use	• An open can of cleaning fluid left around in an office
• Insist upon combustible materials such as papers and envelopes being placed in waste bins and that they are removed regularly for disposal	• A quantity of waste paper piled up in the corner of an office

- Ensure regular maintenance and checking of fire alarms and fire extinguishers
- Arrange regular fire drills for all personnel
- A member of staff should be trained as a fire warden

Hazards to look out for

- Fire alarm/fire-fighting equipment not working when required
- Delay and uncertainty when required to evacuate the building

Note: The local fire brigade will give advice and assistance on all matters relating to fire drills and fire prevention.

First aid

Make sure that all personnel know:

- the name and means of contacting the first aid officer for their department
- the location of the first aid box and facilities

See further details on page 162.

▶ SYMBOLS YOU NEED TO RECOGNISE

Meaning	Symbol	Meaning	Symbol
A general warning and caution for a risk of danger		Safety helmets must be worn	
Caution for a risk of an electric shock		Stack correctly	
No smoking		For use by disabled persons	
Smoking and naked flames prohibited		Fire extinguisher	
Do not use water to extinguish a fire		Assembly point	

Meaning	Symbol
Dangerous substance – harmful by inhalation and if swallowed	
Caution – a risk of fire	
Fire alarm/bell buzzer	or
Fire alarm call point	
Not to be used for drinking water	
Pedestrians prohibited	
No entry	
Direction sign – may be used to indicate fire exit	

Meaning	Symbol
First aid facilities	
First aid treatment	
Kitemark The British Standards Institution approval mark to indicate that goods have been made to the standards laid down by them	
Safetymark The British Standards Institution safetymark to indicate that goods comply with British Standards for safety	
A sample of the product has been independently tested for safety by the British Electrotechnical Approvals Board	BEAB Approved BEAB mark
A symbol used on electrical accessories such as fuses to certify that they have been tested for safety by the Association of Short Circuit Testing Authorities	QUALITY ASSESSED ASTA BS 5750 ASTA safety mark
Fire resistant – having passed the 'match test'	Passed match test

ACCIDENT REPORT FORM

Report of accident or injury to a person at work or on duty and/or a dangerous occurrence
This form must be completed in all cases of accident, injury or dangerous occurrence and submitted to the Safety Officer

---

Injured person's:
Surname BREAKWELL Forenames BARBARA
Title ~~*Mr/Mrs~~/Miss/~~other (state)~~ Date of birth 14.10.78
Home address Flat 9, 200 King Street,
Manchester M2 4WD
Position held keyboard operator
*Employee/~~Student/Contractor/Visitor~~

Date and time of accident 21 November 199-
1500 hrs

Particulars of injury/incapacity
Electric shock
Activity at time of accident/injury
Preparing mail for post
Place of accident/injury
mailroom
Give full details of the accident and any injury suffered and explain how it happened made contact with a loose wire which had come away from the plug of the franking machine, causing an electric shock and state of unconsciousness.
What first-aid treatment was given?
Mouth-to-mouth resuscitation to restore breathing.
Was the injured person taken to hospital? If so, where?
Yes – Manchester General Hospital

State names and positions of any persons who were present when the accident occurred
Paul Brooks, mailroom clerk

Signature of person reporting incident P Brooks
Date of report 21 November 199-
*delete those inapplicable

Fig 13.1 Accident report form

FIRE/EVACUATION PROCEDURE

Instructions to staff

Action to be taken in case of fire or other emergency

Assembly point: FRONT CAR PARK

If you discover a fire:

1 Immediately operate the nearest fire alarm call point

2 Attack the fire, if possible, with the appliances provided but without taking personal risks – ensuring a clear escape route is available at all times

On hearing the fire alarm:

3 The Receptionist on duty will call the Fire Brigade immediately

4 Leave the building and report to the person in charge of the assembly point at the place indicated above, where a roll call will be taken

5 The senior person or authorised deputy on the affected floor will take charge of any evacuation and ensure that no one is left in the area

- USE THE NEAREST AVAILABLE EXIT
- DO NOT USE THE LIFT
(unless specifically provided and indicated as a means of escape for persons with disabilities)
- DO NOT STOP TO COLLECT PERSONAL BELONGINGS
- DO NOT RUN OR PANIC
- IF YOU HAVE VISITORS ESCORT THEM TO THE ASSEMBLY POINT
- DO NOT RE-ENTER THE BUILDING FOR ANY REASON UNTIL THE SAFETY OFFICER OR HIS REPRESENTATIVE GIVES YOU PERMISSION

(Notice for display in premises having a simple alarm system – to be displayed on notice boards, in all rooms and by each fire alarm point)

Fig 13.2 Fire/evacuation procedure

▶ WORKING WITH DISPLAY SCREENS

Potential health problems which may arise from the operation of display screens include:

	Possible remedies
1 Eyestrain caused by glare and reflections from the screen	• sustained keyboarding may lead to a build-up of fatigue but regular short breaks throughout the day should prevent this from happening • avoid siting the display screens in a brightly lit area where the lights are reflected in the screen; but the light must be adequate for reading the copy and the screen image • do not look directly at windows or bright lights • use task lighting specially designed for display screen operation – avoid unshielded fluorescent lights • use the brightness controls to suit the lighting conditions in the office • keep the screen clean, removing dirt and

Problem	Remedy
	'grease' finger marks from it • try moving the screen, desk or source of reflections • consider using an anti-glare screen filter, as illustrated in Fig 13.3 • operators wearing glasses or contact lenses may have to have them corrected to the range of focus required
2 Stress caused by boredom and slow computer response time	• job variation and rotation will help to relieve this
3 Posture fatigue	• use adjustable chairs to provide the correct seat height and back-rest positions as laid down in British Standards Institution specifications • adopt a comfortable and relaxed keying position • adjust the detachable keyboard and tilt the swivel facilities on the screen to suit your own needs
4 Screen flicker	• as a display screen ages it is inclined to develop more faults such as drift and jitter of the images and it is possible that the brilliance control will need to be turned up • screen flicker may affect epileptics but it should be possible to avoid excessive flicker by adjusting the display screen controls • regular servicing is essential to correct deterioration of the visual image
5 Unsatisfactory working environment	• *Space*: make sure that there is adequate space for you and the workstation so that you can move your arms and legs freely (see minimum space requirements on page 117). Your desk should be able to take whatever documents are handled. The use of a copy holder may help to avoid awkward neck movements • *Ventilation/ light/ heat*: check that these are set at comfortable levels. As electronic equipment may dry the air, make provision for the circulation of fresh air or a humidifier • *Noise*: consider methods of sound proofing if noise is a distraction

Fig 13.3 Glare guard filter

The Health and Safety (Display Screen Equipment) Regulations 1992, published by HMSO for the Health and Safety Executive, came into force on 1 January 1993 to implement minimum safety and health requirements for work with display screen equipment. Under these regulations employers are required to:

- Analyse workstations of employees covered by these regulations and assess and reduce risks.
- Ensure workstations meet minimum requirements. Employers have until the end of 1996 to upgrade existing equipment (unless immediate action is necessary to reduce risks). Equipment used for the first time must comply immediately.
- Plan work so there are breaks or changes of activity.
- On request, arrange eye and eyesight tests, and provide spectacles if special ones are needed.
- Provide health and safety training.
- Provide information for employees on what steps have been taken to comply with the regulations.

▶ PROGRESS CHECK

Multiple choice questions

1 The health and safety of office employees is protected by an act passed in:
a 1964
b 1970
c 1974
d 1992

SAFETY SELF-ASSESSMENT GUIDE

Are you safety conscious?
A checklist to discover if you are...

tick if you do

I take reasonable precautions against injury:
- to myself ☐
- to others ☐

I take reasonable precautions to prevent fires from starting ☐

I always close fire doors ☐

I know:
- how and when to raise the fire alarm ☐
- * where the nearest fire extinguisher is kept ☐
- how to use a fire extinguisher (assuming it is required of me) ☐
- what to do when the fire alarm is sounded ☐
- the escape route to use in an emergency ☐
- where my assembly point is ☐
- who takes care of disabled colleagues and visitors in an evacuation ☐

I know what action to take if I find a fault in electrical equipment which seems unsafe for use ☐

I know how to avoid strain when lifting ☐

I know where the first aid box is kept ☐

I know how to summon a firstaider in the event of an accident ☐

I know what action to take and who to contact in an emergency ☐

Are you safety conscious? You are, if you have been able to tick every box. If you didn't tick every box, now is the time to find out the missing information and, if necessary, seek further clarification from your supervisor.

2 The Workplace (Health, Safety and Welfare) Regulations 1992 require floors to be cleaned:
  a whenever the need arises
  b at least once a month
  c every day
  d at least once a week

3 The temperature in offices is not regarded as reasonable if it falls below:
  a 12°C
  b 14°C
  c 16°C
  d 18°C

4 Which of the following do you consider to be a safety hazard in an office?
  a removing an electric plug from its socket
  b standing on steps to reach a book on a high shelf
  c smoking in offices
  d running along the corridor to answer a telephone call in a distant office

5 Fire doors in offices must be kept closed when not in use:
  a on no occasion
  b at all times
  c only in the evenings and at weekends
  d when the fire alarm is sounded

6 The safest way to lift a heavy article from the floor is to:
  a bend your knees and your back
  b bend your knees and keep a straight back
  c keep your legs and your back perfectly straight
  d bend over with your legs wide apart

7 This symbol means:

  a smoking and naked flames prohibited
  b fire exit this way
  c no entry upstairs
  d risk of electric shock

8 When the fire alarm is sounded you should:
  a open the windows and doors in your office
  b switch off and unplug any electrical appliance you are using
  c run as fast as you can to the assembly point
  d use the nearest lift to your office

9 Re-arrange the following tasks in the order in which they should be carried out in the event of finding a fire, with the first at a:
  a leave the building by the shortest route
  b attack the fire with a fire extinguisher
  c telephone for the fire brigade
  d sound the fire alarm

10 Pair the following meanings with the symbols they represent (note that there is a surplus symbol):

Meaning	Symbol
a no smoking	a 
b no entry	b 
c no pedestrians	c 
d no smoking and naked flames	d 
	e 

Short answer questions

State the missing words or phrases:

11 All offices should maintain a/an .... for reporting all office injuries.

12 To work safely you need to be .... to ensure that your office is free from hazards.

13 For safety, a guillotine should be fitted with a/an ....

14 In order to ensure adequate support and reduce fatigue, the height of a typist's chair should be fully ....

15 This sign is used to indicate where .... can be obtained.

Supply brief answers to the following questions:

16 State the four duties placed on employees under the Health and Safety at Work Act:
a ....
b ....
c ....
d ....

17 Give three safe working practices when using equipment:
a ....
b ....
c ....

18 Suggest three 'do nots' when leaving the building in the case of an emergency:
a ....
b ....
c ....

19 Give three possible remedies to avoid eye-strain caused by glare from a VDU screen:
a ....
b ....
c ....

20 All accidents should be recorded in an accident book. State four of the most important items of information which should be recorded:
a ....
b ....
c ....
d ....

Section D COMMUNICATIONS

Communication is the conveying of information or data from one person (the sender) to another (the receiver). It breaks down if one of the parties fails to communicate properly when, for example, the sender communicates wrong or incomplete information or the receiver does not listen or concentrate on the message and fails to grasp its true meaning. The diagrams opposite illustrate the principal methods of communication in business, the first showing written forms of communication and the second, the oral methods, with a brief description of each on page 130.

The choice of which method of communication to use depends on several factors, eg the urgency, length, safety and confidentiality of the message, whether a written record is required and a consideration of the cost involved. The units in this section of the book give the essential factors which must be considered by the office worker when preparing and presenting any form of communication. It is also important to learn to select the most appropriate method and, when writing a letter, making a telephone call or sending a fax, to ensure that the message is clear, accurate and businesslike.

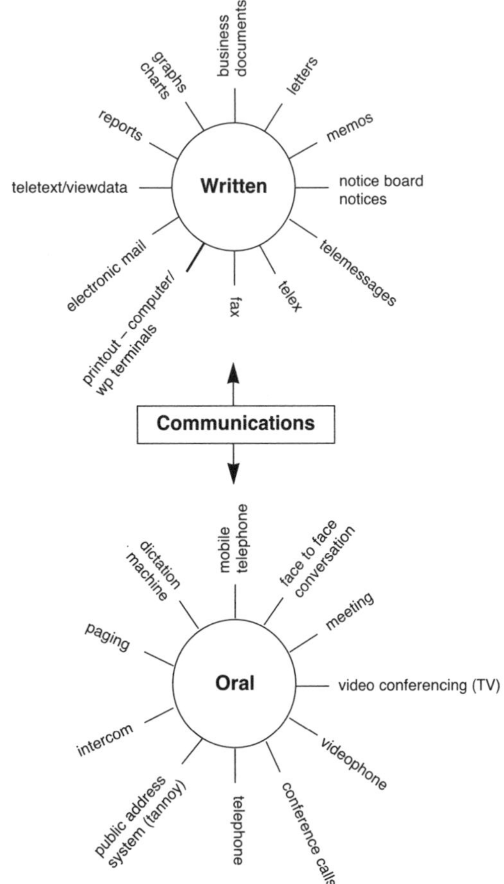

▶ THE ABC OF BUSINESS COMMUNICATIONS

Business documents: printed forms for transmitting data/text
Ceefax: BBC televised information service
Computer terminal/Data services: for transmitting and receiving data/text
Conference calls: A British Telecom telephone service for conferences and meetings
Dictation machine: for communicating to typist
Face-to-face conversation: ideal for personal/confidential matters
Fax: for transmitting replicas of documents any distance with complete accuracy - combines the speed of the telephone with the reproduction facility of the office copier
Graphs/charts: for the visual presentation of data
Intercom: internal oral communication
Letter: written communications of any length
Memo: written communications within an organisation
Meeting: for collecting the views of several people, the information being conveyed by minutes and reports
Mobile telephones: for communicating with people on the move
Noticeboard: a means of displaying information for a large number of people
Paging: for the location of staff as they move around a building
Prestel (Viewdata): a British Telecom televised information service
Public address system (tannoy): for conveying information to a large number of people in a building
Report: communication of written information to aid decision-making
Telemessage: a British Telecom service for transmitting urgent written information
Telephone: for internal and external oral communication
Teletext: ITV 3/4 televised information service
Television-closed circuit: a means of transmitting data within an organisation
Telex (teleprinter): combines the speed of the telephone with the authority of the written word
Videoconferencing: a British Telecom service for closed-circuit television of conferences and meetings
Videophone: provides for people to 'meet' by telephone on a screen face to face
Voice bank: a computerised 'mailbox' for recording messages
Word Processor/Electronic mail: after processing, information is printed or communicated by telephone direct to a correspondent

Unit 14
Oral communication

Competences developed in this unit:

- Process incoming and outgoing telecommunications (NVQ1)
- Supply information to meet specified requests (NVQ1)
- Receive and transmit information electronically (NVQ2)

Office workers spend a large proportion of their time using the spoken word to communicate to others by face-to-face conversations, using the telephone and attending meetings. With thought, care and diplomacy in what they say and how they say it, they can have more influence and, at the same time, establish rapport and goodwill with their colleagues and clients.

Oral communication involves the skills of listening and speaking, both of which are essential if a message is to be successfully conveyed and received. Communication fails if the sender conveys the wrong message, even if the recipient receives it accurately. Conversely, if a message is conveyed accurately and efficiently but the recipient is negligent in listening, there is a breakdown in communication. It is clear that both parties to a communication must be proficient in both listening and speaking. Some important points to consider when receiving and conveying messages are given below.

▶ RECEIVING MESSAGES

- prepare to listen – 'tune in' and focus on what the speaker is saying
- be natural and relaxed but try not to be distracted by others who may be present in the office
- make sure you listen selectively to assimilate the essentials of the message conveyed
- as you listen, concentrate on key words/phrases that will help you to grasp the message
- show interest in the speaker by your expression and by looking at him or her
- be a patient listener and do not interrupt before the speaker has finished
- concentrate on what is being said so that you keep pace with the speaker and do not lag behind – this allows you to consider the implications of what is being said
- if it is essential to remember detailed information such as telephone numbers, names and addresses, reference numbers, etc, write them down in note form as they are given to you – it is also a good idea to note down all important items of information
- ask the speaker to explain anything that is unclear or difficult for you to understand
- be prepared to give the speaker a reaction verbally or non-verbally, if appropriate – a nod or a smile may be all that is required to satisfy the speaker that you are following what is being said

▶ CONVEYING MESSAGES

- organise your thoughts before you speak – prepare a plan of what you wish to say
- present your message logically and clearly
- use simple, concise sentences and avoid unnecessary jargon
- speak clearly at the right volume, tone and pace
- be polite and considerate in what you say
- avoid repeating what you have already said and be sure to keep to the point of the subject under discussion
- develop a rapport with listeners so that they are receptive to your message
- obtain feedback by checking that the recipient has understood your message
- say what you mean and mean what you say!

▶ TELEPHONE

The business student should acquire the ability to answer the telephone confidently and efficiently, chiefly through practice and a thorough knowledge of telephone services and technique. Answering the telephone is an important duty because when you are working in an office you are representing your firm and the tone of your greeting and the manner in which you handle the calls will create a favourable or unfavourable first impression.

It costs nothing and is no trouble to extend a pleasant, helpful and courteous greeting to all callers which, in return, will enhance the company's reputation and help to make its business dealings friendly and cordial.

Answering the telephone

- Answer promptly when the telephone rings and state your name or your firm's name.
- Do not say 'hello' as this wastes time and does not help the caller.
- Try not to keep a caller waiting. If there is likely to be a long delay in making the connection it may be better to ring the caller back, thus saving waiting time on the telephone. This is particularly important if the call is made from a call box where the caller may not have the additional coins.
- Have a message pad and pencil to hand so that you can write down a message.
- You may have to leave the telephone for a while to make an enquiry or collect some information. If so, let callers know how long you expect to be and ask if they would prefer you to call them back. Arrange for calls to be answered for you while you are away.
- When an incoming call has to be transferred from one extension to another, convey the caller's name and request to the new extension so that the caller does not have to repeat the message.
- If there is a delay before a caller can be connected, keep him or her informed of progress.
- If an incoming call is disconnected, replace the telephone receiver so that the caller can re-establish the call as soon as possible.
- If you receive a call which is a wrong number, remember that the intrusion is not intentional and that it is probably just as irritating to the caller as it is to you. You need not apologise but one made by the caller should be accepted politely.
- Always try to greet people cheerfully, even at the end of the day. If you know a caller's name use it when speaking to them.
- Callers who wish to speak to someone who is absent should not be kept waiting but asked whether they would like to:
  a speak to someone else
  b be rung back when the person returns
  c ring again later
  d leave a message

Whatever the answer, the caller's name, firm's name and telephone number should be noted.

Making a telephone call

- Check the correct code and number before dialling. If you are in doubt look it up in the telephone directory and write it down.
- After dialling the number, allow sufficient time for the call to be connected.
- If you make a mistake while dialling, replace the receiver for a short while and then start dialling again.
- When the person answers, say who you are and to whom you wish to speak and their extension number if you know it.
- If you are connected to a wrong number, remember to apologise.
- If a number cannot be dialled, dial 100 and ask the operator to get it for you, stating the number required and your own number.
- A telephone call should be planned in exactly the same way as a business letter. Even before dialling the number you should have any necessary papers at hand. It is also advisable to prepare beforehand a short list of points to be discussed.

Making a telephone call abroad

- Check the correct codes and number and write them down. If you do not know these numbers you can look them up in the international codes section of *The phone book* or obtain them from the appropriate international operator by dialling the number given in the international dialling section of your telephone directory.

- With International Direct Dialling (IDD) you can dial the call yourself. Dial the four groups of digits in the following order:
  a international code (00)
  b country code
  c area code
  d subscriber's number
  If you are not able to dial direct, the call must be placed with the international operator (dial 155).
- Be prepared to wait up to a minute before you are connected because of the long distance involved.
- Bear in mind the time differences for each country. Note that between March and October, British Summer Time is one hour later than GMT (Greenwich Mean Time).

Emergency calls

See page 162.

Telephone charges

British Telecom's charges for dialled telephone calls are based on the following criteria:

- Duration — According to the number of minutes, subject to a minimum charge
- Distance
  1 Local (within 15 miles) – cheapest charges
  2 Regional (15–35 miles)
  3 National (more than 35 miles) – the most expensive charges
- Day and time
  1 Weekend rate
  midnight Friday to midnight Sunday – cheapest times
  2 Cheap rate
  1800–0800 Monday to Friday
  3 Daytime rate
  0800–1800 Monday to Friday – the most expensive times

Savings in telephone costs can be made by telephoning at times when the weekend or cheap rates are applicable.

Telephone tones

Dialling tone A low pitched burr indicates that the equipment is ready for you to start dialling.

Ringing tone A repeated double beat tells you that the number is being rung. Allow two minutes for the number to answer; if there is no reply by then replace the telephone, wait a little while and try again.

Engaged tone A single note repeated at regular intervals usually means the number being called is in use but it can also mean that the equipment is engaged. In either case you should replace the telephone and try again in about five minutes.

Number unobtainable tone A continuous high pitched note indicates that the number is either out of service or spare. If you hear this tone, check that you have the correct number (and dialling code) and then dial again. If you hear the tone again dial 100 and tell the operator what has happened.

'Lines engaged' announcement On some calls you may hear a prerecorded voice saying: 'Lines from . . . are engaged, please try later.' This means that there is overload on the lines from the district mentioned and you should replace the handset and wait a few minutes before dialling again.

▶ TELEPHONE EQUIPMENT AND FACILITIES

Switchboards

Incoming calls will usually be received at a switchboard and routed through an operator to the various extensions. External calls may also be made from the switchboard although it is normal for such calls to be made from the extensions. Modern switchboards, sometimes known as call-connect systems or call distribution systems, incorporate microprocessor technology and are operated electronically to provide fast and efficient communication links, both within the organisation and externally. The facilities provided by digital exchanges may include:

- liquid crystal display on the switchboard giving time, date, number dialled, extension called or a message from an extension
- internal and external calling from all extensions – internal and external calls are distinguished by different ringing signals
- a memory stores the last number called and will reconnect the caller at the press of a button – tedious redialling of engaged numbers is eliminated
- repertory dialling – automatic dialling from a directory of stored 'frequently used' numbers
- ring back when free – an engaged extension rings the caller back when the current call is finished
- A call can be held 'on line' while you make an enquiry by ringing another number or transferring the call to another extension
- group hunting – a call can be diverted to another extension or a group of extensions in order to leave you undisturbed. You can still make outgoing calls and any urgent calls can be returned to you, if required.
- telephone conferences can be arranged with several extension users
- selected terminals can be allowed to interrupt calls to convey urgent messages
- automatic call distribution system in which incoming calls are automatically placed in a queuing system so that the operator can answer them in order
- when connected to recording equipment, all calls can be logged providing a printed record of numbers dialled and the extensions making the calls
- music on hold – music is played to callers while they wait to be connected to their extension
- appointment reminders – an extension is called when it is time to leave for an appointment
- call forwarding – incoming calls are transferred automatically to another venue

Telephone answering machine

If it is necessary to provide a 24-hour telephone service to an organisation, which may be essential for firms receiving communications from all over the world, an answering machine (as in Fig 14.1) may be connected to the telephone or it may be an integral part of a telephone system. A telephone answering machine gives a prerecorded announcement inviting the caller to record a message. The message should give:

Fig 14.1 Automatic telephone answering machine with remote control

	Example:
• The name of organisation	*Fothergill & Company – Solicitors*
• A greeting	*Good evening*
• The reason for the recording	*Our offices close at 5 o'clock from Mondays to Fridays ...*
• Instructions for recording a message	*but if you would like to leave a message, please speak after the bleep, giving your name, address and telephone number and, if you are a client of ours, the name of your solicitor*
• Action to be taken with the message	*Your message will be conveyed to the solicitor concerned in the morning*
• An acknowledgment of the call	*Thank you for calling*

Messages are recorded on magnetic tape and then transcribed and typed on to message sheets the following morning or whenever the staff return to the office. This equipment provides a continuous answering and recording service and is particularly useful for use at lunch time and when the organisation closes for the night.

A remote interrogator is a useful device for people who travel a great deal and who are required to keep in touch with information at their base of operations. It allows a business executive to extract information from an answering machine when away from the office. The interrogator is fitted to the telephone and, by using a special code number, the executive can telephone in to the office and listen to the messages received on the machine. The executive can switch the machine on or off and change the outgoing message from any telephone when away from base.

Some answering machines are used only to supply information to callers, eg dates and times of sales at a retail store, and in these instances they do not provide a recording service for callers.

Voicebank

This is a development of the telephone answering machine using a computerised 'mail box' for recording spoken messages when staff are not available to receive calls in person. It is linked to an existing telephone system and a caller's message can be played back by dialling the voicebank number and keying in a PIN number. A pager may be used to alert the user to a message in the mailbox. Each extension user is allocated a box number which is usually the same as their extension number. Messages can be reviewed, deleted and, if necessary, re-recorded before being transmitted. You can be informed when a message has been cleared by the recipient. Urgent messages can receive top priority treatment by automatically being placed at the front of all other messages in the mailbox. If a message is exceptionally important, the system can be requested to ring the telephone of the recipient at repeated intervals. If a person is away from the office, any messages received can be diverted to another box number. Voicebank ensures that messages are delivered quickly and accurately without the harassment of making repeated telephone calls when people are not available to receive them.

A voice response unit can also be used to handle a variety of routine functions which will supply information and advice to callers. It can answer the call, ask for the caller's identification or order number and then route the call and relevant information to the member of staff who is available to deal with the call.

Loudspeaking telephone

The user of a loudspeaking telephone can make and receive calls without holding the handset. It is useful for small conferences as the people present can all hear what is said by the incoming caller and anyone at the conference can reply.

Cordless telephones

British Telecom's Freelance cordless telephone (Fig 14.2) allows the user to operate the telephone anywhere within 100 metres from the base unit. It can also be used to provide a two-way intercom service between the base system and the handset. Special features of the Freelance cordless telephone include:

- a memory device capable of storing nine 'frequently used' numbers
- a last number re-dial button which saves time re-dialling numbers which are engaged
- a volume control on the handset which enables you to increase the volume when using the telephone in a noisy environment
- a secrecy button so that the conversation cannot be heard on another telephone extension
- the use of security codes to prevent unauthorised access
- a 'call diversion' service which provides for calls to be diverted from an extension to the cordless telephone
- a 'call waiting' service in which the cordless telephone is bleeped when a person is trying to get through to you while you are on the phone.

Fig 14.2 A cordless telephone

Mobile telephones

Mobile radio or cellular telephones provide a means of speedy communication with colleagues and clients when they are on the move. Two-way battery-operated radio telephones can be used to keep in touch with other people operating within a closed circuit, but the advent of cellular phones has extended the area of coverage with the setting up of 'cells', each with their own transmitter in different parts of the country.

A cellular telephone enables you to call an ordinary telephone number or another cellular phone user. You can also receive calls from either source, providing that you are in an area served by your operating network, Cellnet or Vodaphone.

There are three different types of cellular phone:

- **mobile:** one which is permanently installed in a motor vehicle
- **portable:** one which can be used in any situation and is powered by battery
- **transportable:** one which can be used in or out of a motor vehicle powered by a rechargeable battery

The use of a car telephone must never be allowed to distract the driver's attention from driving. The Highway Code states:

1 Do not use a hand-held microphone or telephone handset while your vehicle is moving, except in an emergency.
2 You should only speak into a fixed, neck-slung or clipped-on microphone when it would not distract your attention from the road.
3 Do not stop on the hard shoulder of a motorway to answer or make a call, however urgent.

Pager

This is a device for contacting people when they are away from their offices, using a bleep to let them know they should 'phone a specific colleague. Alternatively, a Number Master allows anyone to send their telephone number to the pager's LCD display, so that the recipient can respond direct. BT's Message Master XL is an alpha-numeric radio pager with the ability to display full text messages of up to 80 characters in length. When a message is received, a tone and flashing light alerts the user that a message has been conveyed. The system operates throughout the UK but the user will select and pay only for the geographic area required. (*See* Fig 14.3.)

Fig 14.3 Pager with alpha-numeric receiver

▶ BRITISH TELECOM TELEPHONE SERVICES

Accurist timeline: a 'speaking clock' for giving the correct time.

Alarm calls: a reminder call service whereby the exchange will ring you at a requested time.

BT direct connect: a service which automatically connects callers to a pre-programmed number when they pick up a remote handset. It provides customers and potential customers with a fast and simple means to make contact with a company without having to dial a number and at no cost to themselves.

Caller display: equipment used with the telephone to register the telephone numbers, time and date of your most recent incoming calls. It enables you to see the phone number of a person calling you before answering the call.

Call forwarding: a service for firms which provides customers with a local number, day or night, and when they ring their calls are automatically redirected to wherever the firm's telephones are manned.

Call return: a free service which tells you the telephone number of the last person who has called you and the time the call was made. The code 1471 is dialled for this service.

Call waiting: a service which lets you know, with a gentle bleep, if someone is ringing your number while you are on the phone. You can arrange for the first call to be on hold while you speak to the second caller.

Charge advisory service: a method of finding out the cost and length of a call.

Collect calls: a service which arranges for a call to be charged to the called subscriber's account.

Directory enquiries: a service for supplying telephone numbers not found in a directory.

Freefone 0800: a service which enables customers, clients, agents or employees in the UK to telephone an organisation without cost to themselves. It encourages customers to place orders by telephone and it can also be used by representatives and employees to save them the time and trouble of using coins or cards and claiming refunds for calls made to their company. The calls are made by using a special freefone 0800 number. The company is required to pay the normal telephone call charge and the caller pays nothing.

International Freefone 0800: a service which allows customers in many overseas countries to dial firms in the UK direct either free or for no more than the price of a local call. It can also be used with a fax machine number to allow customers to fax their enquiries and orders free of charge. The international 0800 service is available for use in major European markets, USA, Australia, Japan, Hong Kong and Canada.

Lo-call 0345: a service which enables customers, potential customers and staff to phone or fax your organisation over any distance within the UK for the price of a local call. The balance of the call charge is paid by the organisation. It enables companies to maintain a customer service presence in a locality without having to provide the local resources.

Weathercall: a service providing a summary of local weather conditions and forecasts.

▶ PROGRESS CHECK

Multiple choice questions

1 When listening to a message:
- **a** interrupt the speaker at any time of the conversation in order to clarify a point
- **b** be prepared to give the speaker a reaction verbally or non-verbally
- **c** write everything down to aid your memory
- **d** avoid looking at the speaker

2 Which of the following would be suitable for communicating information to a large number of people?
- **a** intercom
- **b** voicebank
- **c** tannoy
- **d** loudspeaking telephone

3 Modern telephone switchboards may be referred to as:
- **a** liquid crystal display boards
- **b** repertory dialling systems
- **c** telephone answering machines
- **d** call connect systems

4 Of the four mentioned below, the cheapest time to make a long-distance telephone call is:
- **a** Monday 1500 hrs
- **b** Tuesday 1230 hrs
- **c** Wednesday 1830 hrs
- **d** Saturday 1000 hrs

5 You have dialled a telephone number and hear a single note repeated at regular intervals. This sound indicates that:
- **a** the number you require is engaged
- **b** the number you require is unobtainable
- **c** the receiver has a mobile telephone
- **d** the receiver's telephone is ringing

6 When making an International Direct Dialling telephone call, which of the following groups of digits would you dial first?
- **a** subscriber's number
- **b** area code
- **c** country code
- **d** international code

7 When receiving an external telephone call which has been routed to your extension by your switchboard operator you would:
- **a** say 'hello' to ensure that the caller is on the line
- **b** state the name of your organisation plus a greeting such as 'good morning'
- **c** ask the caller for his or her name in order to establish immediate communication
- **d** state your name and your position/ department in the organisation

8 Which of the following information would you expect to hear on a telephone answering machine announcement?
- **a** firm's name ....
- **b** time ....
- **c** date ....
- **d** receptionist's name ....

9 In the freefone service the caller:
- **a** makes telephone calls at specially reduced rates
- **b** makes telephone calls without payment
- **c** is credited with the cost of telephone calls
- **d** is charged at the cheap rate for telephone calls made at any time of the day

10 Pair the following lists of words (note that there is a surplus item in the second column):

a voicebank	**a** cellnet
b mobile telephone	**b** records messages
	c redirects calls
c call return	**d** code 1471
d call forwarding	**e** automatic dialling

Short answer questions

State the missing words or phrases.

11 You receive an incoming call. In the process of transferring it, the caller is disconnected. Who should make the call to re-establish contact? ....

12 When making a telephone call check the .... before dialling.

13 Oral communication involves the skills of speaking and ....

14 Cellnet and Vodaphone are operating networks for .... telephones.

15 The code number to use for dialling firms free of charge is ....

Supply brief answers to the following questions:

16 A telephone answering machine gives a pre-recorded announcement. List three items that the announcement should include:
- **a** ....
- **b** ....
- **c** ....

17 Provide three tips for a good telephone answering technique:
- **a** ....
- **b** ....
- **c** ....

18 Give three ways in which to deal with a telephone caller when the person he or she wishes to speak to is engaged on another line:

a ....

b ....

c ....

19 When are the following forms of communication used?

a A noticeboard..
....

b A public address system (tannoy) ....
....

c A graph or chart...................................
....

20 Suggest three telephone services which may be used to encourage customers to place orders with your firm:

a ....

b ....

c ....

Unit 15
Written communication

Competences developed in this unit:

- Respond to correspondence
- Prepare a variety of documents
- Receive and transmit information electronically

(NVQ2)

Written business communications include:

- letters
- memos
- message sheets
- telemessages
- telex
- computer: data services
  e-mail
- fax

▶ BUSINESS LETTERS

The writer of a business letter should always aim to be accurate, clear, brief and courteous. The letter should also be set out clearly and correctly. The numbers in the letter in Fig 15.1 relate to the following points:

1 Date
The date must be typed in order of day, month and year, eg 11 June 19—.

2 Reference
The reference on a letter may consist of the initials of the dictator and the typist such as Our Ref PFC/JH or it may consist of the file reference number such as Our Ref 1427. The reference of the addressee should always be used whenever it is known.

3 Inside name and address
This is the name and address of the addressee. Type the postcode at the bottom of the address and whenever possible on a separate line.

4 Salutation
This is the writer's greeting. It is governed by the relationship which exists between those corresponding, the usual salutations for business correspondence being Dear Sir(s) or Dear Mr Hunt.

5 Heading
If there is a subject heading it should stand out clearly.

6 Opening sentence
This is used to introduce the subject matter of the letter by referring to the previous letter, telephone conversation or meeting or, if there has been no previous correspondence, by referring directly to the subject matter.

7 Body of letter
The sentences and paragraphs in the body of a letter must be arranged so that they appear in logical sequence and so that each aspect is dealt with in a separate paragraph.

8 Subscription (or complimentary close)
This is the closing complimentary remark in a letter and is again governed by the relationship existing between those corresponding and by the salutation already employed. The usual subscriptions for business correspondence are Yours faithfully with Dear Sir(s); and Yours sincerely with Dear Mr Hunt.

9 Description of signatory
The name of the writer and their position in the business are typed below the complimentary close leaving space for the signature, as in the following example:

Yours faithfully

G H Champion
Managing Director

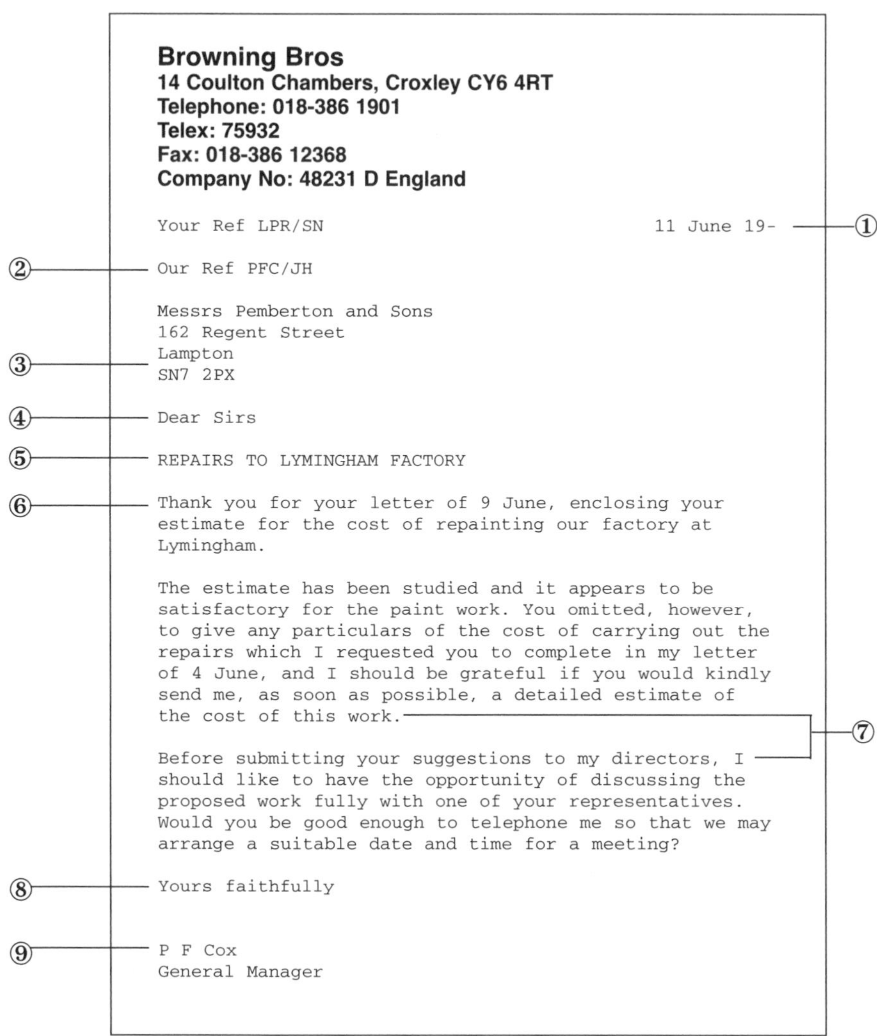
Browning Bros
14 Coulton Chambers, Croxley CY6 4RT
Telephone: 018-386 1901
Telex: 75932
Fax: 018-386 12368
Company No: 48231 D England

Your Ref LPR/SN 11 June 19- ①

② Our Ref PFC/JH

Messrs Pemberton and Sons
162 Regent Street
③ Lampton
SN7 2PX

④ Dear Sirs

⑤ REPAIRS TO LYMINGHAM FACTORY

⑥ Thank you for your letter of 9 June, enclosing your estimate for the cost of repainting our factory at Lymingham.

The estimate has been studied and it appears to be satisfactory for the paint work. You omitted, however, to give any particulars of the cost of carrying out the repairs which I requested you to complete in my letter of 4 June, and I should be grateful if you would kindly send me, as soon as possible, a detailed estimate of the cost of this work. ⑦

Before submitting your suggestions to my directors, I should like to have the opportunity of discussing the proposed work fully with one of your representatives. Would you be good enough to telephone me so that we may arrange a suitable date and time for a meeting?

⑧ Yours faithfully

⑨ P F Cox
General Manager

Fig 15.1 Business letter

▶ MEMOS

Memos are used for internal communication or for writing to representatives or agents in this country or abroad. The salutation and complimentary close are not used and the addressee's name or title is normally sufficient (*see* Fig 15.2).

▶ MESSAGES

Messages from telephone callers or visitors to the office should never be entrusted solely to memory, which may well prove unreliable, and the important facts should be written down while they are being received. The following important points should be noted:

- The date and time of the call or visit.
- The name of the person for whom the message is intended.
- The caller's name, address and telephone number.
- Precise details of the message received.

The message should be repeated back to the caller to make sure that it has been taken down correctly. Fig 15.3 is an example of a typical message sheet. The message should either be

MEMO

To: Training Manager | Date: 8 January 199-

From: Office Manager | Ref: P1436

NEW FAX MACHINE

The new fax machine will be installed on 21 January and the manufacturers have agreed to provide an instructor to train the staff in using it. The instructor will attend from 1030 to 1200 hrs on Wednesday, 22 January, and I would like at least one representative from each department to attend the training course.

Can you please make the necessary arrangements with the departmental heads for members of their staff to attend.

Fig 15.2 Memo

MESSAGE FOR

Mr G Clifton

WHILE YOU WERE OUT

Mr D Hobbs

Of Snows Business Forms Ltd, Manor House Avenue, Millbrook, Southampton SO9 4WA

Telephone: 01703 777711

Telephoned		Please ring	✓
Called to see you	✓	Will call again	
Wants to see you	✓	Urgent	

Message: He would like to make an appointment to see you do discuss a new range of computer stationery which has been designed to meet your needs.

Date 5 October 19- Time 1345

Received by *S Bates*

Fig 15.3 Message sheet

typed or written with a pen. As soon as it has been recorded it should be placed on the executive's desk so that it can be seen immediately on his or her return.

▶ GUIDELINES FOR WRITING MESSAGES AND CORRESPONDENCE

- plan what you are going to write – jot down the points you wish to make and arrange them in logical order
- make sure that what you write is clear and can be understood by the recipient
- use the correct style and tone of writing to suit the circumstances of the communication
- write your communication in the appropriate format and layout, eg message form, memo, letter or report
- use correct grammar
- spell and punctuate accurately
- use words which convey the correct meaning and avoid unnecessary jargon
- take care to avoid emotive or provocative language
- use sentences which are simple and concise
- group your points into paragraphs and grade them so that they follow in correct sequence with each paragraph leading systematically to the next – if appropriate, use paragraph headings
- when typed, check your work carefully to ensure that there are no errors in it
- always try to be courteous and helpful in your writing

▶ CHECKING PRINTOUTS AND TYPESCRIPT

A document, despatched to a customer or client, with undetected errors not only creates a poor impression of the organisation but can create serious problems. Checking (or proofreading as it may be called) is, therefore, of great importance and cannot be stressed too much. The following hints for efficient proofreading might help you in this work:

- the printed copy must be checked word for word with the original (see Fig 5.4 for an example original). If possible, do this with another person: one person reading from the original and the other person checking the printed copy
- concentrate on checking the make-up of each word or set of figures – it is impossible to check accuracy by skimming through phrases or sentences
- at the same time as looking for errors, check that the content makes sense to you
- watch out for these errors – indicated by the following numbers in Fig 15.5
  1. typographical errors
  2. spelling errors
  3. punctuation errors
  4. grammatical errors
  5. incorrect use of capital letters
  6. mis-reading figures (when there are totals check that these are accurate)
  7. transposition of words
  8. omissions
- mark the errors lightly in pencil in the margin for the necessary corrections to be made

▶ TELEMESSAGES

British Telecom's electronic hard copy messaging service combines telecommunications with postal delivery. Telemessages can be sent at any hour of the day or night from a telephone, fax or telex machine, but for next-day delivery they must be sent by 2200 hrs. To send a message by telephone, dial 190 and ask for 'Telemessage'. A printed message is then delivered by first class post next morning. Specially designed telemessages may be used for messages of congratulation and good wishes, printed on attractively designed greetings stationery.

▶ TELEX

The telex system provides a very quick means of written communication by teleprinters among over 70,000 subscribers of the British Telecom Telex Service in the UK and more than two million businesses around the world. A teleprinter (as in Fig 15.6) combines the speed of the telephone with the authority of the written word. A printed copy of the message is available at both the sending and receiving teleprinters. The telex service is available day and night and mes-

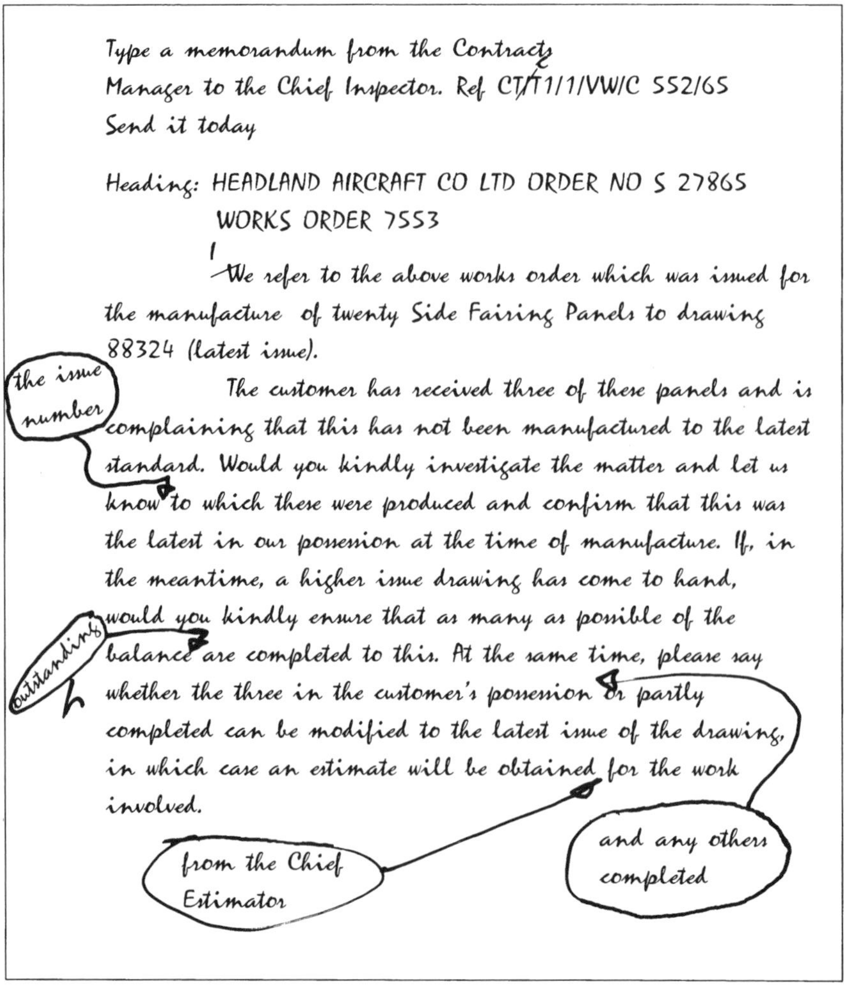

Type a memorandum from the Contracts
Manager to the Chief Inspector. Ref CT/T1/1/VW/C 552/65
Send it today

Heading: HEADLAND AIRCRAFT CO LTD ORDER NO S 27865
WORKS ORDER 7553

We refer to the above works order which was issued for the manufacture of twenty Side Fairing Panels to drawing 88324 (latest issue).

The customer has received three of these panels and is complaining that this has not been manufactured to the latest standard. Would you kindly investigate the matter and let us know to which these were produced and confirm that this was the latest in our possession at the time of manufacture. If, in the meantime, a higher issue drawing has come to hand, would you kindly ensure that as many as possible of the balance are completed to this. At the same time, please say whether the three in the customer's possession or partly completed can be modified to the latest issue of the drawing, in which case an estimate will be obtained for the work involved.

the issue number

outstanding

from the Chief Estimator

and any others completed

Fig 15.4 Original

sages may be transmitted to a subscriber even though their teleprinter is unattended, provided it is switched on.

A standard rental charge is made for the provision of the necessary equipment and for hiring the line to the telex exchange, although telex machines may also be purchased from manufacturers. Telex charges are based on the distance between the calling and called subscribers' telex centres and the duration of the calls.

Electronic teleprinters use microprocessors which have memories allowing telex messages to be stored and sent automatically at fast speeds when required. Messages can be edited, in a similar way to using a word processor, allowing the operator to insert, correct or delete parts of a message and rearrange the text, with the aid of a visual display screen. Messages can be stored in the machine's memory and presented to the operator on the screen, while the teleprinter continues to receive incoming messages or transmit other outgoing messages. Copies of the messages transmitted and received are produced by the printer.

MEMORANDUM

From: Contracts Manager Ref: CT/C1/1/VW/C552/65

To: Chief Inspector Date: 1 April 19--

(6) HEADLAND AIRCRAFT CO LTD
ORDER NO. S27865
7553 WORKS ORDER 7335

I refer to the above Works Order which was issued for the manufacture of twenty Side Fairing Panels to drawing 88324 (latest issue).

(4) The customer has received three of these panels and is complaining *pl* (1)
there have that this has not been manufactured to the latest standard. Would you kindly investigate the matter and let us know the issue number to which these were produced and confirm that this was the latest in
(7) our possession at the time of manufacture. If, in the meantime, a higher issue drawing has to come hand would you kindly ensure that
trs as many as possible of the balance outstanding are completed to this.

(3) At the same time please say whether the three in the customer's possession and any others completed or partly completed can be *lc* (5)
modified to the latest issue of the Drawing, in which case an
Sp estimate will be obtained for the work involved.
(2) *omission* (8)

Fig 15.5 Checked typescript from original

Fig 15.6 An electronic teleprinter

Other features of the electronic teleprinter include:

- storing incoming messages in the memory when the printer is in use and printing them out as soon as it is free
- printing the time and date automatically on all outgoing messages
- storing standard paragraphs and phrases in the memory for recall when required
- transmitting the same message automatically to multiple addresses
- automatically redialling an engaged number until it is free to receive the message
- storing frequently used numbers in the memory for short-code calling

With the use of a 'mailbox' facility, telex messages can be operated directly from an electronic typewriter, word processor or computer – giving many more people access to telex communications. The messages received can be read on a VDU screen or printed out on a printer.

Operating procedure

The procedure for operating a telex teleprinter is as follows:

1 The operator keys in the correspondent's telex number (obtainable from the United Kingdom Telex Directory).
2 The correspondent's answerback code (an abbreviated name) must appear on the teleprinter before any further action can be taken to indicate that the receiving telex is ready to receive the message.
3 The operator's answerback code is typed in.
4 The operator types the message or transmits a message stored in the memory.
5 The operator repeats the answerback code to indicate the end of the message to the recipient.
6 Correspondent's answerback code must appear at the foot of the message to confirm that the full message has been transmitted.

When autocall facilities are used this procedure is carried out automatically at any time of the day or night without an operator present.

Preparing messages for telex

Because telex charges are based on the time of transmission, messages should be condensed as much as possible, but without making them unclear and ambiguous.

A message for transmission by telex should contain the following:

- correspondent's telex number
- sender's answerback code
- date and time (if not automatically printed)
- message containing the important points:
  - ○ no salutation and complimentary close
  - ○ omit non-essential words and phrases
  - ○ use common abbreviations where appropriate
  - ○ repeat important numerical data in words
  - ○ reduce the description of sender to the minimum words required
- Repeat sender's answerback code

An example of a telex message is given in Fig 15.7.

Features of telex:

- it provides an instant written communication which is ideal for many business purposes
- it is a reliable means of communication for messages of a technical or quantitative nature
- foreign languages can be translated more easily in the written form provided by telex
- it can be used to receive messages when the office is closed, particularly useful for communications from overseas
- it can be used for the transmission and receipt of computer data and telemessages

▶ FAX

Fax (facsimile) machines use the telephone to transmit, within seconds, any form of printed, typed or handwritten matter, drawings, diagrams and photographs from one location to another. Replicas of documents can be sent any distance with complete accuracy by combining the speed of the telephone with the reproduction facility of the office copier.

Operation of the equipment is simple and in the more sophisticated models loading is automatic; the originals to be transmitted are

```
493876    WINTON G
342689    SYSTEMS G
1-JAN-9-   11.30.10
REF 9342
URGENT

PLEASE DELIVER ORDER NO. 1876 FOR 100 (ONE HUNDRED)
ALUMINIUM PULL-HANDLES (CAT. NO. 2230) ASAP.

THESE ARE REQUIRED FOR URGENT EXPORT CONSIGNMENT.

CONFIRMATION OF DESPATCH REQUESTED BY RETURN

KEITH ASH

342689    SYSTEMS G
493876    WINTON G
```

Fig 15.7 A telex message

stacked in a loading tray and after making telephone contact with the recipient, the operator presses the start button and the copies are transmitted automatically. Copies can also be received automatically without requiring the services of an operator. An important advantage over telex is that the input material does not have to be typed, and complicated and detailed orders can be sent with complete accuracy. Other applications for this equipment include the distribution of engineering drawings to branches; gaining access to records stored centrally at head office; and transmitting advertisement copy to printers.

Advantages of Fax machines over telex are:

- any originals can be sent, whether they are drawn, typed or photographed
- no lengthy training is required to operate equipment
- errors are eliminated and no intermediate checking is necessary
- the overall cost is less because of the fast transmission speed (scanning device 'skips' white areas of original)
- small portable machines are available which can be plugged into any telephone
- it is possible to transmit a signed copy of the original document to give it authenticity

Figure 15.8 is an illustration of a high speed plain paper fax machine. The machine can store up to 50 pages in its memory and the paper tray holds 500 sheets which reduces the risk of paper running out while the fax is receiving messages unattended. It allows the user to send and receive faxes at the same time. The automatic document feeder can hold as many as 15 sheets. There is a photocopying function which allows duplicates to be taken easily and quickly. Activity reports maintain a record of all transmissions made.

▶ FAXMAIL

This is a high-speed Royal Mail fax service for the transmission of documents between more than 110 Faxmail centres in the UK and over 40 countries abroad. Documents, including line drawings and diagrams up to A4 size may be handed in to certain post offices for direct transmission to another centre. At the destination the copy is delivered to the recipient,

Fig 15.8 A fax machine

either the same day or next day, depending on the option selected.

Greeting cards with a facsimile handwritten message can also be sent by Faxmail for delivery the same day by courier.

Fax users can also use this service by faxing their documents with a header sheet to the Electronic Mail Centre on Freefax 0800 181154.

▶ INTEGRATED SERVICES DIGITAL NETWORK (ISDN)

ISDN is British Telecom's digital dial-up public network offering integrated voice, data, images and video conferencing communications. The following are some typical applications of ISDN:

- data file transfer
- faxing documents
- voice communication
- video conferencing and desktop conferencing

Manufacturers have created a new generation of equipment to capitalise fully on the capabilities of ISDN but special terminal adapters can also be used to make use of existing equipment.

The UK ISDN network is also connected to many overseas countries, including France, Germany, USA, Hong Kong, Australia and Japan.

Costs involve installing a single ISDN line, a quarterly rental charge and usage of the line on a time basis, similar to installing a conventional phone line. It provides so much more than the phone with its facility to move files from computer to computer, send faxes and print-quality text and photographs, transmit stock control barcodes and maintain remote video surveillance of premises.

▶ PROGRESS CHECK

Multiple choice questions

1 If you required a permanent record of a communication you would need to use:
a paging
b Ceefax
c intercom
d telex

2 Which of the following would provide the quickest delivery of an urgent message?
- **a** memo
- **b** fax
- **c** first class letter
- **d** telemessage

3 A written communication between two departments of a company would be made by:
- **a** letter
- **b** intercom
- **c** memo
- **d** viewdata

4 An answerback code appears in a telex message to indicate that:
- **a** the recipient's telex is ready to receive the message
- **b** the recipient's telex is engaged
- **c** there is a message waiting to be answered
- **d** the recipient has the answer to your question

5 Which of the following should be included on a memo?
- **a** salutation
- **b** date of communication
- **c** telephone number
- **d** complimentary close

6 The equipment which combines the speed of the telephone with the reproduction facility of the office copier is called:
- **a** telex
- **b** videophone
- **c** teletext
- **d** fax

7 A telemessage is transmitted from the sender to British Telecom by:
- **a** telephone
- **b** telegram
- **c** pager
- **d** datapost

8 Teleprinters used in the telex service may be:
- **a** rented from the Post Office
- **b** bought from the Post Office
- **c** rented from British Telecom
- **d** bought from Cable & Wireless plc

9 Re-arrange the following in the order in which they should appear in a business letter, with the first at a:
- **a** salutation
- **b** references
- **c** complimentary close
- **d** description of signatory

10 Pair the following lists of words (note that there is a surplus item in the second column):

Communications	**Functions**
a telex	**a** transmission of replicas of documents
b fax	**b** internal written communications
c intercom	**c** internal oral communications
d memo	**d** mass communication
	e urgent written communications abroad

Short answer questions

State the missing words or phrases:

11 After dialling, the telex operator expects to receive a/an ....

12 A letter starting with 'Dear Sir or Madam' should end with 'Yours ....

13 A teleprinter combines the speed of the telephone with the authority of the ....

14 Electronic teleprinters use .... which have memories.

15 The letters ISDN stand for ....

Supply brief answers to the following questions:

16 List three ways in which a firm may receive information:

a ....
b ....
c ....

17 The following methods may be used to write to a firm's branches at home and overseas:

a ....
b ....
c ....

18 List three advantages of transmitting information by fax:

a ....
b ....
c ....

19 What is the difference between each of the following?

a telex ....
b telemessage ....
c teletext ....

20 Give three tips for writing business correspondence:

a ....
b ....
c ....

Unit 16
Mail services

Competences developed in this unit:

- Receive and send mail (NVQ2) – in conjunction with Unit 8 Incoming and outgoing mail

Royal Mail offers a wide range of services for the despatch of mail to destinations in the UK and abroad and a summary is given below. Full information and prices for each of the services are given in the *Mail Guide*. Current rates of postage are also supplied in comprehensive guides for inland and overseas post and these should be available in the mailroom for quick reference. Area Customer Service Centres may be contacted for information and advice about mail services.

▶ INLAND LETTERS AND CARDS

Letters and cards may be sent by first or second class services. The Post Office endeavours to deliver first class mail on the next working day after collection and second class within three working days after collection. The class of a letter is determined by the amount of postage paid and no written indication is necessary. A letter posted unpaid or underpaid, except in the business reply or freepost services, is treated as second class and is charged on delivery with the deficit of the second class postage plus a small fee.

▶ MAILSORT

A contract can be arranged with Royal Mail to allow discounts on letters posted in bulk, ie a minimum of 4000 items, which have been presorted by postcodes. Exceptionally, a minimum of 2000 letters will be accepted for a discount, provided they are all for delivery within one postcode area and are all posted within the same postcode area. To qualify for a discount the items must normally be of the same size, shape and weight and at least 90 per cent of the addresses must have postcodes.

This service may be used for the following categories of mail:

Mailsort 1 for first-class mail:
target delivery the next working day

Mailsort 2 for second-class mail:
target delivery within three working days

Mailsort 3 for non-urgent second-class mail:
target delivery within seven working days

▶ DOOR-TO-DOOR DELIVERY SERVICE

This service provides for the delivery of unaddressed material on a door-to-door basis with the normal mail to any area from a single post code sector up to the whole country. No stamps are required and items can be enveloped or unenveloped.

▶ SPECIAL DELIVERY

Urgent letters can be sent by the Special Delivery service, which guarantees next-day delivery by 1230 hrs to most UK destinations. Items posted on Friday or Saturday are guaranteed delivery on Monday. A special delivery fee is payable in addition to first-class postage. To confirm delivery of a Special Delivery, Registered or Recorded Delivery package it is necessary to make a local telephone call to 0645 272100 and quote the 13-digit number on the receipt. The label overleaf is used for this service.

▶ RECORDED DELIVERY

The Recorded Delivery service is designed for the correspondent who may require not only proof of posting but also proof of delivery. It is especially suitable for despatching documents of little or no monetary value for which proof of delivery may be required in a court of law. Compensation is limited to £25 for loss or damage and items of greater value should be sent by the Registered or Registered Plus services.

A special fee is payable for this service which is in addition to first or second-class postage. If the sender wishes to obtain an advice of delivery an additional fee is payable. The advice of delivery contains a signature from the delivery address, but not necessarily that of the addressee.

The procedure for preparing and despatching a Recorded Delivery package is the same as for registered mail, as given in points 1 to 5 of page 35. Confirmation of delivery can be arranged by telephoning 01645 272100 and quoting the 13-digit number on the receipt. Recorded Delivery certificate posting books may be used to save time when posting large quantities of packages.

▶ REGISTERED LETTERS

See page 35.

▶ BUSINESS REPLY

Under this service a person who wishes to obtain a reply from a client without putting them to the expense of paying postage may enclose an unstamped reply card, lettercard, envelope folder or gummed label of a special design. The user may also incorporate in newspaper advertisements and other publications a special design to be used as an address label or folder. The client can post the card etc in the ordinary way but without a stamp and the addressee will pay the usual first or second class postage together with a fee for each item. A Royal Mail licence is necessary for the business reply service.

▶ FREEPOST

A person who wishes to obtain a reply from a client or a member of the public without putting them to the expense of paying postage may include in their communication or advertisement a special address which includes the word 'FREEPOST'. The reply bearing this address can then be posted in the ordinary way but without a stamp and the addressee will pay postage on all the replies that are received. The freepost service can be used by anyone who obtains a licence. It can be used with both first- and second-class post when a pre-printed envelope, card or form is the response device, but only second-class post is permitted when customers respond by writing the freepost address on their own stationery.

This service can be used to attract a response not only through the press but through television and direct mail. The postage plus a small fee on each item is paid by the addressee.

▶ NEWSPAPERS AND MAGAZINES

A special application of Mailsort (page 151) called Presstream is available to publishers who have large quantities of magazines and periodicals to dispatch. In this service they pay lower prices in return for postcode sorting before posting using a mailsort database.

▶ PARCELS

The following UK Parcelforce services are available for the delivery of parcels up to 30 kg at the different delivery times given below.

Service	Delivery time	Inclusive cover for loss or damage (per parcel)
Datapost	Guaranteed next morning with money back guarantee in the event of late delivery	Up to £500
Parcelforce 24	Guaranteed next working day with money back guarantee in the event of late delivery	Up to £500
Parcelforce 48	Guaranteed within two working days with money back guarantee in the event of late delivery	Up to £500
Parcelforce Standard	Normally within three working days	Up to £20*

*It is necessary to obtain a certificate of posting (available free of charge) as evidence of despatch should the need arise to make a claim

Confirmation of delivery by telephone or in writing can be arranged with all services.

The compensation fee parcel facility provides a higher level of compensation for the Parcelforce Standard service. By paying this fee, a parcel can be insured against loss or damage during transit up to a maximum value of £500. The sender must complete a certificate of posting with the addressee's name and address, and the amount of compensation required, and hand this certificate to the post office counter clerk together with the parcel, fee and postage. The clerk then initials and date stamps the top portion of the certificate of posting and returns it to the sender. Posting lists may be used, instead of separate certificates of posting, when posting a large number of parcels.

Under the Parcelforce Datapost service consequential loss from £100 to £5000 per consignment is included. A consequential loss is a loss to the sender arising out of some failure in the Parcelforce service and is over and above the actual value of the articles lost, damaged or delayed, eg in the case of manufactured or sample goods delayed or damaged in the post, this could result in the consequential loss of sales and profits.

▶ POSTAGE FORWARD PARCEL SERVICE

The postage forward parcel service enables a company to receive parcels from customers without prepayment of postage; the postage, with a small fee on each parcel, is paid by the addressee. A licence to use this service must be obtained from Parcelforce. This service is designed primarily to meet the needs of companies who wish to obtain a parcel from a customer without putting the customer to the expense or trouble of paying postage.

▶ INTERNATIONAL POSTAL SERVICES

Swiftair

Swiftair is a special high speed overseas letter post which delivers airmail letters at least one day earlier than those sent by ordinary airmail. The red swiftair label should be stuck on the envelope in the top left-hand corner, and when posting it should be kept separate from other correspondence to ensure prompt delivery. Mail requiring more urgent delivery should be sent by the Parcelforce Datapost service (see page 153).

Airmail letters, cards and parcels

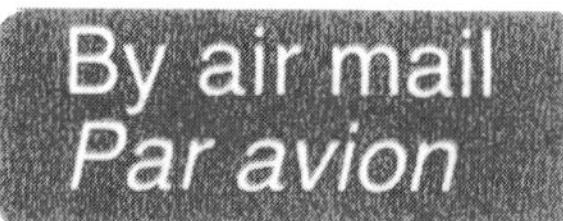

These are sent by air and blue airmail labels should be stuck on the packages to ensure that they are delivered promptly.

Aerogrammes

These may be sent to any address in the world. They must not contain enclosures and must be written on either the stamped forms which are obtainable from post offices or on privately manufactured forms on which the postage may be prepaid, either by means of the necessary postage stamp or by a franking machine impression.

Europe

Business letters, packets (up to 2 kg in weight) and cards are sent by airmail and are usually delivered within two to four days in cities. Letters and postcards to the EC up to 20 g are charged at the same rate as inland first-class letters.

Airstream

Large business users sending at least 2 kg of airmail per day may take advantage of the Airstream contract service, in which Royal Mail arranges to collect mail, complete the documentation, stamp the packages and post them.

Surface mail

Surface mail is the cheapest way of sending letters and cards abroad but delivery to some countries can take up to 12 weeks.

Printflow

Printed papers up to 5 kilo in weight may be sent abroad by airmail or surface mail at reduced rates of postage by the Printflow service. Printed papers include newspapers, magazines, directories, calendars, photographs, books and non-personalised mailshots.

There are three different types of Printflow service, allowing the sender to select the best combination of speed and cost for their particular needs:

- PRINTFLOW AIR — used when speed of delivery is a major consideration
- PRINTFLOW AIRSAVER — for a less expensive but moderately fast delivery service outside Europe
- PRINTFLOW SURFACESAVER — used for optimum ecoomy when speed of delivery is not essential

Overseas small packets

This service provides for the transmission of goods, whether dutiable or not, in the same mails as Printflow which, as a rule, travel more quickly than parcels. The sender must write their name and address on the outside of the packet and must write the words *Small packet* in the top left-hand corner on the address side of the packet. Small packets may be sent by air mail or surface mail. The packets may be sealed and contain personal correspondence if it relates to the contents being sent.

Airpacks

Prepaid, specially manufactured airpacks for

European and Worldwide destinations may be used for sending goods weighing up to 500 g by airmail. Additional postage has to be paid for heavier weights. A customs (C1) label is incorporated on the front of the packaging and must be completed by the sender.

▶ PARCELS

The following international parcel services are offered by Parcelforce.

- INTERNATIONAL DATAPOST — For urgent parcels of documents or goods. Guaranteed express deliveries can be made to some 200 countries and territories worldwide with moneyback guarantees in the event of late delivery. An inclusive charge covers compensation, consequential loss and collection from the sender's premises.
- INTERNATIONAL STANDARD SERVICE — For less urgent delive-ies to Europe from three working days and the rest of the world from five working days. The charge includes compensation.
- INTERNATIONAL ECONOMY SERVICE — Use for optimum economy. Delivery to Europe from 10 working days and the rest of the world 20 working days.

The Parcelforce charges, guaranteed delivery times, weight and size allowances, prohibitions and import licence requirements for each country are listed in the *Parcelforce International User Guide*. This guide can also be used to look up time zones, working days, dialling codes and contacts, eg Overseas Chambers of Commerce, for most countries abroad. All merchandise must be accompanied by three signed copies of commercial invoices to verify the value of the contents. Advice on customs documentation requirements for international parcels can be obtained from the Simpler Trade Procedures Board (SITPRO). Tel: 0171 2871814.

▶ CUSTOMS DECLARATION FORMS

All packets posted to countries outside the EU at the letter rate of postage and containing goods, whether or not dutiable in the country of destination, must be declared to customs. If the value of the goods does not exceed £270, a green label (form CN22) is sufficient, but for goods in excess of £270 a form CN23 plus a green label should be completed.

Customs requirements for parcels are given separately for each country in the *Parcelforce International Users Guide* and any advice on customs documentation requirements for international parcels can be obtained from the Simpler Trade Procedures Board. Tel: 0171-287 1814.

▶ INTERNATIONAL REPLY COUPONS

International reply coupons, obtainable from post offices, enable anyone sending a letter abroad to prepay a reply, ie instead of enclosing a stamped addressed envelope, the sender encloses a reply coupon which is exchangeable for postage stamps at post offices abroad.

▶ PRINTED POSTAGE IMPRESSIONS

An alternative to franking and stamping mail for organisations which send average daily mailings of over 250 items or average annual postage expenditure of £12,000 is to send their mail with printed postage impressions (PPIs). They can be used for large quantities of identical inland or international letters or packets at first- or second-class postage. Envelopes, labels or wrappers are pre-printed and may be used for regular or occasional postings. Royal Mail invoices the user for the cost of the postage after the items have been dispatched.

▶ PRIVATE BOXES

Instead of the mail being delivered in the

ordinary way a private box may be rented at a post office for the reception of postal packets 'to be called for' by the renter or their agent. The box must be taken for a definite address in the postal district in which the service is required and letters and parcels addressed to the renter must bear their full address and include the private box number, eg:

John Payne Enterprises plc
PO Box 149
21 Bolton Street
BLANKTOWN
BN8 3AP

By means of this service the renter can obtain mail before the normal delivery time. Correspondence is handed over only on production of a check card.

▶ POSTE RESTANTE

Poste restante means post waiting. To assist travellers with no fixed address, correspondence and parcels may be addressed to them at any main post office. The words 'Poste restante' or 'To be called for' must be included in the address. At the expiry of two weeks (one month for a packet originating abroad) postal packets are treated as undeliverable. To ensure delivery to the right person addressees must produce evidence of their identity when calling for mail.

▶ LATE POSTING FACILITY

Registered letters, first-class letters and recorded delivery packets are accepted in travelling post offices at railway stations up to five minutes before the departure times of the trains on payment of a fee in addition to the postage fee. The fees must be affixed in stamps before a letter is presented at the station.

▶ REDIRECTION OF POSTAL PACKETS

Letters, registered packets, postcards and newspapers are retransmitted by post without additional charge provided the packet is unopened and reposted not later than the day after delivery, Sundays and public holidays not being counted. If an adhesive label is used to indicate the new address the name of the original addressee must not be obscured otherwise the packet will be liable to surcharge as unpaid.

Registered and recorded delivery packets must not be dropped into a letter box but must be handed over the counter of a post office.

Redirection of mail by Royal Mail

If a person or business moves from one address to another, redirection of letters and other postal packets is undertaken by Royal Mail and Parcelforce at various rates depending on the period of redirection required. Forms should be completed and sent to the Royal Mail Redirection Centre and Parcelforce Customer Care Unit serving the old address.

▶ SELECTAPOST

This service is provided by Royal Mail for mail to be sorted into specified categories such as departments before it is delivered.

▶ RED STAR PARCEL DELIVERY SERVICE

Parcels are carried by train for delivery on the same day or overnight. They must be handed in to a railway station at least 30 minutes before the chosen train leaves and they are then available to be collected at the destination station 30 minutes after the train's arrival. Alternatively, a door-to-door courier service can be arranged with collection from the sender's premises and delivery to the consignee's address for same day or overnight despatch.

An International Delivery Service combines the use of road, rail and air transport for urgent delivery of parcels to addresses in countries around the world. There are also many private delivery firms offering courier services for express delivery of parcels.

▶ PROGRESS CHECK

Multiple choice questions

1 Which Royal Mail service would give you compensation for an expensive article lost in the post?
  a special delivery
  b certificate of posting
  c recorded delivery
  d registered post

2 The Royal Mail service which enables a company to pay the postage on letters and cards received from its correspondents is called:
  a selectapost
  b freepost
  c special delivery
  d datapost

3 A poste restante letter is:
  a one addressed to the local head postmaster
  b one addressed to a post office for collection by a person travelling around the country
  c one delivered to a letter box mounted on a post at the end of a long drive
  d one addressed to an overseas visitor for collection at an airport

4 The recorded delivery service provides:
  a proof of posting only
  b proof of delivery only
  c proof of posting and delivery
  d proof of communications on recorded tapes

5 The part of the recorded delivery form in Fig 16.1 is:
  a a receipt which is kept by the sender
  b retained by the post office as a record of the package
  c affixed to the package which is given to the addressee
  d included with the contents inside the package

Fig 16.1

6 If you receive a letter for a person who has moved to another address you can redirect it free of charge provided that:
  a the addressee has completed the Royal Mail form requesting redirection of postal packets
  b it is unopened and reposted not later than the day after delivery
  c it is unopened and a certificate of posting is obtained from the local post office
  d it is opened and an adhesive label is used to indicate the new address without obscuring the original address

7 Which of the following is the fastest method of posting a letter abroad?
  a swiftair
  b airmail
  c airpack
  d aerogramme

8 The Royal Mail service which sorts incoming mail is called:
  a datapost
  b mailsort
  c freepost
  d selectapost

9 Pair the following lists of words (note that there is a surplus item in the second column):

Facility	Postal Service
a high-speed delivery to Far East	**a** Presstream
b UK overnight delivery	**b** Swiftair
c despatch of magazines	**c** Freepost
d UK replies paid	**d** Recorded delivery
	e Datapost

10 Pair the following lists of words (note that there is a surplus item in the second column):

Article	Method
a legal document	**a** airmail
b books	**b** registered
c letter to Uganda	**c** Printflow
d jewellery	**d** recorded delivery
	e special delivery

Short answer questions

State the missing words or phrases:

11 Poste Restante on an envelope means the letter will be collected from the ....

12 The Household Delivery Service provides for the delivery of .... on a door-to-door basis.

13 The service used by publishers to dispatch newspapers is called ....

14 Parcels up to a maximum weight of .... may be sent by the Parcelforce Standard Service.

15 International reply coupons are used when writing letters abroad for ....

Supply brief answers to the following questions:

16 Name the three principal Parcelforce services:
a ....
b ....
c ....

17 State the categories of mail which are handled by each of the following services:
a Mailsort 1 ....
b Mailsort 2 ....
c Mailsort 3 ....

18 State for what purpose each of the following services would be used:
a Freepost: ....
....
b Recorded delivery ....
....
c Postage forward parcel: ....

19 Name three of the fastest overseas services:
a ....
b ....
c ....

20 List three labels used with postal services:
a ....
b ....
c ....

Unit 17
Receiving and assisting visitors

Competences developed in this unit:

- Receive and assist visitors
- Monitor and maintain the security of the workplace (NVQ2)

When you are receiving visitors or telephone calls on behalf of your firm you are creating that 'all-important' first impression. The caller gains a favourable impression when:

- The reception office is tastefully furnished and tidy. Decorative plants enhance the appearance of an office.
- The receptionist or secretary is pleasant, polite, helpful, smart and well spoken.
- The visitor is made welcome and well looked after; to ensure this:
  - invite them to sit in an easy chair while waiting
  - supply them with an appropriate newspaper/journal to read
  - if there is a delay, apologise and offer a cup of coffee or tea and keep them fully informed of the position
- A record is kept of callers expected and callers received (a register of callers or visitors' book will normally be compiled – see Fig 17.1).
- Visitors are introduced correctly to the firm's representative by announcing their name, title and company clearly. Give the visitor's name before the name of your firm's representative, but when introducing a man and a woman it is courteous to announce the woman's name first.
- The receptionist uses the visitor's name during conversation with them. The efficient receptionist or secretary will know by name the visitors who call regularly.
- The receptionist is tactful and helpful when a visitor (without an appointment) cannot see the person requested. In such cases arrangements are made for the visitor to see someone else or another appointment is arranged on a mutually agreed date.
- The receptionist has a thorough knowledge of the organisation, its activities and personnel and can supply information to visitors without having to consult others.

Date	Name of caller	Organisation	Time of arrival	Referred to
19- May 1	J R Chivers	Twyford Timber Supplies Ltd	1015	P Ridley
" 1	B Spear	Compton College of FE	1045	P S Adams
" 1	P G Clark & T Moon	Office Technology plc	1110	K Pratt
" 1	A R Manning	Midland Bank plc	1500	R A Lawes

Fig 17.1 Register of callers

- Full information is immediately available concerning the organisation as well as local hotels, train/air services, telephone nos, etc.

Visitors from another firm may introduce themselves by offering the receptionist a business visiting card such as the one in Fig 17.2 which provides their name, firm and position in the firm. If no card is offered, the receptionist should make a note of these details.

The receptionist should retain the card as it provides the relevant information for informing the appropriate member of staff of the visitor's arrival and for making the necessary introduction. The information from the cards may also be entered on visible index strips or a computer for quick reference.

▶ TELEPHONE

In a small to medium-sized organisation the receptionist will normally also be responsible for operating the main switchboard and tannoy (see Unit 14). This will involve receiving all incoming calls for the organisation, which have to be carefully and tactfully handled. For example, on receiving an offensive, indecent or menacing call, it is advisable to cut off the caller immediately without giving the company's name in the usual way. If such calls continue the receptionist should inform the security officer and the police. If a telephone call is received stating that a bomb has been planted on the premises, as much information as possible should be obtained from the caller, such as:

- location of the bomb
- the time it is expected to go off
- any circumstances concerning the motive for the bomb
- the identity of the caller

It is important to make as many notes as possible of the conversation and try to detect the nationality and any accent of the informer. Immediately after the call the following steps should be taken:

1 inform the security or safety officer and the police (dial 999)
2 assist the security or safety officer to take the necessary precautions until the police arrive to take charge of the situation

▶ RECEIVING PARCELS

While goods received for production will normally be delivered to the Goods Received Section, parcels for other departments are usually delivered to the Reception Office. They may be accompanied by a delivery or consignment note (see example of a delivery note, Fig 2.9 on page 20). The person delivering the parcel will normally require a signature to acknowledge receipt of the delivery. Before signing, the receptionist should check that:

SYSTEMS FURNITURE plc
Office furniture for the modern office

Leonard A Scott
Home Sales Manager

Brookfield Industrial Estate, Twyford, Westshire TD3 2BS

Tel: 0193 384192   Telex: 342689   Fax: 0193 219673

Fig 17.2 Business visiting card

- the parcels are addressed to the company
- the number of parcels is correct, as stated on the delivery note
- the parcels are not damaged in any way – any damage must be noted on the delivery note returned to the driver, as well as on the copy retained.

▶ SECURITY

The receptionist, with the assistance and surveillance of security staff, controls the access of visitors to the offices and the process of recording their names in a register of callers is a method of checking them in.

The following methods may also be used:

- Issue all employees with photo-identity cards to be worn at all times.
- Use coded electronic cards incorporating pre-programmed number combinations or computerised cards for staff to operate door locks, allowing only those authorised to enter premises – cards may carry an employee photo ID which is photographically or digitally reproduced.
- Issue visitors and contractors with passes to be worn at all times.
- Keep a record of all permanent and temporary passes issued.
- Arrange for visitors to be met and returned to the reception office by their hosts.
- Employ security officers to control the admission of visitors and contracting staff.
- Use a closed-circuit television (as in Fig 17.3) for surveillance of buildings – a time-lapse video system offers 24-hour surveillance, and the input from up to 16 video cameras can be recorded on one tape, providing up to seven days' recall.
- Install public address equipment throughout the building to enable emergency announcements to be made to all occupants.

Fig 17.3 Closed-circuit television security system

When handling confidential information:

- Never leave confidential records lying around when you leave your office – be sure to lock them away when they are not in use.
- Place confidential records in a folder so that they are not immediately visible to an onlooker.
- Classify and control confidential, private or secret records by marking them accordingly.
- Position your desk in such a way that visitors to your office will not be able to read confidential documents while they are being processed – if this information is displayed on your word processor screen, it may be necessary to scroll it away temporarily when visitors are present.
- Supervise visitors so that they are never left alone at any time in your office.
- If confidential documents have to be reproduced on a copier, it may be desirable for you to do this to ensure that the contents are not disclosed to others.
- If asked for confidential information by an unauthorised person, use tact and diplomacy to evade the question and explain that you have no authority to supply such information and that enquiries should be made elsewhere.
- Take care when supplying confidential information on the telephone that the caller is authorised to receive it.
- Avoid confidential telephone information being overheard by others – this may entail ringing back when you are alone in your office or transferring the call to a more private office.
- Any confidential or secret documents no longer required should not be put in the waste paper bin but destroyed in a shredder or incinerator.

- Take as much care over confidential computerised data and recorded data on dictation machines as you would with documents.
- Inform your manager immediately of any breaches of security you see or which are brought to your attention.

▶ SECURITY OF COMPUTERISED DATA

See page 101.

▶ EMERGENCY SERVICES

The receptionist has a key role to play in the communications for emergency services, such as sending for ambulances and reporting fires. See Unit 13 for details of safety, fire and evacuation procedures.

Emergency telephone calls

It is vital to understand clearly the procedure for making an emergency telephone call as in time of trouble a call efficiently conducted could be a vital factor in saving life.

For the fire brigade, police, ambulance and other emergency services dial 999 unless you are told otherwise. It is important to remember that you are connected first to an operator who will put you through to the emergency service required. When the operator answers give:

1 the name of the emergency service required
2 your telephone number

When the emergency service answers give:

1 the address where help is needed
2 all other information for which you are asked

▶ GUIDELINES FOR FIRST AID

- be aware of the need for safety at all times
- know where the nearest first aid box and facilities are
- know how to contact the named first aider when an accident or illness occurs
- know how to send quickly for a doctor or an ambulance in major accidents or illnesses (see above)
- know how to help an injured person by:
  - making the casualty as comfortable as possible (but do not attempt to move them until you know what is wrong)
  - ensuring that the casualty can breathe freely (allow plenty of fresh air into the room)
  - disconnecting the electric power as quickly as possible in the case of an electric shock
  - keeping the casualty warm by wrapping them in blankets or coats for treatment of shock
- know that first aid treatment apart from simple procedures, such as the above, should only be applied by qualified first aiders
- complete an accident report form (as in Fig 13.1) in accordance with the organisation's policy

▶ SOURCES OF INFORMATION FOR THE RECEPTION OFFICE

Source	*Provides details of:*
The organisation	
● Internal telephone index	internal telephone numbers of staff
● Organisation chart	staff positions and their sections and departments
● Company sales leaflets and pricelists	details and prices of company's products
● Company's house journal	company activities and news
Telecommunications	
● Phone books	telephone numbers, addresses, postal codes and dialling codes
● Yellow pages	telephone numbers and addresses grouped under the headings of trades and professions
● The European Business Directory	telephone numbers fax numbers and addresses for companies in EC countries
● British Telecom Telex directory	telex numbers and answerback codes

Source	*Provides details of:*
• British Telecom Fax Directory	fax numbers
Visitors	
• Register of callers	visitors to the organisation
• Business visiting cards	visitors to the organisation
• Receptionist's desk diary	appointments made for visitors
Travel	
• AA/RAC Handbooks	road maps, hotels, etc
• Railway Timetables	train times
• Chambers World Gazetteer	location of places, names of towns, etc throughout the world
General	
• English Dictionary	words: their meanings, pronunciation, spelling
• Secretary's Desk Book	secretarial services and sources
• Local Town Guides	local services and facilities, street maps, hotels, etc
• Teletext and Viewdata Services	see page 182

▶ OTHER DUTIES OF THE RECEPTIONIST

In addition to the duties already discussed in this unit, the receptionist will normally be required to do or to assist with the following:

- Receive and relay messages (*see* page 131)
- Operate: a telephone answering machine (*see* page 134)
  a fax machine (*see* page 146)
  telex equipment (*see* page 146)
- Make appointments and enter them in a diary (*see* page 92)
- Arrange refreshments for visitors
- Organise car parking facilities for visitors
- Update organisation charts and internal directories
- Organise temporary cover of reception desk
- Arrange flowers and displays in the reception area

▶ PROGRESS CHECK

Multiple choice questions

1 A visitor who arrives at reception to see an executive without an appointment should be:
  a turned away and asked to make an appointment
  b shown straight into the executive's room
  c asked to wait while the executive is consulted
  d asked to see the executive's deputy

2 If you were making a telephone call from outside London to the number shown below, which sequence of numbers would you dial?
  Telephone: 0171 325 8162/8163
  Extension: 2143
  a 0171 325 8162 8163
  b 2143 0171 325 8162
  c 0171 325 8162
  d 0171 325 8162 2143

3 When making an emergency '999' telephone call you should first give the operator:
  a your own name
  b the location where help is needed
  c details of the emergency service required
  d your firm's name

4 A business visiting card gives details of:
  a the visitor's name and their company's name
  b the visitors' names and the reasons for their calls
  c train times and hotel addresses for an executive visiting firms
  d an appointment made for a visitor

5 Which of the following services would you use if you needed to make an international telephone call?
  a ADC **c** STD
  b PBX **d** IDD

6 When an incoming telephone call has to be transferred from one extension to another:
a ask the caller to ring again on another line
b take the necessary action swiftly and do not repeat the caller's name and request
c take a message from the caller to save time and prepare a message sheet
d convey the caller's name and request to the new extension

7 When making a telephone call the correct code can be found in the:
a phone book
b answerback code directory
c post code directory
d Mailguide

8 The document which you sign and use to check the parcels delivered at the reception desk is the:
a goods received note
b delivery note
c remittance advice note
d despatch note

9 Pair the following sources of information for receptionists with the contents (note that there is a surplus item in the second column):

Reference source	Contents
a organisation chart	**a** staff telephone numbers
b register of callers	**b** visitors' names and companies
c house journal	**c** visitors' appointments
d desk diary	**d** staff locations
	e company's news and activities

10 Pair the following lists of words (note that there is a surplus item in the second column):

Caller's request	Department referred to
a details of a job vacancy	**a** sales
b request for a catalogue and price list	**b** accounts
	c personnel
c Customs and Excise official to discuss VAT	**d** works
	e buying
d sales representative with details of a new product	

Short answer questions

State the missing words or phrases:

11 A receptionist will record the name of all visitors in a/an ....

12 One duty of a receptionist is to make .... and enter them in a diary.

13 A visitor from another firm may introduce himself/herself by offering the receptionist a/an ....

14 Any damage to a parcel delivered to the reception office should be ....

15 When the emergency service answers in a 999 emergency telephone call you should state ....

Supply brief answers to the following questions:

16 List three duties of a receptionist:
a ....
b ....
c ....

17 List three sources of information which are used by a receptionist:

a ....

b ....

c ....

18 Give three reasons why the reception desk should be near the main entrance:

a ....

b ....

c ....

19 Suggest one reference source for the reception office for information about each of the following:

a The organisation ....

b The visitors ....

c Travel arrangements ....

20 List three steps which should be taken to safeguard confidential information:

a ....

b ....

c ....

Unit 18
Travel arrangements

Competences developed in this unit:

- Arrange travel for persons
- Book accommodation for a specified purpose

(NVQ2)

▶ HOW TO PLAN

It is important when making arrangements for travel and accommodation that careful and systematic planning is done to ensure that action is timely and nothing overlooked. Checklists of the action to be taken are helpful as a reminder of jobs to be done. Figures 18.1, 18.2, 18.3 and 18.4 show appropriate checklists for inland travel, booking accommodation, using the services of a travel agent and foreign travel.

Itinerary

Note that an itinerary (as shown in Fig 18.5) gives:

1 Name(s) of travellers.
2 Total and individual dates.
3 Departure and arrival times of trains and aircraft (and flight numbers for air travel).
4 Railway station names or airport terminal numbers (where appropriate).
5 Hotel names, addresses, telephone numbers and fax numbers.
6 Business names, addresses, telephone numbers and names of contacts.
7 All times using the 24-hour clock system to save any confusion which may arise between am and pm.

CHECKLIST FOR INLAND TRAVEL

1 **Agree dates and enter them in the diary** ☐
2 **Book hotel (if required) – see Fig 18.2 on page 167** ☐
3 **Arrange meetings/appointments, as required** ☐
4 **Check confirmation of hotel reservation** ☐
5 **Prepare an itinerary** ☐
6 **Collect air or rail tickets and seat reservations (if required)** ☐
7 **Assemble the following items for the traveller:**
- **itinerary** ☐
- **hotel brochure and confirmation of booking** ☐
- **road map book (if travelling by car)** ☐
- **air/rail tickets** ☐
- **file of correspondence/documents for meetings/appointments, etc** ☐
- **supply of business stationery, including visiting cards** ☐

8 **Discuss any outstanding matters to be dealt with in the office during the period of the visit** ☐

Fig 18.1 Checklist for inland travel

CHECKLIST FOR BOOKING ACCOMMODATION

1 **Check essential details with the person requiring the accommodation and note down the dates, venues, hotels if requested, and their requirements for accommodation.** ☐

2 **Select suitable accommodation which meets the needs of the traveller (reference may be made to one of the reference books listed on page 181, such as the AA Members' Handbook).** ☐

3 **Telephone the hotel to reserve accommodation and ascertain the price. You will need to supply the following:** ☐
- **name(s) of people requiring accommodation**
- **dates and times – specifying clearly the nights for which the room is required and approximate times of arrival and departure**
- **type of room required, ie single, double, twin**
- **method of payment to be used**

4 **Confirm the telephoned reservation in writing by letter or fax and request a confirmation by the hotel.** ☐

Fig 18.2 Checklist for booking accommodation

CHECKLIST FOR TRAVEL AGENT

Information to be supplied when using the services of a travel agent

- **journey dates** ☐
- **countries/places to be visited** ☐
- **airline preference** ☐
- **class of travel, ie first class, executive class (business/club) or economy class (tourist)** ☐
- **smoking or non-smoking seats** ☐
- **car hire** ☐
- **if travelling by car, registration number, type of car and length of car** ☐
- **hotel reservations** ☐
- **insurance** ☐
- **visa** ☐
- **transport to airport** ☐

Fig 18.3 Checklist for using a travel agent

Remember: to keep a copy of the itinery for use in the office and for any others who require information about the traveller's movements.

▶ FLIGHT SCHEDULES

Figure 18.6 is an extract from an airline timetable which you may need to use when planning journeys involving air travel. You should note the following:

- Days of the week are represented by the numbers 1 to 7, ie 1 = Monday, 2 = Tuesday … 7 = Sunday
- The times use the 24-hour clock system. The

CHECKLIST FOR FOREIGN TRAVEL

First tasks

- Agree dates and enter them in diary ☐
- Airline tickets booked ☐
- Insurance arranged ☐
- Hotel booked ☐
- Vaccinations arranged, if necessary ☐
- Visa applied for, if required ☐
- Passport – still current? ☐
- Arrange meetings/appointments abroad ☐
- Business visiting cards printed with information on reverse in language of country visited ☐
- Information about country visited – send for copy of *Hints for Exporters* ☐
- Arrange to be met at foreign airport/hire car ☐
- Apply to AA for international Driving Permit ☐

One week before visit

- Check receipt of airline tickets ☐
- Check receipt of insurance certificate ☐
- Check confirmation of hotel booking ☐
- Check receipt of visa, if required ☐
- Order travellers cheques and currency from bank ☐
- Prepare itinerary ☐
- Book transport to airport in this country ☐

1–2 days before departure

- Collect travellers cheques and currency from bank ☐
- Assemble the following items and hand to traveller: ☐
  - airline tickets
  - insurance certificate
  - vaccination certificate
  - visa
  - passport
  - *Hints for Exporters* booklet
  - travellers cheques and foreign currency
  - itinerary
  - hotel brochure and confirmation of booking
  - international driving permit
  - confirmation of transport arrangements
  - file of correspondence/documents for meetings/appointments
  - supply of stationery for use abroad
  - business visiting cards
- Discuss any outstanding matters ☐

Fig 18.4 Checklist for foreign travel

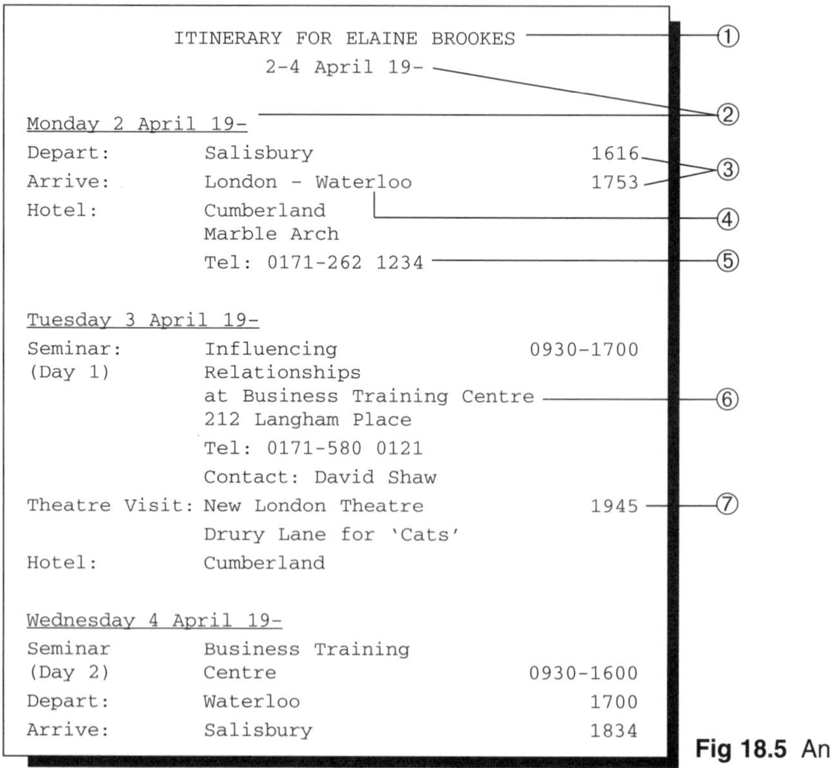

ITINERARY FOR ELAINE BROOKES
2-4 April 19-

Monday 2 April 19-

Depart:	Salisbury	1616
Arrive:	London - Waterloo	1753
Hotel:	Cumberland Marble Arch Tel: 0171-262 1234	

Tuesday 3 April 19-

Seminar: (Day 1)	Influencing Relationships at Business Training Centre 212 Langham Place Tel: 0171-580 0121 Contact: David Shaw	0930-1700
Theatre Visit:	New London Theatre Drury Lane for 'Cats'	1945
Hotel:	Cumberland	

Wednesday 4 April 19-

Seminar (Day 2)	Business Training Centre	0930-1600
Depart:	Waterloo	1700
Arrive:	Salisbury	1834

Fig 18.5 An Itinerary

LON

From To	Days 1234567	Depart	Arrive	Flight number	Aircraft /Class	Stops	Transfer Information Airport	Arrive	Depart	Flight number	Aircraft /Class
FROM LONDON CONTINUED											
▶	**KANSAS CITY**										MC RD RZ
	1234567	1145Ⓝ	1851	BA199	767/JM	1	PIT	1540	1740	BA7231♦	DC9/FY
▶	**KARACHI**										
	1-----7	1000④	0235†	BA123	777/FJM	2	MCT	2245	2359	PK226	AB3/CY
29 Oct–28 Nov	-2-----	1000④	0235†	BA123	767/FJM	2	MCT	2250	2359	PK226	AB3/CY
5 Dec–30 Mar	-2-----	1000④	0235†	BA123	777/FJM	2	MCT	2245	2359	PK226	AB3/CY
	1---5--	1030④	0255†	BA125	767/FJM	1	BAH	2020	2230	GF752	32S/FJC
	---4---	1030④	0355†	BA125	767/FJM	1	BAH	2020	2330	GF752	32S/FJC
	--3----	1600③	0450†	PK782	747/FCY	0					
	----5--	1930③	0820†	PK710	747/FCY	0					
	------7	1930③	1030†	PK788	747/FCY	1					
	-----6-	2030③	0920†	PK756	747/FCY	0					
▶	**KEY WEST**										MC AL HZ
	1234567	1000Ⓝ	1834	BA295	747/FJM	1	MIA	1450	1745	BA7121♦	DH8/Y
▶	**KINGSTON**										
	--3-5-7	1230Ⓝ	1930	BA265	747/JM	1					
▶	**KIRKWALL**										HZ
	12345--	0715①	0955	BA4104	757/M	1	ABZ	0840	0910	BA5752	ATP/M
	-----6-	1300①	1610	BA4772	757§/C	1	EDI	1415	1450	BA8767♦	SH6/Y
	12345--	1400①	1800	BA4782	757/C	1	EDI	1515	1640	BA8767♦	SH6/Y
▶	**KNOXVILLE**										HC RD AL HZ
	12345-7	1145Ⓝ	1849	BA199	767/JM	1	PIT	1540	1735	BA7423♦	100/FY
▶	**KUALA LUMPUR** ⊘ All flights are No Smoking.										
	-2-4-6-	1100④	1005†	BA011	744/FJM	1	SIN	0750†	0915†	SQ106	AB3/PY
	1-3-5-7	1825④	1500†	BA033	744/FJM	0					
▶	**KUWAIT**										RD
	-2-----	0930③	2040	KU182	AB3/FJM	1					
	--3-5-7	1030③	1955	KU102	747/FJM	0					
	1--4-6-	1030③	2025	KU104	AB3/FJM	0					
	--3----	1255④	2250	BA157	767/FJM	0					
	1--4-67	1330④	2325	BA157	767/FJM	0					
6 Dec–31 Jan	--3----	2230③	0825†	KU106	AB3/FJM	0					
▶	**LAGOS**										
	--3-5-7	1100Ⓝ	2035	BA077	747/FJM	1					
	12-4-6-	1200Ⓝ	1925	BA075	747/FJM	0					
▶	**LANSING**										RD
	1234567	1145Ⓝ	1908	BA199	767/JM	1	PIT	1540	1750	BA7091♦	D38/Y
▶	**LARNACA**										
	-----67	0940①	1620	BA662	767/CM	0					
	12345--	2030①	0310†	BA664	757§/CM	0					

156 1 Monday 2 Tuesday 3 Wednesday 4 Thursday 5 Friday 6 Saturday 7 Sunday
♦ Operated by one of British Airways partner carriers. See page 4 for details.
† Next day
‡ Two days later
§ Aircraft may vary

Fig 19.6 Extract from British Airways worldwide timetable

24-hour clock system begins at midnight and continues throughout the day and night for 24 hours, ie 0900 is used for 9.00 am and 2345 for 11.45 pm
- Arrival times are given in the 'local' time, eg a flight leaving London at 1230 and arriving in Kingston at 1930 (local time: 5 hours behind GMT) takes 12 hours

The schedule provides:

- flight numbers, eg 744/FJM = Boeing 747-400 First class, Club World/Business class and World Traveller (Economy)
- number of stops made (passengers do not change planes)
- departure terminal in a circle, eg ① = Heathrow Terminal 1, Ⓝ = Gatwick
- day of arrival, eg † = next day

▶ PROGRESS CHECK

Multiple choice questions

1 The name of the document giving full details of travel and accommodation for a business trip is:
a a business visiting card
b an itinerary
c a checklist
d a visa

2 One of the first tasks to be done when making arrangements for travel abroad would be to:
a prepare the itinerary
b order travellers cheques from the bank
c book transport to the airport in this country
d apply for a visa

3 Which of these tasks in making travel arrangements is out of order?
a book hotel
b arrange appointments
c agree dates for visit
d prepare itinerary

4 Before travellers cheques can be released they must be signed at the bank by the:
a person travelling
b bank manager
c chief cashier of the traveller's firm
d bank cashier

5 Hotels in the UK can be referred to in:
a *Chambers' World Gazetteer*
b *AA Members Handbook*
c *Pears Cyclopaedia*
d *Whitaker's Almanack*

6 Gatwick Airport is represented in the British Airways timetable by:
a Ⓖ
b Ⓝ
c ①
d ②

7 Athens is two hours ahead of GMT. A plane leaves Athens at 1100 and arrives in London at 1300. The journey has taken:
a two hours
b three hours
c one hour
d four hours

8 You may refer to Fig 18.6 to answer this question. The aircraft leaving London for Karachi at 1030 on day 4 will arrive in Karachi on:
a Wednesday
b Thursday
c Friday
d Saturday

9 Application forms for British passports can be obtained from:
a post office
b bank
c customs and excise office
d consulate

10 Pair the 24-hour clock system times with those given for the 12-hour system. (Note that there is a surplus item in the second column)

12-hour clock	24-hour clock
a 8 pm	**a** 8000
b 8 am	**b** 2300
c 11 pm	**c** 1100
d 11 am	**d** 0800
	e 2000

Short answer questions

State the missing words or phrases:

11 Washington, USA is 5 hours .... GMT in the UK.

12 The symbol † in a British Airways Flight Timetable indicates that the plane will arrive ....

13 You should use a .... when making travel arrangements to ensure that nothing is overlooked.

14 The .... system should be used in itineraries to save any confusion between am and pm.

15 GMT stands for ....

Supply brief answers to the following questions:

16 List three documents that are used in inland travel:

a ....
b ....
c ....

17 State three items of information which you should give to a travel agent to make travel arrangements for you:

a ....
b ....
c ....

18 Name three books of reference which may be used in connection with travel arrangements:

a ....
b ....
c ....

19 Put the following three tasks into correct sequence of the order in which they are undertaken for making travel arrangements:
1 prepare itinerary, 2 book hotel, 3 enter agreed date in diary

a ....
b ....
c ....

20 State three methods of payment which may be made by a traveller abroad:

a ....
b ....
c ....

Unit 19
Organising meetings and other events

Competences developed in this unit:

- assist in arrangements for the provision of supporting facilities and materials
- assist in arrangements for the attendance of persons at events
- assist in arrangements for the provision of catering services at events

(NVQ2)

These objectives are broadly based and relate to the organisation of events in general but in this unit our main attention is focused on organising meetings. Organising any type of event, whether it is a business meeting or a social event, will involve you in many of the following tasks:

- noting the decision made about:
  - the purpose of the event
  - the date and time
  - the venue
  - the budget
- preparing a checklist of action to be taken (see Fig 19.1)
- preparing invitations/agenda/leaflets, drawing up a mailing list and distributing the items
- recording receipts and expenses
- obtaining and selecting menus (taking account of dietary needs) and ordering catering services
- organising speakers, guests, entertainment, etc
- planning and preparing facilities and materials, having regard to their security, eg programmes, handouts, visual/aural aids, book displays, floral decorations, etc
- arranging transport and accommodation for speakers, guests, etc
- reception and routing of people at the event, use of name tabs, etc
- drawing up attendance sheets
- arranging for press attendance when requested

After the event:

- ensuring the safe return of all equipment and materials
- comparing actual costs with estimates
- considering and reporting on the feedback of the event

Meetings were referred to in Section D as one of the principal oral methods of communication in business for the purpose of collecting the views of several people. They may also be used:

- to consult on and discuss matters of common interest
- to negotiate, eg a wage award
- to inform staff about new work procedures or update them on other current developments
- to make decisions by democratic means
- to solve problems by pooling expertise
- to plan or monitor progress, eg production
- to investigate occurrences, eg accidents
- to make recommendations to a parent committee or an executive

▶ TYPES OF MEETING

There are many different types of meeting, some of which are formal and others informal.

Formal meetings are those which are prescribed by law, standing orders or constitution and include annual general meetings of shareholders, board meetings, statutory committees, standing committees, etc. They are conducted in a formal manner and in accordance with a set agenda, held on specified dates, presided over by a chairman and with a secretary engaged to record the minutes.

CHECKLIST FOR ARRANGING A MEETING

Ten days before the meeting

Agree date of meeting with chairman and participants unless the date was fixed at a previous meeting (see computerised desk diary planner on page 90 as a means of coordinating dates for meetings) ☐

Book meeting room ☐

Order refreshments (if required) ☐

Enter date of meeting in chairman's diary ☐

Secretary discusses and agrees agenda with chairman ☐

Seven days before the meeting

Secretary notifies participants of arrangements made for meeting with agenda and papers ☐

Secretary prepares the chairman's agenda ☐

The day before the meeting

Collect together the following items required for the meeting:

- spare copies of the agenda ☐
- minutes of previous meeting ☐
- all relevant papers and files, including letters of apology received from people unable to attend ☐
- attendance register or sheet ☐
- any books of reference required, eg standing orders ☐
- stationery: writing paper, notebooks etc ☐

The day of the meeting

Attend early to make sure that the meeting room is ready and bring with you the above items ☐

Place 'meeting in progress' notice on meeting room door ☐

Arrange for participants to sign the attendance sheet ☐

Assist the chairman by providing the information required, ie:

- minutes of the last meeting
- letters of apology
- information from files
- standing orders ☐

The secretary records the details of the decisions reached and the results of any voting which may take place ☐

Comply with the procedures laid down for the security and confidentiality of information ☐

After the meeting, clear the room of all papers and ensure that all files, etc are returned to the office ☐

The day after the meeting

The secretary prepares draft minutes for approval by the chairman ☐

When approved, the Secretary types the minutes in their final form for distribution to participants ☐

The secretary types any correspondence resulting from the meeting ☐

File any papers used at the meeting, the minutes and the correspondence typed since ☐

If a further meeting was planned, note the date in the chairman's diary ☐

Fig 19.1 Checklist for arranging a meeting

Informal meetings are less rigid and may be called at any time and for any reason. A record may or may not be kept of the meeting, but where meetings are called to discuss business matters it is advisable to have a written record of decisions reached. Executive meetings, staff meetings, advisory committees and working party meetings will normally be informal to allow participants to contribute freely without having to adhere to rigid procedures.

▶ THE AGENDA

An agenda, as shown in Fig 19.2, is a programme of the details of the business to be discussed at a meeting in the order in which they are to be taken.

The agenda is sent to all members of the committee or organisation to give them adequate notice, and to enable them to ponder over, prior to the meting, the items of business

```
STAFF WELFARE COMMITTEE

A meeting of the Staff Welfare Committee will be held in
the Boardroom on Friday, 14 October 199- at 1530 hrs

AGENDA

1  Apologies for absence.

2  Minutes of the last meeting.

3  Matters arising from the minutes.

4  Staff canteen: To receive a report from     Paper 1
   the Canteen Manager concerning proposed     attached
   increases in prices.

5  Car park: To consider the working party     Paper 2
   report on a new layout for the car park.    to follow

6  To receive proposals for the staff
   Christmas Dinner.

7  Any other business.

8  Date of next meeting.

K ABRAHAM
Secretary
```

Fig 19.2 An agenda

to be discussed. The period of notice to be given is laid down by the constitution of the organisation and is normally seven to fourteen days. It is customary at committee meetings to arrange at one meeting the date of the next. The agenda usually includes the notice convening the meeting, which contains the day, date, time and place of meeting.

The agenda is prepared by the secretary in consultation with the chairman, and the items of business dealt with at the previous meeting are taken into consideration. The secretary should make a note of any matters requiring the attention of the committee, so that these may be included in the agenda for the next meeting.

Chairman's agenda

A chairman's agenda contains more information than the ordinary agenda, and spaces are left on the right-hand side of the paper for the chairman to make notes. The additional information is added by the secretary to assist the chairman in conducting the meeting efficiently, eg names of members who have sent apologies for absence, any matters arising from the minutes, and any information which has to be considered when reaching decisions.

▶ MINUTES

Minutes, as in Fig 19.3, are a record of the proceedings of a meeting and are kept to preserve a brief, accurate and clear record of the business transacted.

The key factors concerning the taking of minutes:

1 Record the exact wording of resolutions passed or decisions reached with the names of the proposers and seconders

MINUTES OF MEETING:	A meeting of the Staff Welfare Committee was held in the Boardroom on Friday, 14 October 199- at 1530 hrs Present: Miss C Parsons (in the Chair) Mr P L Brown Mrs J Clarke Miss C H Ellis Mr T R Moon Mr J Strong Miss K Abraham (Secretary) Mr F Morris (Canteen Manager)
Apologies:	Apologies were received on behalf of Miss J Tucker and Mr V Williams.
Minutes:	The minutes of the last meeting, which had been circulated, were taken as read and approved and were signed by the Chairman.
Matters arising:	There were no matters arising out of the minutes.
Staff Canteen:	The Canteen Manager submitted a report outlining the current financial position of the canteen. Since October of last year, when the price of meals was last increased, food costs had risen by 20% and he proposed a similar increase in the price of meals in order to meet the extra costs. It was generally felt that, at a time when salary increases were less than 10%, an increase of 20% for canteen meals would be unacceptable. Miss Ellis suggested offering a smaller choice of meals as a possible means of reducing costs. Mr Strong was of the opinion that the firm's subsidy should be increased to meet the higher costs. After much discussion it was agreed to defer increasing prices until the Chairman and the Canteen Manager had had a meeting with the Personnel Manager to seek an increase in the meals subsidy, and the Canteen Manager had considered other means of saving expenditure such as reducing the choice of meals offered.
Any other business:	Miss Parsons stated that the Bridgetown office had adopted flexitime and she considered that the majority of staff at this branch would like to change over to it. Members agreed to seek the view of staff and to report back their findings to the next meeting.
Date of next meeting	It was decided to hold the next meeting of the Committee on Tuesday, 7 November 199-.

Chairman
7 November 199-

Fig 19.3 Minutes

2 Note the main arguments for and against the decisions
3 Write the minutes as soon as possible after the meeting while the discussions are fresh in the mind
4 Write minutes wholly in the third person and in the past tense
5 Be as brief as possible as a summary is required – not a verbatim record
6 Write clearly so that there is no possible doubt about the decisions reached
7 Arrange the items in the same order as on the agenda
8 Prepare a draft for approval by the chairman before typing the final copy

▶ FORMAL MEETINGS

Companies are required by law to hold annual general meetings of shareholders regularly each year and 21 days' notice must be given of the date. These meetings are governed by set procedures laid down in the memorandum and articles of association. The items of business discussed include the declaration of dividends, election of directors and auditors and the presentation and adoption of the company's annual report and accounts for the previous year. Other types of organisation such as clubs, associations and voluntary bodies will also hold formal annual general meetings. The agenda has to be sent to all members of the organisation who are eligible to attend the meeting and will normally include annual reports from the officers, the financial statement and balance sheet and election of officers and committee for the following year.

▶ BUSINESS MEETING TERMS

Ad hoc 'Arranged for this purpose.' An ad hoc sub-committee is appointed to carry out one particular piece of work, such as the arrangements for the visit of a very important person (VIP). These committees are sometimes called special or special-purpose committees

Addendum An amendment which adds words to a motion

Adjournment Subject to the articles, rules or constitution of an organisation, the chairman, with the consent of the members of the meeting, may adjourn the meeting in order to postpone further discussion, or because of shortage of time. Adequate notice of an adjourned meeting must be given

Amendment A proposal to alter a motion by adding or deleting words. It must be proposed, seconded and put to the meeting in the customary way

Casting vote A second vote usually allowed to the chairman, except in the case of a company meeting. A casting vote is used only when there is an equal number of votes 'for' and 'against' a motion

Closure A motion submitted with the object of ending the discussion on a matter before the meeting

Dropped motion A motion that has to be dropped either because there is no seconder or because the meeting wants it to be abandoned

En bloc The voting of, say, a committee en bloc, that is, electing or re-electing all members of a committee by the passing of one resolution

Lie on the table A letter or document is said to 'lie on the table' when it is decided at a meeting to take no action upon the business in it

Majority The articles and rules of the organisation will state the majority of votes needed to carry a motion

Memorandum and articles of association Regulations drawn up by a company setting out the objects for which the company is formed and defining the manner in which its business shall be conducted

Motion A motion must normally be written and handed to the chairman or secretary before the meeting. The mover of the motion speaks on it and has the right to reply at the close of the discussion. The seconder may then speak to the motion only once. If there is no seconder, a motion is dropped and cannot be introduced again. When put to a meeting, the motion becomes 'the question' or 'the proposal', and when it is passed, it is called 'the resolution'. A motion on something which has not been included on the agenda can be moved only if 'leave of urgency' has been agreed by the meeting or if it has been included under the customary item 'any other business'.

Nem Con 'No one contradicting', ie there are no votes against the motion, but some members have not voted at all

Next business A motion 'that the meeting proceed with next business' is a method of delaying the decision on any matter brought before the meeting

No confidence When the members of a meeting disagree with the chair they pass a vote of 'no confidence' in the chair. When this happens the chair must be vacated in favour of a deputy or some other person nominated by the meeting. There must be a substantial majority of members in favour of this decision

Point of order This a question regarding the procedure at a meeting or a query relating to the standing orders or constitution raised by a member during the course of the meeting, eg absence of quorum

Poll Term for the method of voting at an election, usually a secret vote by ballot paper. The way in which a poll is to be conducted is generally laid down in the standing orders or constitution of the organisation

Postponement The action taken to defer a meeting to a later date

Putting the question To conclude the discussion on a motion it is customary for the chairman to 'put the question' by announcing 'The question before the meeting is ...'

Question be now put When members feel that sufficient discussion has taken place on a motion, it may be moved 'that the question be now put'. If this is carried, only the proposer of the motion may speak and then a vote is taken. If the motion 'question be now put' is defeated, discussion may be continued

Quorum The minimum number of persons who must be in attendance to constitute a meeting. This is stated in the constitution or rules of the organisation

Reference back An amendment referring a report or other item of business back for further consideration to the body or person submitting it. If the motion 'reference back' is defeated, the discussion is continued

Resolution A formal decision carried at a meeting. It must be proposed, seconded and put to the meeting in the customary way. A resolution cannot be rescinded at the meeting at which it is adopted

Rider An additional clause or sentence added to a resolution after it has been passed. It differs from an amendment in that it adds to a resolution instead of altering it. A rider has to be proposed, seconded and put to the meeting in the same way as a motion

Right of reply The proposer of a resolution has the right of reply when the resolution has been fully discussed. He is allowed to reply only once, and afterwards the motion is put to the meeting

Standing orders Rules compiled by the organisation regulating the manner in which its business is to be conducted. It may also have the title 'Constitution'

Status quo Used to refer to a matter in which there is to be no change

Sub-committee A sub-committee may be appointed by a committee to deal with some specific branch of its work. It must carry out such functions as are delegated to it by the committee and must report to the committee periodically

Ultra vires Beyond the legal power or authority of a company or organisation

Unanimous When all members of a meeting have voted in favour of a resolution it is said to be carried 'unanimously'

▶ PERSONNEL INVOLVED IN MEETINGS

Chairman (Note the title 'chairperson' is sometimes preferred.) The chairman is appointed by a meeting to:

- manage the proceedings of a meeting and keep order
- approve the items to be discussed on the agenda
- conduct the business according to the agenda and standing orders or constitution; keep the discussion within prescribed limits and allow all points of view to be expressed
- deal with points of order
- guide the discussion and assist the meeting to make decisions by passing resolutions, amendments, etc
- take a vote or poll and declare the result
- sign the minutes and ensure that action is taken, as approved
- close, adjourn or postpone meetings

Secretary Responsible for the meeting arrangements as given on page 173

Treasurer A treasurer is involved when a meeting is responsible for the receipt and payment of money. Duties include:

- presentation of financial reports
- advice to the meeting on financial matters
- submission of audited accounts when required

Convenor A person authorised to call a meeting

Ex-officio A person who is a member of a committee by virtue of office, eg the Canteen Manager may be an ex-officio member of the Staff Welfare Committee

Co-opted A person who serves on a committee as a result of the committee's power of co-option, ie the committee approves of the appointment by a majority vote in order to engage the services of a person who can assist them in their work

In attendance Those who attend a meeting to provide a service such as secretarial, legal, financial, etc, but do not have voting powers

Proxy A person appointed to attend a meeting and vote on behalf of a member who is unable to attend

Teller A person who counts the votes at a meeting

▶ BRITISH TELECOM SERVICES FOR MEETINGS AND CONFERENCES

Conference calls

This service uses the ordinary telephone to provide conference facilities for up to 60 individuals at locations throughout the UK and worldwide on any date and at any time, day or night. It is an efficient and economic way to run meetings without the expense of travel and hotel accommodation.

Videoconferencing

This service links groups of people in different locations by sound and vision. Although an expensive method, it provides the advantages of a face-to-face meeting without including travelling and accommodation costs, and makes better use of people's time. Any documents, models or technical drawings being discussed can be shown in close-up on the TV monitors installed at each location.

Business television

This is a private satellite-based television network that can be used to broadcast messages to staff or customers anywhere in the world. It is ideal for communicating with a large number of people at many venues and may be used for training sessions, company announcements, product launches, staff briefings, etc.

▶ PROGRESS CHECK

Multiple choice questions

1 An agenda is:
- **a** a record of the decisions reached at a meeting
- **b** a programme of business to be discussed at a meeting
- **c** an extract from the standing orders relating to the conduct of meetings
- **d** a report submitted for consideration at a meeting

2 The secretary discusses and agrees an agenda with the chairman:
- **a** the day after the meeting
- **b** the day of the meeting
- **c** the day before the meeting
- **d** ten days before the meeting

3 The secretary assists the chairman at a meeting by:
- **a** providing information required from files
- **b** using a casting vote, when required
- **c** conducting the meeting according to the agenda and standing orders
- **d** signing the minutes of the last meeting

4 An ex-officio member of a committee is one who:
- **a** serves after retiring from office
- **b** attends because of the office held
- **c** counts the votes
- **d** serves as a co-opted member

5 Which of the following telecommunications equipment can be used for conducting meetings?
- **a** voicebank
- **b** teletext

c videoconferencing
d voice response unit

6 Which one of these items is out of order on an agenda?
a apologies
b any other business
c minutes of the last meeting
d matters arising

7 A resolution is carried unanimously when:
a the majority are in favour
b the majority are against
c all are in favour
d all who vote are in favour but some have abstained

8 The minimum number of persons who must be in attendance to constitute a meeting is known as:
a ad hoc
b status quo
c quod vide
d quorum

9 Which of the following has the right of reply when a motion has been fully discussed?
a proposer
b seconder
c chairman
d convenor

10 Pair the two lists of words (note that there is a surplus item in the second column)

Personnel	**Duties**
a chairman	**a** votes on behalf of an absent member
b proxy	**b** counts the votes
c convenor	**c** declares the results of voting
d teller	**d** records results of voting
	e calls a meeting

Short answer questions

State the missing words or phrases:

11 Formal meetings are those which are prescribed by ...., standing orders or constitution

12 The first item on a committee meeting agenda is ....

13 A .... is an additional sentence added to a resolution after it has been passed at a meeting

14 A point of order at a meeting relates to a question about the ....

15 The written record of a meeting is known as ....

Supply brief answers to the following questions:

16 State three sources of information which the secretary of a meeting provides for the chairperson:
a ....
b ....
c ....

17 Give three reasons for holding meetings:
a ....
b ....
c ....

18 State four essential items of information you need to know in order to organise an event:
a ....
b ....
c ....
d ....

19 Name three business meeting terms concerned with ending the discussion of an agenda item:
a ....
b ....
c ....

20 List three of the duties of a meeting chairperson:
a ....
b ....
c ....

Unit 20
Sources of information

Competence developed in this unit:

- Supply information for a specific purpose (NVQ2)

Communication is the means of transmitting facts and figures from one person to another, and an important part of your work in this process is checking the information and knowing where to find it when it is required. You may have to refer to reference books, locate information from computerised services or seek it out from organisations.

▶ REFERENCE BOOKS IN COMMON USE

Information	Source
Abbreviations, initials, acronyms	*Acronyms, Initialisms and Abbreviations Dictionary*
Air services	*ABC World Airways Guide*
Biographies of living eminent people	*Who's Who* *Debrett's People of Today*
Civil servants	*Civil Service Year Book*
Clergymen of the Church of England	*Crockford's Clerical Directory*
Companies: financial data, directors	*The Macmillan Stock Exchange Official Year Book* Dun & Bradstreet's *Who Owns Whom*
Companies: names, addresses and telephone numbers in the EU	*The European Business Directory*
Companies: ownership, subsidiary companies	Dun & Bradstreet's *Who Owns Whom*
Companies: prominent firms in the UK	*Key British Enterprises, The Times 1000 leading companies in Britain and Overseas*
prominent firms in the world	*Principal International Business Exporters' Encyclopedia – the World Marketing Guide*
Directors and their companies	*Directory of Directors*
Employment legislation	*Croner's Reference Book for Employers*
Fax numbers	*British Telecom Fax Directory*
Forms of address	*Black's Titles and Forms of Address*
General information: dictionary, gazetteer, legal data, synonyms and antonyms, office compendium	*Pears Cyclopaedia*
Geographical: spelling and location of places	*Ordnance Survey Gazetteer of Great Britain* *Chambers World Gazetteer*
Governments for countries throughout the world and international organisations	*Statesman's Year Book* *The Times Guide to the European Parliament* *The Europa Year Book*
Information technology	*Croner's IT*
Insurance companies	*Insurance Directory and Year Book*
Legal officers, barristers, solicitors, judges	*Waterlow's Solicitors' and Barristers' Directory*

Information	Source
Local community: services, organisations and town street maps	*Town Guide*
Local government authorities: areas, populations, names of chief officers	*Municipal Year Book*
Manufacturers and suppliers	*Kelly's Business Directory*
Medical practitioners	*Medical Directory*
Newspapers, trade journals	*Benn's Media, Willing's Press Guide*
News reference service	*Keesing's Record of World Events* *Facts on file – world news digest*
Parliamentary verbatim reports	*Hansard*
Postal services: Royal Mail services	*Mailguide*
Parcelforce services	*UK User Guide* *International User Guide*
Printing and writing	*Author's and Printers' Dictionary* *Writers' and Artists' Year Book*
Qualifications, addresses of professional bodies	*British Qualifications*
Road travel, maps, hotels	*Automobile Association Members' Handbook* *Royal Automobile Club Guide and Handbook* *The Times Atlas of the World* *Hotels and Restaurants in Great Britain*
Secretarial services and procedures	*Secretary's Desk Book*
Shipping	*The ABC Passenger and Shipping Guide* *Lloyds International List*
Telephone numbers: general classified by trades and professions	 *Phone books* *Yellow pages* *Thomson Local Directory*
Telex numbers and answerback codes	*British Telecom Telex Directory* *Telex Answerback Directory*
Train times	*Regional Train Timetables* *Great Britain Passenger Railway Time Table*
Travelling abroad: advice to business executives	*Hints to Exporters*
Words and their spellings, meanings, derivations and pronunciations	*Dictionary*
Words: synonyms and antonyms	*Roget's Thesaurus of English Words and Phrases*
World affairs, British and foreign embassies, UK sovereigns, royal family, peerage, cabinet ministers, members of parliament, Bank of England, law courts, churches, order of precedence in Great Britain, EU, United Nations	*Whitaker's Almanack*

▶ A GUIDE TO FINDING INFORMATION IN REFERENCE BOOKS

- If a reference book is not available at your workplace, try the local library where most of these reference books will be kept in the reference section.
- Check first in the library catalogue of books held on card, microfiche or computer, to find out whether the book you require is

stocked and, if so, where it is kept. If you look in the title A-Z catalogue you will find the classification number of all books held by the library. The Dewey decimal classification numbers, which are used in most libraries, contain three digits followed by a decimal point and further digits to represent particular subject areas, eg 651.189 for a book on office services. General reference books such as Whitaker's Almanack use the primary classification number 030.

- If the book you require is not in stock, ask the librarian whether there are alternative books which may provide the same information.
- When you have found the book, check the date of publication (usually on the reverse of the title page) to see if the book is a recent edition, otherwise the information it provides may be out of date.
- Look first at the contents page at the front and the index at the back to find the page number where the information can be located.
- When you have located the correct page, write down the relevant information and its source, ie the reference book title and its page, on a piece of paper: it is unwise to rely on remembering important facts. It may be possible, subject to copyright law, to take a photocopy of a particular page if you require detailed information.
- If you cannot find a reference book on the subject you require, there may be some information about it in one of the major specialist encyclopaedias (Classification Number 030).
- Even current editions of reference books cannot provide recent developments and changes and if you require the most up-to-date information you will need to refer to newspapers, journals or online databases which are available at most libraries. See also the information services provided by videotex below.

▶ COMPUTERISED INFORMATION SERVICES (VIDEOTEX)

Quick access to a wide range of information through a television receiver is now available by using the BBC and ITV teletext services or the British Telecom viewdata service. The teletext services of Ceefax (BBC), ITV3 and ITV4 transmit pages of written data to television sets by means of coded electronic pulses. The British Telecom viewdata service Prestel uses the telephone network to connect the user's television receiver with the computer supplying pages of data. The page of information required is selected by a remote controlled push button handset connected to a specially adapted domestic television receiver.

To look up the latest share prices on Ceefax BBC2, the handset is operated as follows:

- press the text button to reveal the main categories and their page numbers, ie Finance (200), Sport (300), Weather (400)
- key in 200 to reveal the finance headlines and page numbers for the major categories in finance, ie Key market pointers at a glance (201); Share prices: A–G (221), G–S (222), S–Z (223); Latest foreign exchange rates (252/253)
- key in the relevant number for the shares required

If you know the page number you can omit Stage 2 and proceed straight to the required page.

These services provide information on such topics as foreign and London stock market reports, share prices, foreign exchange rates, commodity prices, weather maps, train and air services, news headlines, entertainment and sport, food guide, guides to manufacturing and service industries, government information and reference information of all kinds.

Prestel is an interactive system as users can send messages both to each other on a special computer and to information providers using response pages. Goods can be ordered by Prestel and hotel rooms, theatre seats, etc can be booked from your own television set.

Messages may be sent and received by the Prestel Mailbox Service. Subscribers have their own 'mailbox' which is used for receiving and transmitting their messages. Telex messages may also be sent and received via a Prestel mailbox.

A special financial information service, called Citiservice, is provided by British Telecom for investors, traders, financial advisers and business executives who require a knowledge of immediate market conditions. It provides instantaneous updating of prices in real time as well as on-line investment services, such as automatic portfolio valuations and electronic share ordering. Dedicated data lines connect the Citiservice Computer Centre direct to exchanges, banks and brokers around the world, providing a continuous flow of financial data 24 hours a day.

Private viewdata systems supply specialised information to restricted user groups, eg farming, travel, stock exchange, law, local government, etc. Access may be via Prestel or directly through the public telephone network.

▶ ORGANISATIONS

Organisation	*Information supplied*
Bank	banking and foreign currency
British Telecom	telecommunications
Chamber of commerce	local businesses, trade matters
Consulates	visas
County council/district council	local government matters
Customs and Excise	value added tax
Driver and Vehicle Licensing Centre, Swansea SA99 1AN	driving licences
Her Majesty's Stationery Office	government publications
Information bureau	local services and events, hotels
Inland Revenue	income tax
Job centre/careers office/Training Commission	employment and training matters
Library	reference information of all kinds: books, newspapers, journals, etc
National Television Records Office, Bristol BS98 12L (or post office)	broadcast receiving licences
Parcelforce National Enquiry Centre	parcel post
Post office	postal information, motor taxation
Regional passport office	passports (application forms from local employment offices and post offices)
Royal Mail Customer Service Centre	Royal Mail services
Social Security Department	national insurance
Travel agent British Rail Airport AA/RAC offices Tourist offices	travel information

▶ GRAPHS AND CHARTS

Line graphs, bar charts and pie charts are effective means of presenting data so that it can be read and interpreted easily and trends identified.

Line graphs

Figure 20.1 is an example of a line graph which compares the sales of systems desks with the sales of executive desks. Note the following when constructing a line graph or interpreting data from one:

- the title describes the content of the line graph
- the time scale, in this case six months, is displayed along the bottom horizontal line (or axis)
- the scale of the financial data is given on the vertical line at the side – '0' takes the bottom line position and the largest sum the top line

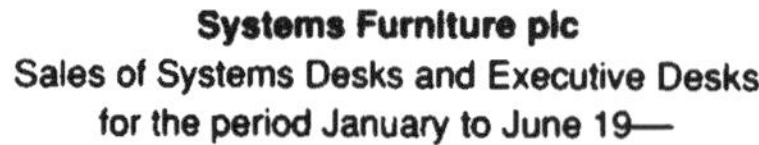

Systems Furniture plc
Sales of Systems Desks and Executive Desks
for the period January to June 19—

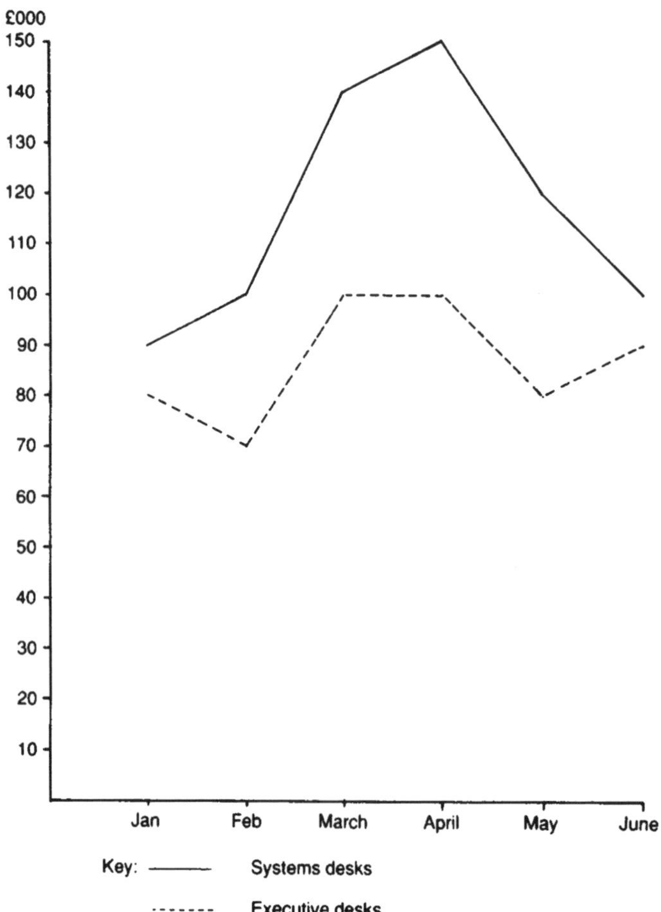

Fig 20.1 Line graph

- different colours may be used for the lines of the graph but if colour work is not practicable, contrasting black lines such as a continuous and a dotted line may be used, as in this example
- the key is important to explain what the different lines represent

Bar chart

Bar charts are also effective means of displaying comparative data. They are similar in many respects to line graphs, except that individual bars instead of continuous lines are used for each month or other period. Figure 20.2 is an example of a bar chart showing the same data as in the line graph. The following points should be noted concerning this example:

- the title, the vertical and horizontal axes and the key are similar to those used for the line graph
- different colours or various black and white forms may be used to distinguish the bars
- the bars should be of equal width

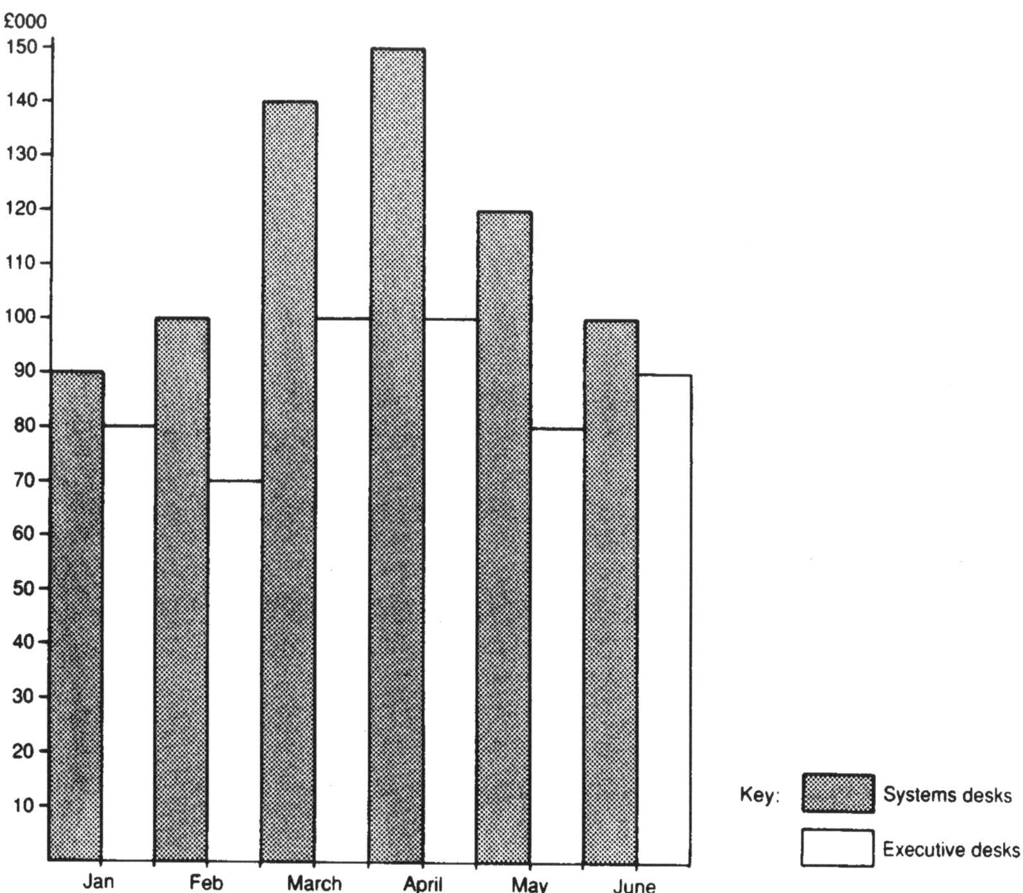

Fig 20.2 Bar chart

Pie charts

A pie chart formed by a circle is another method sometimes used to display information in pamphlets, journals and posters. The full circle represents the total amount of the sum involved and the various amounts which make up the total are shown as 'slices' cut into the 'pie' in proportion to the whole. The pie chart in Fig 20.3 illustrates how revenue from sales for June 19- was apportioned. Note that the total circle represents £400,000 and that the cost of wages, £100,000, takes up a quarter of the circle or 90° of the circumference (the distance round the circle = 360°).

Computer graphics

Special graphics applications can be carried out on a computer, and graphs (similar to those in Figs 20.1, 20.2 and 20.3) can be displayed on a VDU and printed out. A light pen can also be used as a drafting aid for plotting images on the screen.

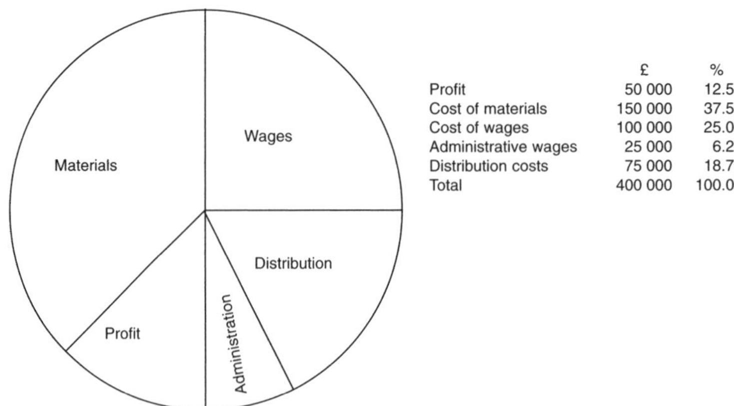

	£	%
Profit	50 000	12.5
Cost of materials	150 000	37.5
Cost of wages	100 000	25.0
Administrative wages	25 000	6.25
Distribution costs	75 000	18.75
Total	400 000	100.00

Fig 20.3 A pie chart

▶ PROGRESS CHECK

Multiple choice questions

1 *Crockford's Clerical Directory* contains information about:
- **a** office administrators
- **b** members of parliament
- **c** clergymen
- **d** directors

2 Her Majesty's Stationery Office supplies:
- **a** government reports
- **b** stationery and forms for government returns
- **c** telephone directories
- **d** Mailguides

3 In which of the following books would you find the location of a town in a foreign country?
- **a** *Parcelforce International User Guide*
- **b** *AA Members' Handbook*
- **c** *Lloyds List International*
- **d** *Chambers World Gazetteer*

4 Information about the EU can be found in:
- **a** *Municipal Year Book*
- **b** *Whitaker's Almanack*
- **c** *Stock Exchange Official Year Book*
- **d** *International Who's Who*

5 The month when sales peaked at Systems Furniture plc, as shown in Fig 20.1, was:
- **a** January
- **b** February
- **c** March
- **d** April

6 Which of the following would you use to find the names and addresses of a number of prominent British companies who manufacture greenhouses?
- **a** *Yellow Pages*
- **b** *Key to British Enterprise*
- **c** *Directory of British Associations*
- **d** *Who's Who*

7 The British Telecom viewdata service is called:
- **a** Ceefax
- **b** Prestel
- **c** 4-Tel
- **d** ITV3

8 From which of the following would you obtain travellers' cheques?
- **a** bank
- **b** post office
- **c** railway station
- **d** Customs and Excise

9 Pair the following lists of words (note that there is a surplus item in the second column):

Reference book		**Information on**	
a	*Kelly's*	**a**	newspapers
b	*Roget's*	**b**	foreign embassies
c	*Whitaker's*	**c**	manufacturers
d	*Willing's*	**d**	solicitors
		e	synonyms

10 Pair the following lists of words (note that there is a surplus item in the second column):

Organisation		**Function**	
a	Customs and Excise	**a**	Foreign currency
b	Post Office	**b**	Income tax
c	HMSO	**c**	Government publications
d	Inland Revenue	**d**	Franking units
		e	VAT

Short answer questions

State the missing words or phrases:

11 The publisher's name and address of a well-known magazine can be found in ....

12 Words are arranged .... in *Roget's Thesaurus of English Words and Phrases.*

13 *Lloyd's International List* contains information about ....

14 You would need to contact the local .... office for advice on income tax.

15 .... classification numbers are used in most libraries for classifying and arranging books.

Supply brief answers to the following questions:

16 List three videotex services:
a ....
b ....
c ....

17 Name three types of information which are given in *Whitaker's Almanack*:
a ....
b ....
c ....

18 List three books of reference relating to information about companies:
a ....
b ....
c ....

19 Suggest where you would obtain information about each of the following:
a Government publications: ....
b Visas: ....
c VAT: ....

20 Which reference books would you look in for information about:
a Doctors: ....
b Solicitors: ....
c Civil Servants:....................................

Section E
STUDENT'S GUIDE TO ASSESSMENT

The methods used to assess your performance in office procedures/practice will vary depending on the examining board selected but this brief guide will outline the different forms of assessment and highlight some of the errors you should avoid.

The following are examples of some of the assessment techniques you may encounter:

Incourse assignments	**Examinations (time-constrained)**
case studies	case studies
intray exercises	intray exercises
oral work	multiple choice questions
working in a team	short answer questions
ability profile	structured written questions
research / information gathering	data response, ie comprehension of data supplied
production tests	open book questions, ie using reference material in the examination room
integration with other subjects	
work experience tasks	
use of information technology	

Some examining boards use a combination of incourse assignments and an examination, while others base their assessment entirely on assignments or an examination.

The National Council for Vocational Qualifications has influenced the examination syllabuses of the different examining boards and they now have more standardisation in line with the competences which are included at the beginning of each of the units in this book. The emphasis is placed on testing the practical application of knowledge and not just how much of it you can remember.

► ASSIGNMENTS

A varied selection of assignments and the relevant NVQ performance criteria are provided in *Practical Office Procedures*, the companion to this book. You should aim to achieve the standards given in these criteria in all of your assignment work. The following are some further tips to help you gain the highest possible grades in your assignments:

- plan your approach to an assignment so that you produce a logical, clear and well laid out answer
- the aim is not to produce an 'examination type' essay but an efficient document or piece of work which would be acceptable in business
- use information from up-to-date sources such as newspapers, journals, reference books, videotex – but remember to name and date the source
- use a variety of methods of presentation, eg written, audio and visual; if you use manufacturers' leaflets be selective and relate them to your task
- take the opportunity to use a computer/word processor whenever possible to assemble and present your work
- state your conclusions clearly and give your reasons for them

- avoid irrelevant information – a bulky assignment containing pamphlets, copied notes, etc, many of which are unrelated to the task, will only serve to frustrate the assessor and have an adverse effect on the result
- always seek assistance when necessary and take full advantage of advice from your tutor or anyone who is in a position to help you

▶ EXAMINATIONS

An examination is usually the culmination of one or two years' work in the subject and you will want to do your best in this 'final hurdle' towards gaining the qualification, so here are some 'do's' and 'don'ts' on examinations:

Do

Before the examination

- revise from your course work folder and textbook making brief notes of key terms, definitions, principles and examples. The short answer questions will be helpful for revision
- get to know the style of examination paper, ie:
  - ○ type of questions
  - ○ compulsory questions
  - ○ number of questions to be answered
  - ○ what you can bring into the examination, eg dictionary, calculator
- practise answering the questions in the time allowed, eg if the examination lasts two hours and you have to answer five questions carrying equal marks, allocate twenty minutes for each question, allowing you ten minutes reading and preparation time at the beginning and ten minutes reading and checking time at the end

The day before the examination:

- collect together the equipment needed, making sure that your pens have adequate refills
- check the venue of the examination and the journey necessary to reach it
- rest and be refreshed so that you will be on top form for the next day

The day of the examination:

- allow yourself adequate travelling time so that you arrive at the examination room relaxed and ready to perform well
- when you are given the examination paper read it carefully noting:
  - ○ any compulsory question
  - ○ how many questions have to be answered
  - ○ the questions you intend to answer
  - ○ the time you have allocated for each question to enable you to pace your work evenly and complete all of the work required

Don't

- revise without concentrating on the major points to remember, eg in buying and selling revise the purpose of the different documents, the information they provide, their distribution and relationship with other documents
- assume that the examination will take the same form as your coursework
- leave your revision to 2 or 3 days before the examination as cramming at this late stage could do more harm than good
- revise until the early hours of the morning: cramming and loss of sleep will only serve to make you dull and confused on the day of the examination
- rely on arriving 5 to 10 minutes before the examination is due to start, especially if you are travelling in rush hour traffic
- rush into answering the first question on the paper - time taken to plan your approach methodically is time well spent

Do

- use your time wisely throughout the whole examination
- use a dictionary (if permitted) whenever you are in doubt about the spelling of a word
- be efficient and business-like:
  - number each answer clearly
  - use main headings and sub-headings if appropriate
  - if you are asked to supply a list, display it with numbers or letters
  - use the layout specified in the question, eg memo, letter, report
  - keep to the point and answer the question as set: no more, no less
- use realistic examples to illustrate your answers and, if appropriate, make use of diagrams
- apply the particular circumstances stated in a case study and make reference to the personnel involved, their departments, positions, etc
- during the final 10 minutes of the examination check your answers to make sure that they are accurately written and make any corrections neatly

Don't

- try to finish early – it is not a race and there is no prize for finishing first – you may even lose marks by rushing your work
- write out the question as this is unnecessary and uses up valuable time
- pad out your answers with irrelevant details – over-long answers not only result in insufficient time being available for the remainder of the paper but frustrate the examiner who may lose sight of any good points you have made
- answer more questions than are required

► A SUGGESTED APPROACH TO ANSWERING EXAMINATION QUESTIONS

Multiple choice questions

- Read all of the possible answers taking care not to be diverted from the correct answer by a distractor.
- Eliminate the answers you know are wrong, so that your final choice is reduced to just one or two answers.
- Don't spend a long time on a question you find difficult but carry on with the next question, returning to the difficult question later.

Written questions

Analyse the requirements of a question by underlining the key words, eg list, compare, explain, etc.

Examples:

'*Explain the uses and advantages of voice banks.*'
There is no need to explain what they are, but give their uses and their advantages.

'*What books and equipment would you need to control the petty cash float? Explain the purpose of each item on your list.*'
Here you are required to list the items such as petty cash book, vouchers, cash box etc and explain, ie give the reasons for their use.

'*Complete an invoice from the following data ...*'
A practical form-filling question in which you are required to enter the essential data on an invoice form and make the necessary calculations. The examiner will give you credit for work which is accurate, relevant and neat, eg use a ruler to underline totals. Be careful to check your calculations and remember that trade discount is deducted and VAT (based on the discounted amount) added. Ensure that every business document is dated.

'*What is the difference between recorded delivery and registered post?*'
The key word in this question is 'difference' which means that you must compare the two items – their uses, provision for compensation, security measures, etc. For example, registered post is used for sending articles of value for which adequate compensation would be payable if they were lost, whereas recorded delivery is used for posting items of little or no monetary value in which proof of posting and delivery may be required.

Practical Office Procedures contains a wide range of tasks for you to use as assignments or as preparation for examinations. I am tempted to conclude by wishing you 'good luck' in your examination but if you have worked hard during your course and you have revised thoroughly, as suggested above, you will not need to be lucky to gain the success you deserve.

Answers to progress checks

▶ UNIT 1

Multiple choice questions

1 c **2** c **3** c **4** b **5** c **6** d **7** a **8** b
9 cadb **10** bcae

Short answer questions

11 information
12 copying and printing
13 owns
14 production/works
15 politely
16 **a** job description
b advertisement
c application form or curriculum vitae
17 Examples:
a Builder
b Insurance company
c Hotel
18 Examples:
a Greater specialisation
b Opportunities for staff development
c More advanced technology
19 Examples:
a Clear, accurate and efficient communication
b Friendly and polite manner
c Accepted standards of dress and appearance
20 Examples:
a Job title
b Department
c To whom accountable

▶ UNIT 2

Multiple choice questions

1 d **2** b **3** b **4** a **5** dbac **6** c **7** a
8 a **9** bdca **10** cdba

Short answer questions

11 statement
12 cash discount
13 credit note
14 advice note
15 added to
16 **a** Trade discount is deducted on invoice; cash discount is deducted when payment is made.
b Cash discount is given for payment within a stated period; trade discount does not depend on time.
c Trade discount may be given to encourage bulk buying; cash discount encourages prompt paying.
17 **a** catalogue and price list
b quotation
c estimate
18 **a** Accounts Department: checking invoice
b Stores section: entering goods on stock records
c Buying Department: confirmation of goods arrival
19 Examples:
a quantity of goods multiplied by rate per article
b calculation and deduction of trade discount
c calculation and addition of VAT
20 **a** To find out prices, delivery dates, terms of payment, etc for ordering goods.
b A written request to the seller to supply goods.
c Documentary evidence of goods purchased and amounts charged for entering in accounts.

▶ UNIT 3

Multiple choice questions

1 d **2** a **3** a **4** c **5** a **6** d **7** d **8** a
9 b **10** deab

Short answer questions

11 receipts or cash sales
12 inventory
13 stock or stores requisition
14 stock control card or bin card
15 minimum stock level
16 **a** The largest quantity of stock which should be held at any one time to avoid over-stocking.
b The smallest quantity of stock which should be maintained to prevent stocks from running out.
c The level at which stock should be re-ordered.
17 **a** controls quantities of stock issued to avoid pilferage.
b ensures that stocks are maintained at minimum levels without affecting production.
c minimises capital tied up in stock.
18 **a** centrally situated for easy access.
b controlled by one person.
c well organised with clear labelling, for easy identification and control of stock.
19 **a** minimises capital allocated to stock.
b minimises space occupied by stock.
c avoids deterioration or goods becoming obsolete.
20 **a** current stock levels.
b when minimum stock levels are reached.
c stock valuations.

▶ UNIT 4

Multiple choice questions

1 a **2** a **3** b **4** c **5** c **6** a **7** b **8** c
9 d **10** bcea

Short answer questions

11 receipt
12 bank account
13 transcash
14 BACS (Bankers automated clearing service)
15 PIN (Personal identity number)
16 **a** to make cheques more acceptable.
b to purchase goods on credit.
c to withdraw cash from an autobank cash machine.
17 **a** registration
b postal orders
c cash on delivery
18 **a** drawer – person who signs cheque and whose account is charged.
b drawee – bank on which cheque is drawn.
c payee – person to whom cheque is made payable.
19 Examples:
a Do not leave spaces for other words or figures to be added.
b Write the word 'A/c Payee' in the crossing.
c Always use a pen.
20 Examples:
a One cheque used for several creditors.
b Safer – no need for payee to call at bank.
c Speedier clearing/payment.

▶ UNIT 5

Multiple choice questions

1 b **2** c **3** a **4** b **5** b **6** d **7** b **8** d
9 b **10** dabe

Short answer questions

11 petty cash
12 the cash book page number
13 petty cash voucher
14 analysis
15 imprest
16 Examples:
a petty cash voucher number
b date
c amount including VAT

17 **a** The imprest is allocated to petty cash account.
b Payments are made for small items.
c At end of period, money spent is reimbursed to restore imprest.

18 **a** stationery
b postage
c travelling expenses

19 **a** total paid £7.99
b stationery £6.80
c VAT £1.19

20 **a** a signature of the person who spends the money as documentary evidence of the transaction
b the second signature from a supervisor who authorises the expenditure to be made.

▶ UNIT 6

Multiple choice questions

1 b **2** c **3** d **4** b **5** b **6** a **7** b **8** b
9 b **10** c

Short answer questions

11 piecework
12 time they leave work
13 pay as you earn
14 P11
15 net pay
16 Examples:
a unemployment
b sickness
c retirement

17 **a** savings
b social club
c union dues

18 Part 1: Sent to Tax office by former employer.
Part 2: Given to new employer by employee, who keeps it.
Part 3: Given to new employer by employee, who sends it to Tax office.

19 **a** PAYE – Table A
b PAYE – Table B
c National Insurance Contributions Table A

20 **a** Employee's code number.
b Total gross pay since beginning of tax year.
c Total tax deducted previously in current tax year.

▶ UNIT 7

Multiple choice questions

1 c **2** a **3** d **4** a **5** c **6** b **7** a **8** b
9 cdba **10** deba

Short answer questions

11 numerical
12 something
13 upright/vertically
14 miscellaneous
15 visible card
16 Examples:
a Document has been passed for filing.
b Document is placed in the correct file.
c Document is placed in the correct chronological sequence.

17 Placed in the section of the cabinet for the secondary title, stating the name or position in the cabinet where the file can be found.

18 **a** 1 Basle
2 Berlin
3 Budapest
b 1 Lisbon
2 London
3 Londonderry
c 1 St Albans
2 Seville
3 Shanghai

19 **a** file name/number
b name of person who borrowed the file
c department of borrower

20 **a** saves space
b film is more durable than paper
c quicker retrieval of data

▶ UNIT 8

Multiple choice questions

1 c **2** b **3** d **4** b **5** a **6** d **7** c **8** d
9 bcde **10** ecda

Short answer questions

11 remittances book
12 circulation slips
13 private, personal or confidential
14 first and second class packages
15 shredder
16 **a** Use a circulation slip for distributing document to all departments concerned.
b Ask department responsible for major part of document to deal with it and consult others concerned.
c Use a copier to make copies for each department concerned.
17 **a** letter is signed
b address on envelope is checked with address on letter
c correct enclosures are enclosed, where appropriate
18 Examples:
a unusual shape or size
b wires attached
c oil or grease marks on cover
19 Examples:
a saves time
b better security
c easier to plan future requirements
20 Examples:
a franking machine
b folding machine
c package tying machine

▶ UNIT 9

Multiple choice questions

1 b **2** c **3** a **4** d **5** c **6** c **7** b **8** c
9 b **10** cbda

Short answer questions

11 checklist
12 plan of action or personal development plan
13 matters are not overlooked
14 VDU
15 time
16 **a** top priority – must be done during the day
b try to do it during the day
c could wait for another day, if necessary
17 Examples:
a diaries
b follow-up systems
c year planner charts
18 Reminders of, for example:
a appointments and meetings
b work deadlines
c files to be followed up
19 Examples:
a identify your role and personal development objectives
b draw up an action plan to achieve objectives
c agree personal development with your supervisor
20 **a** name of person calling
b name and address of the business
c telephone number of contact
d nature of business
e time of appointment
f date of appointment

▶ UNIT 10

Multiple choice questions

1 c **2** b **3** a **4** d **5** c **6** d **7** a **8** b
9 b **10** ceba

Short answer questions

11 Security or confidentiality
12 Daisy wheel, ink jet or laser jet
13 Visual display unit
14 8
15 Manually operated user signal encoder
16 Examples:
a CPU
b VDU
c Keyboard
17 **a** one alphabetical or numerical symbol – 8 bits
b a subdivision of an item of information – employee number
c information relating to several files which can be used by several programs
18 Examples:
a keep back-up copies of disks
b staff required to use passwords
c codes used for document files, known only to users

19 Examples:
- **a** keyboard
- **b** OCR
- **c** MICR

20 Data must, for example, be:
- **a** obtained fairly and lawfully
- **b** accurate and, where necessary, kept up-to-date
- **c** held for no longer than necessary

▶ UNIT 11

Multiple choice questions

1 b **2** b **3** d **4** d **5** a **6** a **7** c
8 d **9** cdab **10** caeb

Short answer questions

11 replicas
12 jogger
13 collator
14 faxing
15 desktop publishing
16 Examples:
- **a** copying incoming letters required for several departments
- **b** making overhead transparencies
- **c** preparing offset litho masters

17 Examples:
- **a** adjust exposure control
- **b** check if toner requires replenishing
- **c** replace original with one of a better quality

18 **a** scanner
- **b** computer
- **c** laser printer

19 **a** fuses working
- **b** check cables and plugs
- **c** refer to manual 'trouble shooting' tips

20 Under the 'fair dealing' provisions you are permitted to make one copy only of an agreed maximum amount of any published material, but you are not permitted to copy a substantial part of it.

▶ UNIT 12

Calculations:

1 25520.18
2 1847.49
3 1148
4 437289.55
5 **a** 9968 **b** 24564 **c** 69776
6 15.285
7 £11.92
8 £160.92
9 £137.08
10 £1078.65

▶ UNIT 13

Multiple choice questions

1 c **2** d **3** c **4** d **5** b **6** b **7** d
8 b **9** dcba **10** ceda

Short answer questions

11 accident book
12 orderly and tidy
13 guard
14 adjustable
15 First aid treatment
16 **a** take reasonable care for the health and safety of themselves and of other persons who may be affected by their acts or omissions at work
- **b** follow safety practices
- **c** co-operate with their employer in promoting and maintaining health and safety
- **d** refrain from interfering with or misusing anything provided for health and safety of themselves or others.

17 Examples:
- **a** know how to stop electric supply in an emergency
- **b** avoid having a trailing flex from a socket to a machine
- **c** report faulty or damaged equipment without delay

18 Examples:
- **a** use the lift
- **b** stop to collect personal belongings
- **c** run or panic

19 Examples:
- **a** regular short breaks
- **b** do not look directly at windows or bright lights
- **c** use brightness controls to suit the lighting conditions

20
- **a** injured person's name
- **b** date, time and place of accident
- **c** name of witness
- **d** nature and cause of injury

▶ UNIT 14

Multiple choice questions

1 b **2** c **3** d **4** d **5** a **6** d **7** d
8 a **9** b **10** badc

Short answer questions

11 caller
12 code and telephone number
13 listening
14 mobile radio or cellular telephones
15 0800
16 Examples:
- **a** name of firm
- **b** reason for the recording
- **c** instructions for recording a message

17 Examples:
- **a** speak clearly
- **b** be polite and cheerful
- **c** answer promptly

18 Examples:
- **a** wait until the person is free to speak
- **b** speak to someone else
- **c** be rung back when the person is free to speak

19
- **a** displaying information for a large number of people over a period of time
- **b** conveying urgent information to a large number of people in a building
- **c** displaying visual data

20
- **a** Lo-call 0345
- **b** freefone 0800
- **c** call forwarding

▶ UNIT 15

Multiple choice questions

1 d **2** b **3** c **4** a **5** b **6** d **7** a
8 c **9** bacd **10** eacb

Short answer questions

11 answerback code
12 faithfully
13 written word
14 micro-computers
15 Integrated Services Digital Network
16 Examples:
- **a** letter
- **b** telephone
- **c** fax

17 Examples:
- **a** memo
- **b** fax
- **c** electronic mail

18 Examples:
- **a** any originals can be transmitted
- **b** errors are eliminated as no intermediate checking is necessary
- **c** simple to operate

19
- **a** British Telecom teleprinter service
- **b** British Telecom hard copy message service
- **c** Computer-based information services (Ceefax and ITV3)

20 Examples:
- **a** use correct style and tone
- **b** use words which convey the correct meaning
- **c** use sentences which are simple and concise

▶ UNIT 16

Multiple choice questions

1 d **2** b **3** b **4** c **5** c **6** b **7** a
8 d **9** beac **10** dcab

Short answer questions

11 Post office
12 Unaddressed material
13 Presstream

14 30 kg
15 Prepaying a reply
16 **a** Parcelforce standard
b Datapost
c International Datapost
17 **a** first class mail
b second class mail
c non-urgent second class mail
18 **a** to enable customers to reply without payment
b to provide proof of posting and delivery
c to enable a company to receive parcels from customers without prepayment of postage
19 **a** Swiftair
b International Datapost
c Airmail
20 **a** Airmail
b Recorded Delivery
c Special Delivery

▶ UNIT 17

Multiple choice questions

1 c **2** c **3** c **4** a **5** d **6** d **7** a **8** b
9 dbec **10** cabe

Short answer questions

11 register of callers
12 appointments
13 business visiting card
14 noted on the delivery note returned to the driver, as well as on your copy
15 the address where help is needed and any other information requested
16 Examples:
a receive and direct visitors
b control the access of visitors to the offices
c receive parcels delivered to the firm
17 Examples:
a internal telephone index
b business visiting cards
c local town guide
18 Examples:
a security reasons – to save visitors having to walk through other offices
b convenience of receiving goods
c provide advice/information for callers
19 Examples:
a organisation chart
b register of callers
c AA handbook
20 Examples:
a lock documents in cabinets when not in use
b mark 'confidential' on documents
c destroy unwanted confidential documents in a shredder or incinerator

▶ UNIT 18

Multiple choice questions

1 b **2** d **3** c **4** a **5** b **6** b **7** d **8** c
9 a **10** edbc

Short answers questions

11 behind
12 next day
13 checklist
14 24-hour clock
15 Greenwich Mean Time
16 Examples:
a itinerary
b visiting card
c rail ticket
17 Examples:
a journey dates
b insurance required
c places to be visited
18 Examples:
a *AA Members' Handbook*
b Airline Timetables
c *Hints for Exporters*
19 **a** 3 **b** 2 **c** 1
20 Examples:
a travellers cheques
b foreign currency
c credit/charge cards

▶ UNIT 19

Multiple choice questions

1 b **2** d **3** a **4** b **5** c **6** b **7** c **8** d
9 a **10** caeb

Short answer questions

11 law
12 apologies for absence
13 rider
14 meeting procedure or a query relating to standing orders or constitution
15 minutes
16 Examples:
- **a** minutes
- **b** extracts from files
- **c** standing orders

17 Examples:
- **a** democratic decision-making
- **b** informing staff about new developments
- **c** consultation

18
- **a** purpose
- **b** date and time
- **c** venue
- **d** budget

19 Examples:
- **a** closure
- **b** next business
- **c** reference back

20 Examples:
- **a** approve agenda items
- **b** deal with points of order
- **c** sign minutes

▶ UNIT 20

Multiple choice questions

1 c **2** a **3** d **4** b **5** d **6** b **7** b
8 a **9** ceba **10** edcb

Short answer questions

11 *Benn's Media* or *Willing's Press Guide*
12 according to their meaning
13 Shipping
14 Inland Revenue
15 Dewey decimal
16
- **a** Ceefax
- **b** ITV3
- **c** Prestel

17 Examples:
- **a** British and Foreign Embassies
- **b** EU
- **c** United Nations Organisation

18 Examples:
- a *The European Business Directory*
- b *Who Owns Whom*
- c *Key British Enterprises*

19
- **a** Her Majesty's Stationery Office
- **b** Consulates
- **c** Customs and Excise Office

20
- **a** *Medical Directory*
- **b** *Waterlow's Solicitors' and Barristers' Directory*
- **c** *Civil Service Year Book*

Index

absent files and cards 74
accident reports 120, 123
Accurist timeline service 137
addressing envelopes 81,109
addressing mail 80
advertisements 6
advertising jobs 6
advice notes 18
aerogrammes 154
agenda 173
airmail 154
airpacks 154
airstream 154
alarm calls 137
Alliance & Leicester Giro 37
alphabetical filing 68
answering the telephone 132
answers to progress checks 192
applying for jobs 8
appointments 92
assessment guide 188
autobank cards 43

bank
  giro credit summary 40, 42
  payments 38
  statements 39
Bankers Automated Clearing Service (BACS) 40
bar
  charts 184
  coding 31
binding equipment 108
booking
  accommodation 167
  procedures 92
  British Telecom telephone services 137
BT direct connect 137
bursters 108
business
  letters 140
  reply 152
  television 178
  units 2
  visiting cards 160
buying 12

calculators 114
call
  forwarding 137
  return 137
  waiting 137
caller display 137
cash
  cards 43
  discount 16
  on delivery 36
catalogues 14
central government 4
central processing unit 97
centralisation of office services 2
chairman's agenda 174
charge
  advisory service 137
  cards 43
cheque cards 43
cheques 39
choosing a supplier 15
chronological filing 70
circulation
  of documents 80
  slips 80
  clock cards 53
closed-circuit television security system 161
coining analysis 62
collators 107
collect calls 137
collection of mail by Post Office 83
combined alphabetical and numerical filing 69
commercial organisations 2
communications 129
compact disks 97
compensation fee parcels 153
computer applications 100
computerised data security 101
computerised procedures
  banking 44
  buying 24
  desk diary planner 90
  document management system 71
  filing 72, 73
  graphics 185
  information services 182
  sales 24
  stock control 30
  text processing 100
  wages 62
computer systems and terminology 97
conference calls 178

copiers 105
copyright law 111
cordless telephones 135
credit
  cards 43
  notes 22
  transfers 40
cross reference slips 74
current account 38
curriculum vitae 8
customs declaration forms 155

data
  hierarchy 99
  protection 101
  storage and retrieval 73
datapost 153
Data Protection Act 1984 102
decollators 108
deductions working sheet (form P11) 56
delivery notes 18
desktop publishing 107
despatch notes 18
diaries 89
direct debiting 41
directory enquiries 137
display screens 124
door-to-door delivery service 151
duplicators 105

electronic
  calculators 114
  filing systems 71
  mailing equipment 82
  teleprinters 144
  timestamp machines 80
emergency telephone calls 162
estimates 15
Europe: letters 154
examination, preparation for 189
expense claim forms 44

fax machines 146
faxmail 147
file retention policy 73
filing 68
fire
  evacuation procedure 124
  precautions 120
firm offers 15
first aid 121, 162
First Direct account 38
floppy disks 102
flight schedules 167
folding and inserting machines 84
follow-up system 91
formal meetings 175
franking machines 82
freefone 137
freepost 152

geographical filing 69
Girobank
  payments 37
  transcash 37
glare guard filters 125
goods received notes 18

hardware 97
health and safety 117
Health and Safety at Work Act 1974 117
holding companies 3

imprest system 47
income tax 53, 55
  deductions working sheets 56
  tables 57, 58
incoming mail 78
indexing 75
induction courses 8
industrial organisations 2
inland
  cards and letters 151
  travel arrangements 166
inserting and mailing equipment 84
integrated services digital network 148
internal structure of organisations 4
international
  datapost 155
  Freefone 0800 telephone service 137
  reply coupons 155
internet 100
interpersonal relationships 5
inventory 30
invoices 19
itinerary 166, 168

job
  applications 8
  descriptions 7

keyboards 97

laptop computers 99
laser intelligent copiers 106
late posting facility 156
lateral filing 70
letter opening machines 79
letters
  construction of 140
  of enquiry 12
  postage for 151
levels of responsibility 4
library, use of 181
line graphs 183
linked current and savings account 38
local
  area network 100

government 4
Lo-call 0345 137
loudspeaking telephone 135

magnetic planning board 91
mail services 151
mailing equipment 82, 84
mailsort 151
maintenance of equipment 108
manufacturing organisations 2
meetings
arrangements for 173
personnel 177
terms 176
types of 172
memos 141
messages 131, 141
methods of paying wages 62, 64
microfilm
reader/printer 72
storage 71
minutes of meetings 174
mobile telephones 136
mouse 97
multi-functional copier, fax and printer 106
multinational companies 3

national giro 37
national insurance 54, 55
national insurance contribution tables 60
numerical filing 69
newspapers 153

office
functions 1
services 1
worker's role 6
oral communication 131
orders 17
organisation charts 5
organisations
information services 183
size of 4
types of 2
outgoing mail 81
overseas
parcel services 155
postal services 154
small packets 154
telephone calls 132
travel arrangements 168

pagers 136
parcels 81, 153
partnerships 3
pay advice slips 53
pay-as-you-earn (PAYE) 53
paying-in books 35
payroll 62
pen computer note pads 99
pension/superannuation contributions 53
personal development 88
petty cash 47
petty cash vouchers 47
pie charts 185
plan filing 71
planning 89
planning control boards 91
plastic year planners 91
postage
accounts 83
forward parcel service 153
postal
orders 36
services 151
poste restante 156
presstream 153
Prestel mailbox 182
price lists 14
printed postage impressions 155
printers 97
printflow 154
printout checking 143
private
boxes 155
limited companies 3
proof reading 143
public limited companies 3
purchase
invoices 20
requisitions 12

quotations 14

receipts 34
receiving/recording payments 34
reception 159
recorded delivery 152
redirection of mail 156
Red Star Parcel Delivery Service 156
reference books 180
register of callers 159
registration 35
remittances books 78
reprography 105
requisitions 12

safe working practices 119
salaries 51
sales
enquiries 12
invoices 21
security 47, 101, 161
selectapost 156
self-service cash card 43
service organisations 2
shared resources (computers) 100
small packets 154

software 98
sole traders 2
sources of information 93, 162, 180
special delivery 151
spreadsheets 98
stand-alone computers 100
standing orders: bank 41
statements 23
statutory
  maternity pay 54
  sick pay 54
stock
  control 28
  control cards 28
  lists 28
  requisitions 12
subject filing 69
surface mail 154
suspicious postal packets 79
Swiftair 153
switchboards 133

telecommunications 132
telemessages 143
telephone
  answering 132
  answering machines 134
  charges 133
  equipment 133
  making calls 132
  tones 133

teletext 182
telex 143
tenders 15
text processing terms 101
time recording 51
trade discount 16
transcash 37
travel
  agent checklist 167
  arrangements 166
typescript checking 143

value added tax (VAT) 20
vertical filing 70
video conferencing 178
videotex 182
visible card record systems 74
visual display units (VDU) 97
voicebank 135

wages 51
weathercall telephone service 137
wide area networks 100
Workplace (Health, Safety and Welfare)
  Regulations 1992 117
work planning and scheduling 888, 89
written communication 140

year planners 91